Housing Demography

Social Demography

Series Editors
Doris P. Slesinger
James A. Sweet
Karl E. Taeuber
Center for Demography and Ecology
University of Wisconsin–Madison

The Causes of Demographic Change:
Experimental Research in South India
John C. Caldwell, P. H. Reddy, and Pat Caldwell

Procedural History of the 1940 Census of Population and Housing
Robert M. Jenkins

Population Growth and Economic Development: Issues and Evidence
Edited by D. Gale Johnson and Ronald D. Lee

Thailand's Reproductive Revolution:
Rapid Fertility Decline in a Third-World Setting
John Knodel, Aphichat Chamratrithirong, and Nibhon Debavalya

Housing Demography:
Linking Demographic Structure and Housing Markets
Dowell Myers, Editor

Gentrification and Distressed Cities:
An Assessment of Trends in Intrametropolitan Migration
Kathryn P. Nelson

A Community Transplanted: The Trans-Atlantic Experience of a
Swedish Immigrant Settlement in the Upper Middle West, 1835–1915
Robert C. Ostergren

Prolonged Connections:
Rise of the Extended Family in Nineteenth-Century England
and America
Steven Ruggles

Housing Demography

Linking Demographic Structure and Housing Markets

Edited by
Dowell Myers

THE UNIVERSITY OF WISCONSIN PRESS

The University of Wisconsin Press
114 North Murray Street
Madison, Wisconsin 53715

3 Henrietta Street
London WC2E 8LU, England

5 4 3 2 1

Printed in the United States of America

Library of Congress Cataloging-in-Publication Data

Housing demography: linking demographic structure and housing markets
    edited by Dowell Myers.
      336 pp.   cm.—(Social demography)
    Includes bibliographical references.
      1. Housing—United States.   2. United States—Population.
    I. Myers, Dowell.   II. Series.
    HD7293.H5838   1990
    3635'0973—dc20
    ISBN 0-299-12550-5   90-50094
    ISBN 0-299-12554-8 (pbk.)   CIP

Contents

Figures

Tables

Preface

This book was a long time in gestation. Long before I began to plan the chapters and enlist contributors, I worried about a problem. Why is there such a gap in the social science literature between the analysis of population and that of housing data? The decennial census of population and housing consists of two halves analyzed by different sets of researchers. Demographers, who have the strongest tradition of census-data analysis, have by and large ignored the housing portion of the data. Conversely, economists, geographers, and urban planners interested in housing have underemphasized the population portion of the data.

Over the past decade I increasingly encountered researchers who had explored connections between population and housing, each contributing different insights toward bridging the great divide. But each of these explorations was isolated, working from different disciplinary bases, and disconnected from other efforts. Given the lack of citations to one another's work, it is apparent that explorers along the population-housing interface have been unaware of one another's successes.

The book before you represents an effort to bridge the gap between the separate analysis of population and housing. I seek to define a shared set of objectives for researchers in the field, urging the organization of a more self-conscious paradigm. To identify the field—one focused on the union of population and housing analysis—I propose a new descriptor and label: "housing demography."

When I first ventured the term "housing demography" a dozen years ago, one of my professors at the Massachusetts Institute of Technology dissuaded me, chuckling that people might get the wrong idea, seeing images of procreating houses. Suitably chastened, I set aside the term for a decade while continuing my research along the interface of population and housing. I conceived or found a number of different research designs for linking population and housing. Some designs started from a population base and some from a housing base; some focused at the national level and some at the neighborhood level.

Along the way I discovered other investigators using other research designs they had invented to pursue particular questions linking population and housing. No one had a label for this style of research; worse, few seemed to recognize any underlying commonalities that might integrate these disparate investigations. When I revived the term "housing demography" a couple years ago, offering it to my fellow investigators in this realm, it was readily accepted as a description sorely needed for our shared activities.

Appropriately, the book is a collected work. There is a great diversity of vantage points from which researchers have explored the relation between population and housing. Against the backdrop of a common framework that I posit for housing demography in the Introduction, it is interesting to view the particular mode of analysis followed by these key innovators in the field. All the chapters are original research products prepared especially for this volume.

I owe a special debt of gratitude to the contributors, for it was their enthusiasm and encouragement that spurred me forward with the project. I have the longest association with George Masnick and John Pitkin, both of whom I met back in the mid-1970s as a student at M. I. T. George taught me much of what I know about household and social demography; John's research focus caused me to link these ideas to the economics of housing consumption. The forecasting team of Pitkin and Masnick has served as an inspirational model for how the techniques and concepts of housing demography can be brought into practical service.

Several other contributors have influenced me over a longer period of time. Bill Baer's interest in the housing stock, and its relation to household occupancy and planning policies, influenced me long before I joined his faculty as a colleague. Several years ago Pat Gober and I found a mutual interest in how household size varies across the housing stock and across neighborhoods of a city. This intellectual resonance was more vital than she may recognize, because it encouraged me to link national-level housing and demographic analysis to more fine-scale intraurban analysis.

In different ways each of the remaining contributors helped me forge a unified conception of housing demography. Over the years, lessons of residential mobility stressed by Eric Moore and Bill Clark have underscored this dynamic aspect of the population-housing interface. Jim Sweet's penchant for social demographic analysis with large-scale data sets includes more of an emphasis on households, and even housing, than is typically found among demographers. His example has encouraged my thinking along these lines. Daphne Spain's work for the U.S. Census Bureau and elsewhere has also been an encouragement, because it has linked issues of race and gender to housing outcomes. Most recently, Ken Chew's analysis of household formation and industrial structure has broadened my thinking about housing demography to include the local economic base.

Finally, Hal Kendig deserves note for his impact on my confidence to assert a paradigm of housing demography. Hal has an urban planning degree, as I do, but has crossed over into gerontology and now integrates several dimensions in his thinking. His synthesis links life course analysis with housing analysis, similar to George Masnick's perspective, but grounded in an urban development context. Hal's thinking emphasizes the integration of several key themes composing housing demography, and his independent discovery of this synthesis adds moral support to the idea of an incipient paradigm with a broader base of attraction.

The book would not have taken shape as readily without the support of the University of Wisconsin Press. Jim Sweet is not only a contributor but also co-editor of the Press's series on social demography. His encouragement helped immensely with the formation of the book. Elizabeth Steinberg and her editorial staff at the University of Wisconsin Press smoothly moved the book to finished form. In particular, Robin Whitaker performed a marvelous job with the copy editing, helping to tie together the many chapters in a uniform format.

I have placed such great emphasis on the moral support the book has received from different individuals because the project was not encouraged with any direct funding. All the contributors accomplished their chapters without any honoraria or other support directly related to the book's planning. In the competition for scholars' scarce time, it is remarkable that this book could fare so well. I am both grateful and amazed that this "labor of love" may finally reach completion.

Along the way I borrowed research time from several sources, not the least of which came from the normally crowded schedule of a teaching professor. My research with Alan Doyle for Chapter 5 was supported by the computer resources of the Population Research Center at the University of Texas at Austin. In my writing and editing I have also made use of general summer research time supported by the School of Business of the University of Wisconsin at Madison.

My part in this book is dedicated to my mother, Ruth Dowell Myers, because she always encouraged me to have confidence in doing things differently.

D.M.

Housing Demography

1 *Dowell Myers*

Introduction: The Emerging Concept of Housing Demography

The close connections between housing and demography have been long neglected. Until recently, the two topics were pursued by different groups of researchers who did not communicate. Recent events have broken that barrier, opening a fertile new field of investigation, a hybrid we term housing demography in this volume.

In the past, demographers have emphasized fertility and the structure of household groups in which the vast majority of the population lives, but they have traditionally stopped short of investigating how the search for accommodation in housing units affects those households. On the other hand, economists, geographers, and urban planners have explored housing as a key component of urban structure, but they have rarely examined the demographic details of who lives in those housing units.

Recently there has been mounting evidence of linkage between housing and population studies. Demographers have begun to investigate the interaction between household compositional processes and housing choices within the city. Economists and housing forecasters have also exhibited strong interest in this relationship. Meanwhile other researchers from a number of social science disciplines have been exploring the role of demographic factors in residential mobility, gentrification, and neighborhood change.

Dowell Myers is Associate Professor in the School of Urban and Regional Planning, University of Southern California, Los Angeles, California 90089-0042.

Thus far, applications of the new integration have been scattered across a wide range of social science journals and professional studies. This fragmentation of research has inhibited advances in the field, leading to rediscoveries and reinventions of relationships and concepts. Also, individual researchers have been restricted, for practical reasons, to fairly narrow slices of the broader housing demography field. Lacking a shared, comprehensive vision of the scope of the field, individual work on manageable subtopics may not be designed for productive and efficient linkage to others' work on related subtopics.

The goal of this book is to help organize a more coherent and productive paradigm for researching the interaction of housing and population. We pursue that goal through several specific objectives. First, we have assembled for this book a diverse selection of original research efforts that illustrate different types of inquiry probing the population-housing interface. The authors approach their topics from the disciplinary bases of demography, economics, geography, sociology, and urban planning.

More than presenting individual research efforts in this new field, we aim to draw together contributions from diverse sources, enhancing the hybridization process. The growth of a rich theoretical base for this new field is stimulated by cross-fertilization of research ideas stemming from the authors' richly varied traditions.

A further objective of the book is to highlight potential interconnections explicitly within the broad field of housing demography. Researchers are likely to benefit by seeing their own work cast in the context of other research. Several authors propose far-reaching conceptual models that potentially embrace one another's contributions. For example, Patricia Gober's geographic analysis of neighborhood changes seeks to relate these to life course changes in the population at large, the latter of which is also examined by James Sweet's chapter on changing household composition. As another example, in William Baer's analysis of changes in the physical housing stock, he goes so far as to seek direct parallels to mortality and morbidity processes in population analysis.

Theory-building is a major objective of the book. Each of the authors presents a brief statement as background to research reported in his or her chapter. And in this introductory chapter, as editor I have presented my own synthesis of theoretical concepts forming housing demography. Together with theoretical statements by the chapter authors, the book collects a rich set of concepts to guide further research.

With this book we strive to provide a platform for subsequent exploration of the population-housing interface. At the very least, we seek to give these explorations some identity, by providing them with a common name, housing demography, by drawing together dispersed investigations, and by highlighting underlying commonalities.

This introductory chapter previews the contributions of the chapters by each of the authors. Some explanation is required for why the particular set of chapters has been selected for this collected work. To place these in better context, we will first review the different types of studies falling within the domain of housing demography. Various efforts have probed the interface between population and housing from different vantage points and with different purposes.

We begin by addressing the mystery of why housing and demographic analyses have remained separate for so long. Given our claim that research of the interface between population and housing has importance, we owe an explanation for why this has been neglected. And given our claim that a new field of housing demography is now emerging, we must explain the forces prompting the new integration of population and housing research.

A Mysterious Separation

It is puzzling why housing and population have been relatively disconnected in analyses for so long. Housing and population are intimately related by the fact that the vast majority of the population resides in household living groups sheltered in housing units. In fact, the definition of a household is that it occupy a separate housing unit, and thus the number of households equals the number of occupied housing units. Beyond this simple equation lie many familiar relationships: different types of households live in different types of housing units.

The long-time separation of demography from housing is even more remarkable given the fact that so many data have been jointly collected in the decennial censuses of population and housing. As we will describe, the availability of a joint data base is of particular consequence for the development of research and theory in housing demography.

Once it seemed housing and demography were more closely allied. In the 1950s and early 1960s a number of works appeared by demographers and sociologists that addressed housing topics. Major landmarks include Duncan and Hauser's *Chicago: Housing a Metropolis* (1959) and Rossi's *Why Families Move* (1955). In that era economists' and planners' work on housing also included attention to demographic factors, as witnessed by Winnick's *American Housing and Its Use* (1957), Grigsby's *Housing Markets and Public Policy* (1963), Maisel's (1966) research on household formations and housing behavior, and David's housing chapter in *Family Composition and Consumption* (1962).

Reasons for the Separation

The climate of the times was important for encouraging this early association of demographic and housing research. The late 1940s and early 1950s were a period when the nation was seeking to recover from a decade and a half of depression and war. During this period housing construction lagged behind household growth (the difference made up by converting existing structures into multiple units). The return of GIs and the onset of the baby boom created awareness of a housing shortage and concern for family formation. In this climate it is not surprising that housing and family factors may have been viewed as more closely related. Investigators' attention was turned to this linkage when research studies were funded, both federally and locally, to investigate housing patterns and problems related to families.

By the mid-1960s suburban construction had eased concern about a housing shortage for the middle class, and new concerns emerged, principally about race and inequality of the disadvantaged. The new awareness about racial segregation and economic inequality seemed to supplant earlier concerns about more mundane relationships between families and housing. In this changed climate, demographers fell away from attention to housing.

In addition to the effects of the prevailing social and political climate, two other major explanations can be cited for the historic separation of population and housing analysis (Figure 1.1). One of the most important factors has been the obstacle imposed by limitations of the available data. Despite the wealth of data collected by the decennial censuses of population and housing, at least until the 1970s most researchers relied primarily upon standard published census reports. Housing questions were tabulated in separate reports or in separate sections from the population questions. (For example, census tract books contain a series of "P" tables, followed by a series of "H" tables.) Consequently, researchers could not easily use census data to explore housing-demographic relationships.

Indeed, all the early research cited above that linked population and housing questions made use of special-purpose data sets; hence, one person's work could not be easily replicated or extended by others. Without ready access to suitable data, the research tradition was stymied in development.

The third explanation for the historic separation is a set of institutional factors involving divisions of academia and the agendas of funding agencies. Housing is an interdisciplinary resarch topic not central to any one field in academia. Architecture, urban planning, geography, home eco-

Separation	Relinkage
Changed social climate: end of postwar middle-class family housing crisis, replaced by concern for race and equality	*Changed social climate:* affordability crisis for middle class and publicity of impacts of baby-boom generation
Obstacles of data limitations: publication of separate tables for housing and population data	*Joint housing-population data bases:* better tables and access to microdata records; advent of the Annual Housing Survey
Institutional barriers: divisions of academia and separate agendas of funding agencies	*Rise of applied research:* greater interest in urban research and applied demography; freedom from disciplinary constraints

Figure 1.1 Reasons for Separation and Relinkage of Demography and Housing

nomics, and urban economics, among others, each have addressed housing to some extent. However, this subject has been relatively absent from sociology and demography. Focusing on issues of population growth and structure central to their paradigm, demographers have not explored the linkage of demographic variables to nondemographic behaviors. Faculty members seeking tenure must publish research on topics acceptable to the most prestigious journals in the field, and sociology or demography journals have not traditionally welcomed housing topics.

The power of disciplinary peer pressure is well illustrated in an auto-biographical note Peter Rossi prefaced to a new edition of his seminal study *Why Families Move* (1980). A graduate student in sociology at the time, Rossi explains that he embarked upon this study with financial support from the Housing and Home Finance Agency, with sponsorship by Robert K. Merton, and with intellectual guidance from urban land economists associated with Columbia University's Institute for Urban Land Use and Housing Studies. Often asked why he ceased to work on the subject of residential mobility after so successful a completion of his study, Rossi (1980: 17–18) explains: ". . . the monograph was received with a distressing lack of enthusiasm from my sociological colleagues. One review berated me for turning into the 'Kinsey of the moving industry.' Another stressed the 'fact' that we all 'knew' that residential mobility was mainly a manifestation of social mobility and hence that my monograph was simply all wrong. . . . My colleagues either sneered at the book because of its crass empiricism or simply disputed its findings, and hence further pursuit of an understanding of residential mobility might drive me deep into professional obscurity." Subsequently, Rossi turned his mind to other topics more approved by his peers in sociology.

The eventual recognition received for his insightful work came from other disciplines, principally geography and economics.

Sources of federal funding also exercise a divisive influence, because different agencies approve proposals judged consistent with their mandates. Housing generally has been viewed as the province of the Department of Housing and Urban Development, although proposals with marginal emphasis on housing variables may be funded by other agencies. A particular factor has been the National Institute of Health's funding of the most influential population research centers. Housing has been a low-priority concern of NIH, and its research funds have exercised a powerful gravitational pull toward the central issues of fertility and mortality. Also, foundations concerned with "the population problem" have steered demographic research toward international studies of population growth and structure. Social reseearch on marriage and family behavior may be approved because it relates closely to fertility, and migration is sanctioned because it is one of the traditional demographic components and it shapes the age structure that generates fertility. In contrast, housing has a very slight relationship to fertility and is not a traditional demographic variable.

The influence of tradition is considerable. Even where demographers and sociologists have ventured into such topics as intraurban migration or city-suburb differentiation, housing factors are largely ignored because they are not present in the traditional literature that serves as source of precedent and theory. It bears remembering that the traditional literature was burdened by the earlier division in the published census data. Had housing data been linked with the population data, how might the theory-building process have yielded more support for including housing variables? Theories dating from an earlier era, hampered by earlier data limitations, continue to exercise an intellectual drag on current research.

Forces Relinking Population and Housing

In the past few years an incipient union has begun to form between demography and housing. Housing professionals have become increasingly aware of the importance of "demographics" for understanding their field. Also, real estate and business interests have begun to stress the need for better data about the populations in small areas of cities. The nature of the local housing stock—both existing housing units and those being built—is essential for understanding local populations. Demographers have increasingly opened their ranks to professionals trained in business, real estate, urban planning, and other disciplines. These professionals have sought to learn how demography can help them make better decisions. In turn, demographers have sought lessons in how the urban context and economic conditions can impact issues of traditional concern to them.

Several different forces since the mid-1970s have encouraged a re-linking of population and housing analysis (Figure 1.1.) Foremost, the social and political climate has changed once again. The "housing affordability crisis" emerging in the 1970s brought renewed attention to the issue of housing for the middle class. Related to this is the emergence of "gentrification," a new word to describe a radical reversal of urban decline in some neighborhoods (Laska and Spain, 1980; Nelson, 1988). This was the most publicized and dramatic housing change occurring in many urban areas, unsettling prior assumptions about the urban order. More generally, research on the residential mobility process attracted increasing attention among urban economists and urban geographers, introducing influential members of these disciplines to the importance of demographic variables (Goodman, 1978; Quigley and Weinberg, 1977; Moore, 1972).

At the same time, much greater awareness about population issues also emerged. The maturation of the baby-boom generation created substantial impacts on behaviors concentrated in specific age groups: for example, schooling, entry into the labor force, and entry into the housing market. So pronounced were the aggregate impacts of the baby-boom generation, that awareness of demography and family formation issues was promoted far beyond the boundaries of professional demography.

The result of this growing awareness was to broaden the appeal, the problem-relevance, of research linking social demography, urban population patterns, and housing, with the result that old boundaries were made less rigid. The search for knowledge of these changes, or solutions for newly developing problems, has led more persons to cross these boundaries. Thus, for example, geographers and urban planning researchers have begun to inquire about demographic changes in gentrifying neighborhoods (Gale, 1986), others have sought new insights into urban population structure (Alonso, 1980; Morrill, 1988), and economists have studied demographic effects on housing demand (Sternlieb and Hughes, 1986; Hendershott, 1988).

Two further changes have encouraged linkage between population and housing. Increasing availability of data bases linking housing and population variables has permitted scholars to explore relationships in ways never before possible. Special-subject reports issued from the 1970 and 1980 censuses in the United States provided extensive cross-tabulations of housing and demographic variables for the nation, and the series of reports *Metropolitan Housing Characteristics* made available published tables of joint demographic and housing characteristics for each metropolitan area. The barrier between the two halves of the census was lowered even further in the 1970s when researchers gained easy access to individual census records on computer tape, both for national and county-group samples, thus permitting unlimited cross-tabulation of housing and population variables. Parallel improvements have occurred in Canadian Census data bases (Miron, 1988: 14–16; Harris, 1987).

Of special note in the 1970s was commencement of the Annual Housing Survey (supervised by HUD's Division of Housing and Demographic Studies). This data base linked even greater housing information with demographic records for household members, and also added two longitudinal dimensions: information on the prior residence of movers entering the housing unit sample; and a file structure permitting analysis of changes over time occuring to both housing units and occupants. The national survey was converted to a biannual time frame after 1981 and renamed the American Housing Survey. In addition, in a series of metropolitan surveys, much smaller samples in some 35 cities were surveyed every three to four years on a rotating basis.

As a result of these data advances, in just a decade a body of work has emerged seeking to integrate demographic variables with housing research (and vice versa). The fruit of this work is featured in this book, and some credit must be given to the easing of data constraints.

The final factor leading to closer integration of housing and demographic research has been the explosive rise of business demography and other forms of applied demography. Whenever this research has been focused within urban areas (as opposed to a national-level focus), housing variables have loomed large as important explanatory variables. Housing is an important factor for classifying neighborhoods in sales-potential models, and it is key for preparing updated population estimates (via the housing-unit method). Much greater use of housing variables may be achieved; thus far, applied resarchers have been proceeding by trial and error, without benefit of much guidance from the traditional demographic literature or other theory. Ironically, this lack of theory may have enabled applied researchers to consider usage of housing variables more than others who are constrained by prior theory and disciplinary boundaries.

The time is at hand for more formal consideration of the linkages between population and housing. A good many researchers have discovered particular relationships, but these have yet to be organized into a coherent body of scholarship. The intent of this book is to examine some of these relationships, presenting a sampling of the newest work related to housing demography. Now that some of the former constraints separating population and housing have been eased, it remains to be seen whether a coherent intellectual basis can be developed for linking population and housing.

The Domain of Housing Demography

The emerging linkage of housing and demography has been spontaneous and experimental, not guided by a clear theory of how that linkage should proceed. It would be useful to have reference to a conceptual framework that encompasses the range of potentially related work. This introductory chapter seeks a classification model, or typology, for different types of studies that have explored the interface between population and housing. I will highlight underlying commonalities and stress potential interconnections.

Two Sides to the Interface

The interface between population and housing may be approached from either side. Using a population base we may inquire, What are the housing characteristics associated with different subgroups of the population? Alternatively, using a housing base we may inquire, What are the population or household characteristics of occupants in different types of units? The decennial census even asks some parallel questions for these two different bases. For example, the migration question asked of persons (Where did you live five years ago?) is paralleled by an occupancy-duration question (How long has the housing unit been occupied by the present household?).

Population-based Inquiry
The population-based inquiry is most common, answering questions such as: How likely are persons of a given age, income, and household size to live in particular types of housing units? For example, many investigators have explored the incidence of household formation (headship rates) or homeownership (ownership rates) across population subgroups. Although this would seem to be a decidedly demographic approach to research of the interface, it is also the approach most commonly adopted by economists (see, for example, Campbell, 1966; Carliner, 1975; Leppel, 1987).

Housing-based Inquiry
Alternatively, researchers have used a housing-unit base from which to explore the interface. From this perspective they have inquired about

the population characteristics of different types of housing units, exploring for example the variation of average household size or population age across the housing stock. Although this approach seems decidedly nondemographic, the major example of the approach is in fact demographers' housing-unit method of local population estimation (Smith and Lewis, 1983). With knowledge of the housing stock characteristics we can estimate the expected characteristics of occupants.

Importance of Geographic Scale
Both perspectives may be required for full understanding of the interface. An argument can be constructed that the linkage between population and housing is two-tiered, with the causation reversed between the tiers (Myers, 1987a,b). At the national or metropolitan level, population characteristics lead to demand for different types of housing. But at the local level, it is the presence of housing units of different types that induces population of different types to locate there.

The question of geographic scale thus becomes the deciding factor in explaining what approach researchers typically take toward investigation of the population-housing interface. Demographers, economists, and others who analyze national-level data sets are prone to use a population base for analysis. Demographers, geographers, urban planners, and others who analyze intraurban variations with local data are more prone to use a housing-unit base for analysis.

Demographers engaged in national-scale research have been able to ignore housing variables entirely, because these have little impact on their key concerns of fertility, mortality, and migration. But housing variables loom in importance for research of intraurban patterns, because housing types are distributed so unevenly across the urban landscape. Location within the city may not be as important as the key intervening variable: type of housing unit. For example, age-specific fertility rates are likely to be much higher in neighborhoods of single-family homes than in one-bedroom apartments. Mortality rates are likely to be much higher in nursing homes than in single-family homes. And migration rates within the city consist of residential moves directed for housing reasons, unlike long-distance moves, which are controlled by economic or career decisions.

Thus we might conclude that urban demography has much more to gain from including housing variables than does national-level demography. Yet the local-level analysis only exposes weaknesses latent, but disguised, in larger-scale analyses. All households live in housing units. The information on these housing characteristics is a relatively untapped resource for explaining household structure and other demographic behavior.

The Emerging Concept

The concept of housing demography is broad, including not only the housing behavior of populations but also the formation and composition of housing stocks. The concept integrates household compositional processes, mobility between housing units, location in urban subareas, and housing market characteristics. This integration is conceived within a longitudinal framework of population change, individual life course behavior, housing consumption adjustments via mobility processes, housing market changes, and changes within neighborhoods or other spatial subareas.

Three underlying precepts seem common to much research in the domain of housing demography. First, the housing demography concept places emphasis on *interconnections*. The housing stock and resident population are linked together, at the household level and in the aggregate. These interconnections include demographic, economic, temporal, and spatial dimensions, and are elaborated below.

Second, housing-demographic behavior is conceptualized within a temporal framework emphasizing *longitudinal processes*. Demography emphasizes the evolution of populations over time, viewing populations as aggregates of individual life histories and emphasizing processes of birth, death, and transformation between states. Because of housing units' durability and long life spans, housing stocks also may be viewed in this longitudinal perspective, observing their construction and change over time and studying the parallel dynamics of households occupying and moving through the units. Research emphasis on the timing of life course events and residential mobility processes serves to link individual histories to aggregate patterns of change.

A third precept is important for research of housing and population behavior in small areas. The immobility of housing units leads to an emphasis on *spatial patterns*. Houses are differentiated by type and fixed in space, and they attract particular types of households matched to their attributes. Thus we may argue that housing provides the essential substructure for small-area demography (Myers 1987b).

Dimensions of the New Field

A wide range of studies has explored the population and housing interface from either the population or housing-unit base. Although the goal of much research in this field is to define interconnections among population and housing processes, yielding a great variety of research, the field

of housing demography can be usefully classified with respect to four
foci:
- household formation and composition;
- housing choices;
- housing construction and inventory change; and
- spatial patterns and consequences.

The first and last of these types of study include both population- and
housing unit–based research, whereas the second is exclusively population based, and the third is exclusively housing unit based. Each type of
focus is briefly summarized below. Following that we will consider how
different research traditions have stressed interconnections among these
separate dimensions of housing demography.

Household Formation and Composition
The first dimension, housing formation and composition, overlaps substantially with a subfield of demography known as household demography and embraces other aspects of social demography as well. Whereas
most housing research begins with the behavior of households, the logi-
cal prior concern in this type of research is with the formation of households from a population. A focus on population brings analysts clearly
within the realm of demography, opening connections to other demographic behaviors.

Not only the formation of households but also their composition is of
concern in housing demography. Aggregate patterns of household composition have been changing markedly in recent years and are of interest for
many reasons. Major trends include the decline in household size, growth
in nonfamily households, declining presence of children, increase in
single-person households, rising numbers of elderly households, and the
surge in young renting households and first-time homebuyers.

From a population base, we may study how households are formed
and then how household composition affects their housing choices. In
turn, we may inquire how formation and composition are affected by the
supply of housing available. Alternatively, from a housing-unit base, we
may inquire how characteristics of the stock (such as size and type of
unit) induce occupancy of different types of households (defined by age
or family composition).

Housing Choices
Housing choices represent the second dimension of housing demography. Housing units provide not only shelter for households but also their
very definition, by virtue of the fact that people live in household groups
defined as separate, occupied dwelling units. The variety of different

housing units parallels, to a degree, the variety of different household types, although past associations have been weakening in recent years. Housing choices are most often defined along three dimensions: tenure (owning or renting), structure type (single-family, multifamily, or mobile home), and size of unit. The most common choices occur at key intersections of these three dimensions: for example, the large, owned single-family home, or the small, rented apartment. However, the past decade has witnessed a proliferation of housing choices—for example, condominiums have brought homeownership to small apartments, and the increasing quality of mobile homes has closed the gap with traditionally constructed single-family homes.

Attention to the nature of housing choices discloses an added dimension to demographic behavior that can be explored with demographic models applied to available data bases. The benefit of a demographic perspective on housing choices is the greater sensitivity to behavioral processes. Not only does a demographic perspective open a window on the dynamics of household formation and composition, it also adds a sharper awareness of temporal dynamics as individuals trace a path through a variety of living arrangements along their life courses. When combined with the lessons derived from research on residential mobility and on the economics of housing consumption, a much richer understanding of housing choices is derived.

Housing Construction and Inventory Change

The housing stock is an aggregate identity that parallels the population in many respects. The stock is a population of housing units, alterable through processes of construction, demolition, and conversion. The U.S. Bureau of the Census measures these changes through reports on the "components of inventory change." The housing stock expands in response to increments of demand, and once in place, it provides a continuing supply of residential opportunities for households. Housing choices (demand-side) are better understood in relation to constraints and opportunities of the housing stock (supply-side).

The composition of the housing stock and its processes of change are of keen interest in their own right. Housing makes up the largest single portion of our urban real estate, and the housing industry is a significant factor in the national economy. Many researchers have explored demographic relationships in order to develop better understanding of demand pressures shaping supply changes over the long term. In fact, this relationship is a complex interaction involving reciprocal impacts. Better understanding of the housing stock dimension and how it integrates with the others is an important feature of housing demography.

Spatial Patterns and Consequences

Space has a special importance for housing. Housing units are distributed at fixed locations in space and remain fixed, by and large, for several decades or more. Different types of housing units are distributed unevenly across the city. Each year a new layer of construction is added to the city, typically concentrated in relatively few locations at a time, and the existing stock may be altered by demolitions, conversions, and home improvements. As a result, the spatial distribution of different types of housing units slowly evolves over time.

In contrast to this relative fixity of housing, households move from house to house, and even those remaining in place may change composition rapidly through the aging of their members. The housing characteristics of neighborhoods strongly shape their resident populations. However, a reciprocal relationship also operates: citywide change in household formation and composition leads to change in market demand, which, in turn, shapes both future construction and use of the existing stock. One prominent example of this reciprocal impact is the gentrification, or neighborhood revitalization, process. Apartment construction in the suburbs to house young baby-boom households is another.

Applied demographers concerned with specific locations, such as those employed by business or government, have expressed keen interest in learning more about population dynamics in cities, suburbs, and smaller subareas. The spatial dimension of housing demography promises lessons of important practical significance.

Interconnections in Research Practice

These four dimensions within housing demography are interplayed in different combinations. At least six major types of study can be found within the scope of research we have defined for the housing demography field:

- household demography and life course;
- housing unit method;
- housing demand;
- residential mobility;
- neighborhood change; and
- construction forecasts and inventory change.

Some of these research topics center more closely than others on a single dimension of housing demography. But each of them illustrates important connections to be made across the various dimensions. Figure 1.2 illustrates the major interconnections in specific lines of inquiry.

	Household Formation and Composition	Housing Choices	Housing Construction and Inventory Change
Housing Choices	Household demography and life course Housing demand Residential mobility		
Housing Construction and Inventory Change	Construction forecasts Housing unit method	Construction forecasts Housing demand	
Spatial Patterns and Consequences	Neighborhood change	Residential mobility Neighborhood change	Construction forecasts Neighborhood change

Figure 1.2 Interconnections of Research Topics

Household Demography and Life Course

The research area of household demography and life course has been among the most self-contained of those intersecting the housing demography field. A major research question concerns the household-formation process (Burch, 1980; Michael et al., 1980; Pampel, 1983). Of special note are the independent but parallel efforts of Pitkin and Masnick (1980) and Ermisch and Overton (1985) to model formations based upon family nuclei or minimal household units.

Household demographers have also focused on the size of households (Kobrin, 1976) and the changing composition of families and households (Masnick and Bane, 1980; Sweet and Bumpass, 1987). Housing constraints on household composition are explored by Krivo and Mutchler (1986). And in this volume, Chew brings new contextual factors to bear on the issue of household formation by young unrelated adults: housing prices and the structure of urban economies.

Life course theory contributes a dynamic dimension to household demography by stressing longitudinal processes. Life course studies stress the interdependent timing of such events as leaving home, marrying, entering the labor force, and having children, giving special attention to changes in life course patterns between cohorts (Elder, 1975).

Housing variables have been less often incorporated into this research tradition, although the housing-choice dimension is being increasingly addressed. Kendig (1984a) analyzes retrospective residential histories within an explicit life course framework that integrates housing choices with other demographic events. Morrow-Jones (1988) uses a multistate model to measure the transition from renting to owning over the life cycle. Pitkin and Masnick (1980) construct an innovative cohort model for tracing housing choices over time by persons with different marital and fertility characteristics. Intercohort differences in homeownership achievement and intergenerational effects have been researched by Myers (1982), Henretta (1984), Kendig (1984b), and Chevan (1989). Myers (1985a,b) has stressed the changing role of wives' labor-force careers in homeownership achievement among married couples in different cohorts. Others have linked housing decisions to marriage patterns (Holmans, 1981; Ineichen, 1979) and fertility behavior (Ineichen, 1979; Hohm, 1984; Murphy and Sullivan, 1985). One particular demographic subgroup, the elderly, is the subject of a vast literature exploring its housing conditions, but only rarely has this housing research focused on demographic forces differentiating segments within the elderly (Goldstein, 1988).

Homeownership is a major subject of the studies cited above because of its importance in family asset accumulation and its significance for young adults' standard of living and perceived well-being. The connections to the Easterlin hypothesis are clear-cut and reviewed by Hohm (1984) and Myers (1985a,b), among others. Generational differences in conditions of homeownership achievement vary tremendously and bear close monitoring (see also Levy and Michel, 1985).

To date, however, the household demography and life course research traditions have rarely incorporated questions about either the housing stock or spatial patterns and consequences within urban areas (but see Kendig, 1984a). Instead, the integration of household demography and life course analysis with other dimensions of housing analysis is being urged by practitioners from other research traditions.

Housing-Unit Method
The housing-unit method is widely used in local areas to estimate and project local populations. The method utilizes an identity linking population and housing as the product of occupied housing units and average household size (plus population in group quarters). A method in applied demography, this research area has not benefited from contributions by the larger scholarly tradition in demography (but see Starsinic and Zitter, 1968; Smith and Lewis, 1980, 1983). The relative isolation of this research topic may reflect the demography profession's general lack of concern for small-area demography, urban demography, and intraurban variation.

The housing-unit method could benefit from better understanding of how household composition changes. And this research focus has a pivotal role to play in housing demography as it spans the household demography and housing stock dimensions of the field. Building on practical evidence supplied by Burchell and Listokin (1978), Myers and Doyle in this volume elaborate a systematic method for exploring the interconnections among household composition and housing stock characteristics.

Housing Demand

One of two major ways in which housing choices are expressed is through housing demand. (The other is residential mobility.) This research area is dominated by economists who employ two related research strategies. The first approach estimates demand by means of headship and homeownership rates (Campbell, 1966; Carliner, 1974, 1975; Apgar et al., 1985; Jaffe and Rosen, 1986; Myers, 1987a; Hendershott, 1988), often as a means of forecasting construction requirements. Headship rates are computed as the ratio of the number of heads (or householders) in a population subgroup relative to all persons in the subgroup, typically defined by age, sex, and marital status. Ownership rates are defined as the ratio of homeowners in a subgroup of households relative to all households in the subgroup. This method is consistent with other forms of demographic analysis.

More recently, economists have sought to explain the trends in household formation rates and homeownership rates by incorporating these within an economic decision-making framework. This has led to a second line of studies that utilize econometric modeling to test the effects of housing prices and supply on living arrangements (Smith et al., 1984; Hendershott and Smith, 1985; Goodman, 1986; Leppel, 1987; Haurin, Hendershott, and Ling, 1988).

A key tension between economics and demography concerns which set of variables is primary: do we control demographics and focus on economic parameters, or vice versa? The choice is important because it leads to alternative research designs and different model specifications. Although not their intent, research findings by economists generally have revealed how dominant are the demographic factors of age and marital status, whereas economic factors are shown to have smaller but significant effects. Given the dominant magnitude of the demographic effects, other effects are easily biased if models are misspecified with respect to the demographic factors.

In the present volume, John Pitkin describes a cohort economic model of housing consumption that is cast in a demographic temporal framework, but which estimates econometrically the effect of economic variables. This formulation appears to marry the strongest features of both paradigms.

Research in housing demography benefits from economists' demand research in several ways. First, economists urge analysts to view household formation and composition more broadly, understanding these household decisions within the broader process of housing choice. Most clearly seen in the case of unrelated individuals, when a person chooses where to live, he or she simultaneously considers the desire for companionship or privacy and the desire for type of housing unit, and evaluates the relative cash cost of alternative arrangements, subject to a budget constraint.

A second lesson is that the supply of housing constrains the decisions made by households. Higher vacancies and lower prices encourage smaller households, as does presence of smaller units in the stock.

Conversely, economic studies have stressed how demographically based demand leads to new construction and other changes in the housing stock. As observed earlier in this chapter, metropolitan-wide demographic changes can be used to forecast demand for different types of units, thus leading to adjustments in supply at the local (subarea) level.

In sum, the analysis of housing demand opens up important interconnections within housing demography, not all of which can be easily researched with available data. Nor can we easily address so many factors simultaneously. Nevertheless, it is important to recognize that specific interconnections exist, and for different purposes we would focus on selected aspects of this system.

Residential Mobility
The second way in which housing choices are expressed is through residential mobility. Because housing units are fixed in place, mobility is the relocation process by which households are observed making their choices. This research area is the most multidisciplinary of those contributing to housing demography, including work by sociologists (Rossi, 1955), demographers (Myers, McGinnis, and Masnick, 1967; Speare, 1970; Speare, Goldstein, and Frey, 1975; Chevan, 1971; Morrison, 1971; Long, 1972; Long and Spain, 1978; Zimmer, 1973), geographers (Clark, 1982; Moore, 1972; Golant, 1977), economists (Quigley and Weinberg, 1977; Goodman, 1978), and urban planners (Varady, 1984; Myers, 1983b).

This research topic has contributed several lessons. First, mobility researchers have found that demographic determinants dominate the mobility process, causing researchers to focus on the demographic composition of households, sometimes to the exclusion of housing variables (Frey and Kobrin, 1982). In its fullest expression, residential mobility research ties housing choices and spatial origins and destinations to household demography.

Second, the dynamic aspect of this research deserves special recognition, because mobility is inherently longitudinal and can be made consistent with life course analysis of change over time. Researchers have focused on transition matrices from housing type to housing type, contingent upon type of household (Golant, 1977; Moore and Clark, 1986). Kendig (1984a) demonstrates how to link mobility to a more general life course analysis, and Dahmann and McArthur (1987) pursue similar analysis with panel data from the ongoing Survey of Income and Program Participation.

A further contribution is the connection made with the housing stock and spatial patterns. Mobility researchers have shown the importance of new construction, tracing the resulting vacancy chains across household types (Lansing, Clifton, and Morgan, 1969). Geographers in particular have documented how mobility is expressed across subareas of the city, in response to the distribution of different housing attractions, and causing demographic change to occur in neighborhoods.

Neighborhood Change

Spatial patterns of housing and demographic change have been researched most commonly with reference to the issue of neighborhood patterns and change. These changes are the end result of residential mobility, but the scope is broader because it includes changes in both household composition and housing demand (Myers, 1983a). Neighborhood research seeks an aggregate perspective, but rather than focus on the population aggregate, it emphasizes changes occurring within the housing unit base. In fact, neighborhood research may be the most complex within housing demography, because it integrates all four dimensions.

At the base, housing stock characteristics are important for defining the opportunities available to households in a given spatial area. Either new construction or turnover in existing units creates vacancies for movers to choose among. The factors governing housing choices have been described by housing demand and residential mobility researchers. Prior to these choices, household formation and composition processes generate underlying demographic demand. Metropolitan-wide household changes lead to aggregate changes in demand, with differing implications for the attraction of particular neighborhoods. At the same time, household changes occur at the local level with the aging of residents already occupying neighborhoods (Myers, 1978; Johnson, 1980). Gober (1986a,b) compares household changes across neighborhoods and casts these in light of broader-scale changes in household composition.

Reflecting the two-tiered model described earlier, on the metropolitan scale we often assume that population change drives housing change. Not only must the total size of the stock expand to house the growing numbers of households, but also rapid changes in the types of households demand changes in the types of housing units. Yet at the local level, excepting the few zones currently being developed for the first time, the stock is fixed in place and is altered only very slowly. Thus the local stock constrains the population that can reside there.

Because of this complexity, few studies have adequately addressed these multiple dimensions of housing-demographic interaction in neighborhood research. Recourse is often made to a simple life-cycle model defining stages of neighborhood change (Hoover and Vernon, 1959; Birch, 1971; Bourne, 1981). An alternative method traces cohorts of neighborhoods defined by their decade of development (Duncan, Sabagh, and Van Arsdol, 1962; Guest, 1974). More elaborate matrix representations of dwelling turnover and population change in neighborhoods have been attempted by Moore (1978) among others. And in the present volume, Gober presses for a closer integration of neighborhood and household life course theory.

Construction Forecasts and Inventory Change

The final major research concentration in the housing demography field focuses on the housing stock. This line of research is more self-contained, just as research on household demography and life course, at the other extreme, is relatively self-contained. Yet we have already seen how elements of this research focus may be interconnected with other research questions. Research on the changing housing stock is an important resource contributing to other parts of the housing demography field.

In turn, there are several respects in which this research area can benefit from contributions by other aspects of housing demography. Chief among these are the ways in which changing demand contributes to new construction needs or to remodeling and neighborhood revitalization. Housing forecasters often make use of demographic analysis to project construction requirements (Campbell, 1966; Pitkin and Masnick, 1980; Jaffe and Rosen, 1986; Burns and Grebler, 1986; Myers, 1987a; Morrison, 1988). The various impacts created as the baby-boom generation passes through different age brackets have heightened forecasters' sensitivity to the importance of age and household composition, in addition to total population growth.

A second major area in which demographic analysis has contributed to research on the housing stock is via parallel expression. The housing stock is an aggregate like a population. Both are composed of members with long life spans, born into cohorts, and experiencing change over time. Adams (1970) demonstrates the importance of vintage analysis in housing that parallels cohort analysis in population. Myers (1984) analyzes how housing vintage interacts with turnover processes, changing household characteristics, and remodeling expenditures. In the present volume, Myers presents a temporal model for analyzing the filtering process impacting houses, neighborhoods, and their occupants.

The Census Bureau's method for describing changes in the housing stock is components of inventory change. Although relatively little work has been published on this type of analysis (Dahmann, 1982, 1983; Baer, 1986), it bears distinct parallels to demographic analysis (see also Gleeson, 1981, 1988; Merrett, 1986). In the present volume, Baer describes efforts to measure the mortality and life expectancy of dwelling units. And he shows the rich variation in qualitative changes that may occur to dwellings over time.

The Chapters in This Book

With this introduction to the field of housing demography, the reader is better able to appreciate the chapters selected here. Each is an outstanding example from one of the different branches of housing-demographic research.

The first group of chapters explores issues in household demography, relating these to housing variables among other factors. "Changes in the Life-Cycle Composition of the United States Population and the Demand for Housing," by demographer James A. Sweet, focuses on the changing life-cycle distribution of American households. Sweet reviews the demographic forces causing growth in some life-cycle categories and decline in others. Then Sweet analyzes the relationship of life-cycle stage to housing demand, outlining the pathway that bridges household demography and housing-demand analysis.

"Urban Industry and Young Nonfamily Households," by demographer Kenneth Chew, addresses the variation in household formation rates by young adults who are not married. Utilizing data collected for a large sample of metropolitan areas in 1970 and 1980, Chew searches for factors that can explain why young persons are more likely to live with relatives in some areas and more likely to live in independent households in others. He finds that lower housing prices are one important factor. But his major contribution is to link household formation patterns to the economic base, or industry structure, of different cities. White-collar or knowledge-intensive employment stimulates greater household formation.

"Housing Quality and Affordability among Female Householders," by sociologist and urban planner Daphne Spain, contrasts the experiences of female-headed households with married couples and male householders. Spain reviews the rapid growth of female householders, relating this to differences in income and location. Using data from the American Housing Survey, she then analyzes differences in homeownership achievement, housing affordability, and housing quality. Pronounced differences are found between household types.

"Age-Specific Population-per-Household Ratios: Linking Population Age Structure with Housing Characteristics," by Dowell Myers and demographer Alan Doyle, approaches household demography from a housing unit base. This chapter presents a detailed method for linking the age composition of households to the characteristics of their housing units. The authors explain how this method advances the basic concept of the housing unit method of local population estimation. They also tie the discovered patterns to theories of how households evolve over time in local areas.

The next group of chapters focuses more closely on the question of housing choices, although the demographic makeup of households remains a strong concern. These chapters adopt a life course, or cohort, perspective for explaining housing demand.

"A Life Course Perspective on Housing Attainment," by gerontologist Hal L. Kendig, presents a sweeping integration of household demography and housing choices. The emphasis is on changes in living arrangements and housing accommodations over the lifetimes of individuals. The life course perspective emphasizes housing careers and processes of change over time. Kendig outlines not only the impacts of housing choices on other life aspects but also the aggregate impacts of housing-career behavior on housing markets.

"Cohort Housing Trends in a Local Housing Market: The Case of Southern California," by demographer George S. Masnick, economist John R. Pitkin, and analyst John Brennan, describes an application of Pitkin and Masnick's (1980) cohort method for forecasting housing demand. The authors describe an analysis and projection of the number of households by type of unit and age of householder. This analysis is carried out for the service area of Southern California Edison and subareas. Of particular interest, the chapter contrasts the experiences of three counties with divergent compositions and growth trajectories. A series of graphs depicts how household cohorts' share in different housing types has been rising or falling.

"Housing Consumption of the Elderly: A Cohort Economic Model," by economist John R. Pitkin, integrates housing-demographic concepts with economic theory of housing consumption. Using a cross-SMSA sample observed in 1970 and again in the mid-1970s (with Annual Housing Survey data), Pitkin presents an econometric model of housing choices that is couched within a cohort framework. The analysis reveals strong lagged effects, because the elderly's subsequent choices are largely determined by prior choices. Pitkin also specifies the weaker effects of income and area housing prices in shaping subsequent choices. The chapter provides strong economic support for the cohort method of forecasting housing consumption.

The third group of chapters addresses spatial and temporal issues surrounding the housing stock and patterns of housing choice and household composition.

"Housing and Households in American Cities: Structure and Change in Population Mobility—1974–1982," by geographers Eric G. Moore and W. A. V. Clark, focuses on both stability and change in the structure of residential flows within metropolitan areas. Using the very rich data from the metropolitan files of the Annual Housing Survey, they examine the degree of variability in both the magnitude of flows and the reasons for moving among sectors of the housing market in six cities over three time periods. They find considerable stability in the general structure of flows over space and time, but there is a progressive erosion of the role of voluntary housing adjustment, particularly among renters, as a primary motivator of local mobility.

"The Urban Demographic Landscape: A Geographic Perspective," by geographer Patricia Gober, examines the territorial properties of household size, composition, and change. Gober reviews alternative theories of intraurban residential location and then contrasts these theories with empirical patterns observed in U.S. cities. She exposes a deficiency in the ability of contemporary theory to link national changes in household structure to local area variation and change, much of which corresponds to life course changes in resident households.

"Aging of the Housing Stock and Components of Inventory Change," by planning professor William C. Baer, addresses the demography of the physical housing stock. The components of inventory change used by the Bureau of the Census are analogous to components of population change. Baer reviews the literature on housing depreciation and mortality. He then presents data measuring qualitative changes in the use of units as they age: subdivision, merger, change to a nonresidential use, or demolition. It is important to grasp these changes in the physical stock because they undergird household and population changes. At a very practical level, it bears remembrance that population survey data are derived from a housing-unit sample frame that is subject to the changes Baer describes.

"Filtering in Time: Rethinking the Longitudinal Behavior of Neighborhood Housing Markets," by Dowell Myers, applies the three-dimensional, demographic concept of time (age, period, and cohort) to traditional questions of filtering. Filtering is the well-known longitudinal process by which older houses shift from one user group to another, often "trickling down" from rich to poor. This chapter reassesses traditional theory, exposing the fallacy of interpreting age cross-sections as defining a life-cycle model of filtering stages. Variations in period effects (economic forces, demographic changes, technology changes, and other historical conditions) create distinct differences between the cohorts of dwellings, or vintages, constructed in different eras. The chapter proposes a more explicit temporal conceptual model for analyzing filtering, and outlines its application to specific research problems.

The concluding chapter, "Future Research in Housing Demography," outlines a research agenda addressing 10 different topic areas. Research issues are framed both in relation to the chapters of this book, extending the current boundaries of knowledge, and also in the context of their potential acceptance to agencies sponsoring research.

Summary

The chapters presented here are but a sampling of work related to housing demography. Perhaps another two dozen skilled researchers are active in this field; many of their names are cited in the references that follow.

Each of the authors here has presented his or her own interpretation of housing demography, and the reader will see how wide is the variation. By collecting these disparate contributions and highlighting some underlying theory, the book aims to stimulate growth of a more coherent paradigm.

Through fostering a shared identity—and a common name—the book strives to create a signpost for kindred travelers in this research realm. The nucleus presented here is but a beginning that begs for further research. We hope others may be inspired by these efforts and use them as a platform for building improved investigations in the field of housing demography.

References

Adams, J. S. 1970. The residential structure of midwestern cities. *Annals, Association of American Geographers* 60:37–62.

Alonso, W. 1980. The population factor and urban structure. Pp. 32–51 in A. P. Solomon (ed.), *The Prospective City*. Cambridge, Mass.: MIT Press.

Apgar, W. C., Jr., et al. 1985. *The Housing Outlook: 1980–1990.* New York: Praeger.

Baer, W. C. 1986. The shadow market in housing. *Scientific American* 255(5, November):29–35.

Birch, D. L. 1971. Toward a stage theory of urban growth. *Journal of the American Institute of Planners* 37:78–87.

Bourne, L. S. 1981. *The Geography of Housing.* New York: John Wiley.

Burch, T. K. 1980. The index of overall headship: A simple measure of household complexity standardized for age and sex. *Demography* 17:25–38.

Burchell, R. W., and D. Listokin. 1978. *The Fiscal Impact Handbook.* New Brunswick, N.J.: Rutgers University, Center for Urban Policy Research.

Burns, L. S., and L. Grebler. 1986. *The Future of Housing Markets.* New York: Plenum Press.

Campbell, B. O. 1966. *Population Change and Building Cycles.* Urbana, Ill.: Bureau of Economic and Business Research.

Carliner, G. 1974. Determinants of home ownership. *Land Economics* 50:109–119.

Carliner, G. 1975. Determinants of household headship. *Journal of Marriage and the Family* 37:28–38.

Chevan, A. 1971. Family growth, household density and moving. *Demography* 8:451–458.

Chevan, A. 1989. Growth of home ownership: 1940–1980. *Demography* 26:249–266.

Clark, W. A. V. 1982. Recent research on migration and mobility: A review and interpretation. *Progress in Planning* 18:1–56.

Dahmann, D.C. 1982. *Housing Opportunities for Black and White Households: Three Decades of Change in the Supply of Housing.* Center for Demographic Studies, CDS-80-6. Washington, D.C.: U.S. Bureau of the Census.

Dahmann, D. C. 1983. Racial differences in housing consumption during the 1970s: Insights from a components of inventory change analysis. *Urban Geography* 4:203–222.

Dahmann, D.C., and E. K. McArthur. 1987. *Geographic Mobility and the Life Course: Moves Associated with Individual Life Events.* SIPP Working Paper Ser. No. 8720. Washington, D.C.: U.S. Bureau of the Census.

David, M. 1962. *Family Composition and Consumption.* Amsterdam: North-Holland.

Duncan, B., and P. Hauser. 1959. *Chicago: Housing a Metropolis.* Chicago: University of Chicago Press.

Duncan, B., G. Sabagh, and M. D. Van Arsdol, Jr. 1962. Patterns of city growth. *American Journal of Sociology* 67:418–429.

Elder, G. H. 1975. Age differentiation and the life course. Pp. 165–190 in *Annual Review of Sociology* 1. Palo Alto, Calif.: Annual Reviews.

Ermisch, J. F., and E. Overton. 1985. Minimal household units: A new approach to the analysis of household formation. *Population Studies* 39:33–54.

Frey, W. H., and F. E. Kobrin. 1982. Changing families and changing mobility: Their impact on the central city. *Demography* 19:261–278.

Gale, D. E. 1986. Demographic research on gentrification and displacement. *Journal of Planning Literature* 1:14–29.

Gleeson, M. E. 1981. Estimating housing mortality. *Journal of the American Planning Association* 47:185–194.

Gleeson, M. E. 1985. Estimating housing mortality from loss records. *Environment and Planning A* 17:647–659.

Gober, P. 1986a. How and why Phoenix households changed: 1970–1980. *Annals of the Association of American Geographers* 76:536–549.

Gober, P. 1986b. Homogeneity versus heterogeneity in household structure: The recent experience of twenty U.S. cities. *Environment and Planning A* 18:715–727.

Golant, S. M. 1977. The housing tenure adjustments of the young and the elderly. *Urban Affairs Quarterly* 13:95–108.

Goldstein, A. 1988. How Are the Elderly Housed: New Data from the 1984 Survey of Income and Program Participation. Paper presented at the annual meeting of the Population Association of America, New Orleans.

Goodman, J. L., Jr. 1978. *Urban Residential Mobility: Places, People, and Policy.* Washington, D.C.: The Urban Institute.

Goodman, J. L., Jr. 1986. *Economic Determinants of Household Formations and Living Arrangements.* Working Paper No. 66. Washington, D.C.: Board of Governors of the Federal Reserve System.

Grigsby, W. G. 1963. *Housing Markets and Public Policy.* Philadelphia: University of Pennsylvania Press.

Guest, A. M. 1974. Neighborhood life cycles and social status. *Economic Geography* 50:228–243.

Harris, R. 1987. Describing the geography of housing in Canada: The HIFE files. *The Canadian Geographer* 31:262–267.

Haurin, D. R., P. H. Hendershott, and D. C. Ling. 1988. Homeownership rates of married couples: An econometric investigation. *Housing Finance Review* 7:85–108.

Hendershott, P. H. 1988. Household formation and homeownership: Impacts of demographic, sociological and economic factors. *Housing Finance Review* 7:201–224.

Hendershott, P. H., and M. Smith. 1985. Household formations. Pp. 183–203 in P. H. Hendershott (ed.), *The Level and Composition of Household Saving.* Cambridge, Mass.: Ballinger.

Henretta, J. C. 1984. Parental status and child's home ownership. *American Sociological Review* 49:131–140.

Hohm, C. F. 1984. Housing aspirations and fertility. *Sociology and Social Research* 68:326–363.

Holmans, A. 1981. Housing careers of recently married couples. *Population Trends* 24:10–14.

Hoover, E. M., and R. Vernon. 1959. *Anatomy of a Metropolis.* Cambridge, Mass.: Harvard University Press.

Ineichen, B. 1979. Housing factors in the timing of weddings and first pregnancies. Pp. 127–140 in C. Harris (ed.), *The Sociology of the Family: New Directions for Britain*. Monograph 28. Totowa, N.J.: Rowman and Littlefield.

Jaffee, D. M., and K. T. Rosen. 1986. *The Demand for Housing Units*. New York: Salomon Brothers.

Johnson, D. C. 1980. Age waves in cities. *The Social Science Journal* 17:87–95.

Johnston, R. J. 1971 *Urban Residential Patterns*. New York: Bell.

Kendig, H. L. 1984a. Housing careers, life cycle and residential mobility: Implications for the housing market. *Urban Studies* 21:271–283.

Kendig, H. L. 1984b. Housing tenure and generational equity. *Ageing and Society* 4:249–272.

Kobrin, F. E. 1976. The fall in household size and the rise of the primary individual. *Demography* 13:127–138.

Krivo, L. J., and J. E. Mutchler. 1986. Housing constraint and household complexity in metropolitan America: Black and Spanish-origin minorities. *Urban Affairs Quarterly* 21:389–409.

Lansing, J. B., C. W. Cllfton, and J. N. Morgan. 1969. *New Homes and Poor People: A Study of Chains of Moves*. Ann Arbor: University of Michigan, Institute for Social Research.

Laska, S. B., and D. Spain (eds.). 1980. *Back to the City: Issues in Neighborhood Renovation*. New York: Pergamon.

Leppel, K. 1987. Household formation and unrelated housemates. *The American Economist* 31:38–47.

Levy, F. S., and R. C. Michel. 1985. *The Economic Future of the Baby Boom*. Research report. Washington, D.C.: The Urban Institute.

Long, L. H. 1972. The influence of number and ages of children on residential mobility. *Demography* 9:371–382.

Long, L. H., and D. Spain. 1978. *Racial Succession in Individual Housing Units*. Current Population Reports, P-23, No. 71. Washington, D.C.: U.S. Bureau of the Census.

Maisel, S. J. 1966. Rates of ownership, mobility, and purchase. Pp. 76–108 in Real Estate Research Program (ed.), *Essays in Urban Land Economics in Honor of the 65th Birthday of Leo Grebler*. Los Angeles: UCLA, Real Estate Research Program.

Masnick, G. S., and M. J. Bane. 1980. *The Nation's Families: 1960–1990*. Boston: Auburn House.

Merrett, S. 1986. The required rate of new dwelling construction. *Environment and Planning A* 18:1531–1535.

Michael, R. T., et al. 1980. Changes in the propensity to live alone: 1950–76. *Demography* 17:39–56.

Miron, J. R. 1988. *Housing in Postwar Canada: Demographic Change, Household Formation, and Housing Demand*. Montreal: McGill-Queen's University Press.

Moore, E. G. 1972. *Residential Mobility in the City*. Resource Paper 13, Commission on College Geography. Washington, D.C.: Association of American Geographers.

Moore, E. G. 1978. The impact of residential mobility on population characteristics at the neighborhood level. Pp. 151–181 in W. A. V. Clark and E. Moore (eds.), *Population Mobility and Residential Change,* Studies in Geography No. 25. Evanston, Ill.: Northwestern University, Department of Geography.

Moore, E. G., and W. A. V. Clark. 1986. Stable structure and local variation: A comparison of household flows in four metropolitan areas. *Urban Studies* 23:185–196.

Morrill, R. L. 1988. Intra metropolitan demographic structure: A Seattle example. *Annals of Regional Science* 22:1–16.

Morrison, P. A. 1971. Chronic movers and future redistribution of population: A longitudinal analysis. *Demography* 8:171–184.

Morrison, P. A. 1988. *Demographic Factors Shaping the U.S. Market for New Housing.* Working Paper P-7467. Santa Monica: Rand Corporation.

Morrow-Jones, H. 1988. The housing life cycle and the transition from renting to owning a home in the U.S.: A multistate analysis. *Environment and Planning A* 20:1165–1184.

Murphy, M. J., and O. Sullivan. 1985. Housing tenure and family formation in contemporary Britain. *European Sociological Review* 1:230–243.

Myers, D. 1978. Aging of population and housing: A new perspective on planning for more balanced metropolitan growth. *Growth and Change* 9:8–13.

Myers, D. 1982. A cohort-based indicator of housing progress. *Population Research and Policy Review* 1:109–136.

Myers, D. 1983a. Population processes and neighborhoods. Pp. 113–132 in P. L. Clay and R. Hollister (eds.), *Neighborhood Policy and Planning.* Lexington, Mass.: Lexington Books.

Myers, D. 1983b. Upward mobility and the filtering process. *Journal of Planning Education and Research* 2:101–112.

Myers, D. 1984. Turnover and filtering in postwar single-family houses. *Journal of the American Planning Association* 50:352–358.

Myers, D. 1985a. Wives' earnings and rising costs of homeownership. *Social Science Quarterly* 66:319–329.

Myers, D. 1985b. Reliance upon wives' earnings for homeownership attainment: Caught between the locomotive and the caboose. *Journal of Planning Education and Research* 4:167–176.

Myers, D. 1987a. Extended forecasts of housing demand in metropolitan areas: The coming downturn. *Appraisal Journal* 55:266–278.

Myers, D. 1987b. The Housing Substructure of Small-Area Demography. Paper presented at the annual meeting of the Population Association of America, Chicago.

Myers, G. C., R. McGinnis, and G. S. Masnick. 1967. The duration of residence approach to a dynamic stochastic model of internal migration: A test of the axiom of cumulative inertia. *Eugenics Quarterly* 14:121–126.

Nelson, K. P. 1988. *Gentrification and Distressed Cities.* Madison: University of Wisconsin Press.

Pampel, F. C. 1983. Changes in the propensity to live alone: Evidence from consecutive cross-sectional surveys, 1960–76. *Demography* 20:433–448.

Pitkin, J. R., and G. S. Masnick. 1980. *Projections of Housing Consumption in the U.S., 1980–2000, by a Cohort Method.* Annual Housing Survey Studies No. 9. Washington, D.C.: U.S. Government Printing Office.

Quigley, J. M., and D. H. Weinberg. 1977. Intra-urban residential mobility: A review and synthesis. *International Regional Science Review* 2:41–66.

Rossi, P. H. 1955. *Why Families Move: A Study in the Social Psychology of Urban Residential Mobility.* New York: Macmillan.

Rossi, P. H. 1980. *Why Families Move* (2d ed.). Beverly Hills: Sage.

Smith, L. B., et al. 1984. The demand for housing, household headship rates, and household formation: An international analysis. *Urban Studies* 21:407–414.

Smith, S. K., and B. B. Lewis. 1980. Some new techniques for applying the housing unit method of local population estimation. *Demography* 17:323–340.

Smith, S. K., and B. B. Lewis. 1983. Some new techniques for applying the housing unit method of local population estimation: Further evidence. *Demography* 20:407–413.

Speare, A., Jr. 1970. Homeownership, life cycle stage, and residential mobility. *Demography* 7:449–458.

Speare, A., Jr., S. Goldstein, and W. Frey. 1975. *Residential Mobility, Migration and Metropolitan Change.* Cambridge, Mass.: Ballinger.

Starsinic, D. E., and M. Zitter. 1968. Accuracy of the housing unit method in preparing population estimates for cities. *Demography* 5:475–484.

Sternlieb, G., and J. W. Hughes. 1986. Demographics and housing in America. Population Reference Bureau, *Population Bulletin* 41:1–34.

Sweet, J. A., and L. Bumpass. 1987. *American Families and Households.* New York: Russell Sage Foundation.

Varady, D. P. 1984. Residential mobility in the urban homesteading demonstration neighborhoods. *Journal of the American Planning Association* 50:346–351.

Winnick, L. 1957. *American Housing and Its Use: The Demand for Shelter Space.* New York: John Wiley and Sons.

Zimmer, B. G. 1973. Residential mobility and housing. *Land Economics* 48:344–350.

PART 1
LINKING HOUSING
CHARACTERISTICS WITH
HOUSEHOLD COMPOSITION

2 *James A. Sweet*

Changes in the Life-Cycle Composition of the United States Population and the Demand for Housing

Introduction

In this chapter I examine the relationship between changes in the family life-cycle composition of the United States population and the demand for housing of various types. I begin by reviewing recent trends in the demographic processes which determine the life-cycle distribution of the population (trends in marriage, cohabitation, and fertility). I then discuss recent change in the propensity of persons in various life-cycle positions to maintain a household. These demographic processes determine the distribution of households by family life-cycle stage. Households at different life-cycle stages tend to have different housing needs. Consequently, changes in the family life-cycle distribution affect the housing needs of the population. The next section describes the housing-type distributions of households at different life-cycle stages. Finally, I examine how the life-cycle-specific distribution of housing type changed during the 1970s and how the changing distribution of households by life-cycle stage affected aggregate housing demand.

This chapter is not about housing changes of individuals or families as they move through their family life cycles; it is instead about the relationship between aggregate change in the family life-cycle distribution and

James A. Sweet is Professor of Sociology at the Center for Demography and Ecology, University of Wisconsin–Madison, Madison, Wisconsin 53706.

aggregate demand for housing. Subsequent chapters take up in more detail the housing experience of two important household types: young unmarried adults without children (chapter by Ken Chew) and female householders (chapter by Daphne Spain).

Overview of the Relationship among Demographic Processes, the Family Life Cycle, and Housing Demand

We view the relationship among demographic process, the family life cycle, and housing demand as follows:

—A population has a size and an age distribution, both of which may change over time.

—Cohorts marry (and separate, divorce, become widowed, and remarry) according to an age schedule. They also reproduce according to an age–marital status schedule. All these schedules may, and do, change over time.

—Given the age structure and the pattern of marriage (and separation, divorce, and widowhood) and reproduction, the population has a family life-cycle stage distribution.

—There is a living-arrangements distribution for each life-cycle stage, the most important component of which for our purposes is the propensity to maintain a household (the headship, or householder, rate). These headship rates may change over time.

—The distribution of the population by life-cycle stage and the headship rate associated with each stage determine the life-cycle distribution of householders. It is, thus, useful to think of the population of households as having a family life-cycle stage distribution represented by the life-cycle stage distribution of householders.

—Each life-cycle stage has a unique pattern of housing preferences and choices, related to differences in such things as size of household, economic resources, and "life style." The life-cycle distribution of the population, combined with a set of life-cycle stage-specific housing choices, produces a distribution of households by housing type. (As an example, in this chapter, I will use a housing-type classification that distinguishes between renters and owners and, for renters, among different numbers of units in the structure. Other characteristics of housing could also be considered in the same framework.) Thus, changes over time in the structure of housing demand may result from any of these factors: change in age structure of the population; changes in the rates of marriage, marital disruption, widowhood, and fertility; changes in living arrangements of persons in particular life-cycle stages; and changes in the kind of housing chosen by persons in each life-cycle stage and living arrangement.

The Family Life Cycle

Social demographers have found the "family life cycle" to be a useful way to think about how changes in the rate and age pattern of demographic processes cumulate to affect the life pattern of individuals, as well as the way in which changes in these demographic processes have macro- or societal effects.[1]

What do we mean by the "family life cycle"? Marriage, childbearing, the departure of children from the parental household, and marital dissolution by either separation (and divorce) or widowhood are among the most significant life events of individuals. Frequently, an individual's entire pattern of everyday life is transformed as a result of these life-cycle transitions. (Perhaps retirement from the work force is another similarly important event, but one which is not the result of a family transition.)

Housing changes are often associated with family transitions. In many cases space requirements change as a result of family transitions. Family transitions are also associated with changes in life activities (life style), which may affect the priority placed on various housing and location characteristics. Further, an individual's or family's economic resources and the demands on those resources often change as a result of family transitions.

We are not assuming that there is a single pattern of life-cycle transitions that every member, or even a great majority of the members, of a society makes. There is a great deal of variation in the family life experience of individuals in our society. Some individuals never marry; some experience marital separation and divorce; others marry and live as couples until the death of one spouse. Many persons marry more than once in a lifetime. Some are childless; others have children in varying numbers. In addition, there is variation in the ages at which family transitions occur in the lives of individuals, as well as in the sequencing of these transitions.

We often think of a population's age and sex structure and its marital-status distribution as important characteristics of the demographic and social structure. The distribution of a population with respect to life-cycle stages is also an important structural characteristic, and one which

---

1. Reviews of the family life-cycle literature are found in Young, 1977a, and Rodgers, 1977. Cuisenier and Segalen, 1977, is a collection of papers on various aspects of the changing family life cycle in Western societies. Sweet (1977) discusses the variety of ways that the family life cycle has been used in social demography. The literature on demographic events structuring individuals' lives derives from the work of Paul Glick (see Glick, 1947; Glick and Parke, 1965; Spanier and Glick, 1980; and Norton, 1983). Critiques of the life-cycle concept and its uses include Trost, 1977; Nock, 1979; Spanier, Sauer, and Larzelere, 1979; and Klein and Aldous, 1979. Other applications of the life-cycle concept in social demography include Taeuber and Sweet, 1976, and Winsborough, 1978.

is particularly significant when thinking about housing patterns and housing demand.

Much of the recent literature on the family life cycle deals with the life cycles or life courses of individuals. Life-cycle stage can also be thought of as a characteristic of family households (at least simple nuclear-family households). This is what Glick did in his original work using the concept. Classifying households by family life-cycle stage becomes problematic in the case of complex extended-family households, as well as nonfamily households, because such households may include adult members at very different individual family life-cycle stages. However, because nonnuclear families are quite rare in the United States, and because about 85 percent of all nonfamily households consist of only one member, it seems reasonable to classify these households, as well as nuclear-family households, by the life-cycle stage of the householder.

There is no universally agreed-upon classification of the family life cycle.[2] The life-cycle classification used here differentiates on the basis of the following:

—marital status, distinguishing among the never married, currently married, and formerly married (separated, divorced, widowed, and married with spouse absent for reasons other than separation);[3]

—presence or absence of children age 18 or younger, and age of the youngest child, for the currently and formerly married. (To be precise, households are classified by presence of "own children" of the householder—i.e., biological, adopted, and stepchildren.); and

—age for those with no children under age 18.[4] (I arbitrarily use age 60 as the lower bound for what I call the elderly population.)

Change in the Life-Cycle Composition of the United States Population

Table 2.1 shows the life-cycle stage distribution of the adult population of the United States in 1960, 1970, and 1980. The rate of change in the total

2. There are many classifications of the family life cycle in the literature. In addition to the works cited above, see Lansing and Kish, 1957; McLeod and Ellis, 1983; and Murphy and Staples, 1979.

3. We do not consider unmarried cohabitation in this life-cycle classification. This is a serious limitation, given the current prevalence of cohabitation, especially among young adults. Bumpass and Sweet (1989) estimate that current rates of cohabitation imply that a majority of young persons today will cohabit prior to their first marriages. A significant share of children who appear to be living in one-parent families are actually living with a cohabiting parent. In future work, cohabitation will have to be taken into account in classifying the life-cycle stage of the population.

4. I arbitrarily use the age of the husband to classify married couples. I could have chosen the age of the wife; it would have made little difference.

Table 2.1   Percentage Distribution of the Population Aged 18 and Older, by Family
Life-Cycle Stage, 1960–80

Life-Cycle Stage	1960	1970	1980	Percentage Change in Absolute Number[a]	
				1960–70	1970–80
Never married					
<30	8.5	11.6	15.6	57.1	64.0
30–44	2.5	1.9	2.5	−9.6	56.6
45–59	1.9	1.5	1.1	−7.0	14.0
Married couple with children under age 18 Youngest child's age					
<6	23.1	18.2	14.0	−9.7	−5.5
6–11	10.1	10.7	8.8	22.7	0.5
12–17	7.6	7.7	7.5	17.4	19.2
Married couple, no children under age 18 Husband's age					
<30	2.9	4.1	4.4	64.9	30.2
30–44	3.8	2.6	3.0	−22.8	46.0
45–59	11.5	11.4	10.8	15.3	15.2
Formerly married with children under age 18 Youngest child's age					
<6	0.9	1.1	1.0	37.5	15.0
6–11	0.6	0.9	1.1	65.7	52.1
12–17	0.7	0.8	1.1	38.7	58.1
Formerly married, no children under age 18					
<30	0.9	1.3	1.8	57.6	71.3
30–44	1.6	1.4	2.3	−0.9	102.3
45–59	3.1	3.0	3.1	11.0	24.7
Elderly (age ≥60)					
Never married	1.6	1.7	1.3	19.7	−5.2
Married couple	11.1	11.9	12.4	23.6	27.2
Formerly married	7.5	8.2	8.3	26.7	24.0
Total	100.0	100.0	100.0	15.6	22.3

Note: In this and the following tables, some columns and rows may not add to the exact
total of 100.0 because of rounding.

[a]Percentage change in the number of persons in the life-cycle stage.

number of persons in each family life-cycle category is shown in the last two columns. Focusing on the 1970–80 decade, there was great variation in rates of growth, ranging from a decline of 6 percent in the number of married couples with preschool-age children to an increase of slightly over 100 percent for formerly married persons aged 30–44 with no children in the household. Other categories growing very rapidly during the 1970s (with increases of 40 percent or more) include: never-married persons under age 30; never married persons aged 30–44; childless married couples with husbands aged 30–44; formerly married persons with youngest child aged 6–11; formerly married persons with youngest child aged 12–17; and formerly married persons under age 30 with no children.

Notice also that the 1960s growth rates of many of the life-cycle groups were very different from the 1970s rates.

The first three columns of the table show the percentage distribution of the population by life-cycle stage at several points in time. This table underscores the fact that many of the categories that have experienced rapid growth in the past decade or so remain relatively small components of the total population. For example, the total of the three categories of formerly married persons with children constitutes only about 3 percent of the adult population, even after several decades of rapid growth.

Table 2.1 shows that over the past two decades there has been:
—a large increase in each decade in the proportion of the adult population that is under age 30 and never married. In 1960, 1 adult in 12 was in this life-cycle stage; by 1980 it was more than 1 in 7.
—a large decrease during each decade in the proportion of the adult population that was married with a preschool-age child. This segment of the population decreased from almost one adult in four in 1960 to one adult in seven in 1980.
—little change in the proportion married with school-age children;
—little change during either decade in the proportion of the adult population that was formerly married with children under 18 in the household;
—only a slight increase in the proportion of the adult population that was formerly married, under age 60, with no children under 18 in the household; and
—little change in the proportion of the adult population in the three elderly life-cycle stages.

Demographic Changes Underlying
the Population's Changing Family Life-Cycle Distribution

In this section we review recent changes in the demographic processes underlying the changing life-cycle stage distribution of the population. I

Table 2.2 Actual and Projected Percentage Change in the Population, by Age, for Decades from 1960–70 to 1990–2000

	1960–1970	1970–1980	1980–1990	1990–2000
<5	−16.6	−4.1	16.7	−8.2
5–13	11.2	−15.2	3.6	6.8
14–17	41.9	1.4	−19.8	18.8
18–24	53.2	22.8	−15.0	−4.6
25–34	10.5	48.5	15.8	−16.3
35–44	−4.4	11.8	46.2	15.6
45–64	16.0	5.9	4.4	31.1
≥65	20.6	27.9	23.3	10.2
Total	13.4	11.0	9.6	7.3

Source: Spencer, 1984:table E.

[a]1990 and 2000 numbers are based on the "medium" set of assumptions, which in the case of fertility assumes a cohort total fertility rate of 1.9.

will briefly discuss changes in the age structure and in patterns of first marriage, cohabitation, marital disruption, remarriage, and fertility. Finally, because the effects of these demographic changes on household structure are also influenced by the choice of living arrangements, I discuss changing householder (or headship) rates of the various life-cycle groups.[5]

Age Structure

The age distribution of the population is determined primarily by fertility patterns during the preceding decades. American fertility declined continuously from the late nineteenth century through the 1940s. This trend was reversed in the mid-1940s when we experienced the baby boom—about two decades of rather high fertility. There was a rapid decline in fertility in the late 1960s, and since the early 1970s, fertility has remained at or slightly below the level necessary for the population to replace itself.

Table 2.2 shows percentage changes in the size of each age group from decade to decade. Because of the decline in fertility, children are a smaller proportion of the population now than in the past. In the 1980s

5. Reviews of recent family change include Westoff, 1987; Sweet and Bumpass, 1987; Cherlin, 1981; Thornton and Freedman, 1983; Davis, 1985; and Schoen et al., 1985.

the proportion of the population in the teen ages has declined further. The large baby-boom cohort can be seen gradually aging. Note the very large growth rates of 14–24-year-olds in the 1960s, 25–34-year-olds in the 1970s, 35–44-year-olds in the 1980s, and 45–64-year-olds in the 1990s.

There has been great variation from decade to decade in the growth rates of various age groups. For example, consider 18–24-year-olds, an age group responsible for a large share of new household formation. This age group increased by 53 percent during the 1960s, but during the next decade the increase was only 23 percent. The number of 18–24-year-olds will decline by 15 percent in the 1980s and by 5 percent in the 1990s.

First-Marriage Patterns

During the past two decades marriage ages have increased at a rapid rate.[6] There was a "marriage boom" at the same time as the baby boom following World War II. Marriage ages dropped and remained very low for two decades, with a median first-marriage age for women of about 20 years. Beginning in the mid-1960s, women began to delay marriage, and by the late 1970s their age pattern of first marriage was again very similar to what it had been in the decades before 1940. Marriage ages of men have also risen, but the rise began about a decade later. The rise in first-marriage age has continued for both men and women through the late 1980s.

Americans do not seem to be foregoing marriage entirely. It appears that most young men and women will marry. They will simply do it later in their lives. Rodgers and Thornton (1985) estimate that perhaps 10 percent of recent cohorts will never marry, up from about 5 or 6 percent of the cohorts that preceded them. Blacks are the only subpopulation that appears to be moving toward a high level of nonmarriage. This is especially true of black women; in 1980, for example, 30 percent of 29-year-old black women had never been married.[7]

To get a more quantitative sense of the magnitude of the change in marriage behavior, Table 2.3 shows the proportion of men and women

6. Demographic studies of recent American marriage patterns and trends include Sweet and Bumpass, 1987:chapters 2 and 3; Cherlin, 1981; Espenshade, 1985; Rodgers and Thornton, 1985; and Goldman, Westoff, and Hammerslough, 1984. Several notable sociological studies of marriage patterns include Cherlin, 1980; Thornton and Freedman, 1982; and Waite and Spitze, 1981. For discussions of marriage patterns in other industrial countries see Festy, 1980; and Westoff, 1987.

7. For discussion of the changing patterns of black Americans, see Sweet and Bumpass, 1987:chapters 2 and 3; Espenshade, 1985; and Cherlin, 1981.

Table 2.3.   Percentage of Persons Never Married, by
            Age and Sex, 1960–86

	1960	1970	1980	1986
Women				
Age 19	59.6	70.5	77.6	84.9
21	35.1	44.4	59.7	67.8
24	15.6	19.9	33.5	41.6
29	8.7	9.3	14.6	23.7
Men				
Age 19	87.3	87.8	90.9	94.8
21	63.3	66.4	77.2	83.4
24	33.5	33.8	50.0	57.2
29	15.9	14.2	24.0	31.4

who were never married at ages 19, 21, 24, and 29 at each decennial
census since 1960 and for 1986 (from the Current Population Survey).

Cohabitation

There has been a rapid increase in the number and proportion of young,
unmarried people living together in a cohabiting relationship.[8] In the
absence of a direct count of the number of cohabiting couples, we rely
on estimates made from the decennial census and the Current Population Survey information on household composition and relationship to
householder. (A cohabiting couple is defined as an opposite-sex pair of
unrelated persons living in a two-adult household.) In the 1960 census
there were about 300,000 such couples; this number increased only modestly to about 450,000 by 1970. However, during the 1970s there was a
rapid increase to 1,800,000 in 1980. It appears that the number has
increased further during the 1980s to about 2.6 million couples in 1988.

In the mid-1980s about 2.5 percent of all adults (persons aged 18 and
older), 6 percent of all unmarried adults, and 8 percent of all unmarried
persons aged 18–64 were cohabiting. Cohabiting persons tend to be
quite young. About a third of all cohabiting women were under age 25
and three-fifths were under age 30; men were somewhat older, with

8. Studies of trends and patterns of cohabitation in the United States using census and
Current Population Survey data include Sweet and Bumpass, 1987:chapter 6; and Spanier,
1983. Recent sample surveys have added greatly to our knowledge of cohabitation patterns. See Bumpass and Sweet, 1989; Bumpass, Sweet, and Cherlin, 1989; Tanfer, 1987;
and Thornton, 1988. Studies of cohabitation in other industrial countries include Bennett,
Blanc, and Bloom, 1986; and Balakrishnan et al., 1987.

about a quarter under age 25 and half under age 30. Slightly fewer than half of cohabiting men and women had never been married. In the cross-section about 1 in 6 separated or divorced persons and 1 in 12 never-married persons aged 20–35 was cohabiting. Slightly fewer than a third of cohabiting couples have children living with them.

Marital Disruption

There has been a nearly continuous increase in the rate of divorce for at least the last century.[9] In the middle of the last century 1 marriage in 14 ended in divorce; by the 1920s this proportion had increased to 1 in 6, and by the late 1970s it was 1 in 2. The most recent set of estimates, based on separation rates in 1984, implies that 12 percent of first marriages will end in separation by the 2d anniversary; 23 percent by the 5th anniversary; 36 percent by the 10th anniversary; and 48 percent by the 20th anniversary.

There has been some discussion in the media suggesting that the trend in marital instability has reversed. Some have speculated that a resurgence of family values has begun. In fact, there does not appear to have been a reversal in the trend in marital instability, although the rate of increase has probably slowed. The drop in the absolute number of divorces seems to be due to the decline in the number of marriages, not to a decline in the rate at which marriages of a given duration are disrupting (Castro Martin and Bumpass, 1989).

Remarriage

Most persons who experience the termination of their marriages by separation or divorce remarry.[10] In the 1970s, 46 percent of women remarried within 5 years, and 64 percent within 10 years of separation. For men, the proportions were even higher: 57 and 78 percent, respectively. For both sexes remarriage proportions were higher the younger the age at marital separation (Sweet and Bumpass, 1987: chapter 5). During the 1970s and

9. Demographic studies of patterns and trends in marital disruption include Sweet and Bumpass, 1987:chapters 5–7; Castro Martin and Bumpass, 1989; Cherlin, 1981; Preston and McDonald, 1979; Weed, 1980; and Morgan and Rindfuss, 1985. Differentials in marital stability are described in Bumpass and Sweet, 1972. Recent longitudinal data have contributed to our understanding of the process of marital dissolution. See Mott and Moore, 1979; and Hoffman and Holmes, 1976. For a discussion of marital disruption from the perspective of children, see Bumpass, 1984.

10. Studies of remarriage include Sweet and Bumpass, 1987:chapter 5; Bumpass, Sweet, and Castro Martin, forthcoming; Mott and Moore, 1983; and Glick, 1980.

evidently continuing into the 1980s, the rate of remarriage has declined (Bumpass, Sweet, and Castro Martin, forthcoming).

Because of the high rate of remarriage, the proportion of the population who is currently separated or divorced is relatively small. In 1985 about 1 adult in 10 was either separated or divorced. The fraction varies by age, reaching a peak of about a sixth at ages 40–44.

Fertility

The final demographic factor affecting the distribution of the population by family life-cycle stage is fertility. The general outline of recent fertility change is well-known.[11] The United States had very high fertility for about two decades following World War II. Birth rates began to decline about 1960, and by the mid-1960s the absolute number of births each year was declining. There were over a million fewer births in 1975 than in 1960; the birth rate (general fertility rate) dropped by 44 percent in 15 years. The general fertility rate has not changed much since 1975, although the annual number of births has risen by half a million because of the shifting age distribution as the early babyboomers have themselves reached the prime reproductive ages.

There has been a continuous decline for over a century in the proportion of women with large families. The baby boom was not so much a revival of large families, but a drop in childlessness and one-child families (which were common during the 1920s and 1930s) and an increase in the proportion of two-, three-, and four-children families. Similarly, contemporary low fertility involves a heavy concentration of family size at two children, with the virtual elimination of families of four or more children. There has been, in addition, an increase in the proportion of one-child families and also some increase in childlessness.

Among women aged 18–34 (of all marital statuses) in 1985 the distribution of expected completed family size was:

	Percent
No children	6
1 child	13
2 children	50
3 children	22
4 or more children	10
Total	100

11. Reviews of fertility change in the United States and other industrial countries include Sweet and Bumpass, 1987:chapter 4; Pratt, 1984; Ryder, 1986; Westoff, 1987; Bourgeois-Pichet, 1987; and Bloom and Pebley, 1982.

These changes in completed family size have their effect on household structure and housing demand, by affecting both the average number of persons per household and the number of years that parents have children present.

There is another aspect of fertility change which also has an effect on household structure—the timing and spacing of births.[12] The baby-boom pattern of reproduction involved early marriage and a very young age of mother (or father) at first birth. Subsequent intended pregnancies tended to follow at very short intervals. More recently, there appears to be much more delay of the first birth, and also considerably wider spacing of subsequent births. Consequently, couples, on average, spend more years married, but without children. If cohabiting years were added to married years, this change would be even more dramatic.

Householder (Headship) Rates

The final social trend that is relevant to the life-cycle distribution of households is the propensity of individuals to form households. This is what has historically been called the household headship rate. However, for a variety of reasons, it is now more reasonable to think in terms of a "householder rate." There were two problems with the "headship" concept. First, it was an anachronism. In earlier times, it was common to think of someone as being the "head" of a household—the person in charge—and most people could give an intelligent response to the census-taker's question, "Who is the head of this household?" Nowadays, perhaps because we have become more egalitarian, we no longer think in these terms. The second problem with the headship concept was that the U.S. Census Bureau followed the sexist practice of recoding cases involving married couples (both spouses present), renaming the husband as the head if the woman had been specified as the household head. By the 1980 census, the householder concept replaced headship. The householder is the person in whose name the house or apartment is owned or rented. In cases where there is more than one such person, one of them is selected as the reference person or householder.

Table 2.4 summarizes recent changes in living arrangements of persons in various life-cycle stages in terms of the householder rate. The seven currently married subgroups are not considered because, for many decades, almost all married couples have maintained their own households. Because a married-couple household must include both a husband and a wife, the householder rate for married persons is about 50 percent.

---

12. Studies of the changing timing of fertility include Bloom, 1982; and Bloom and Trussell, 1984.

Table 2.4   Householder (Headship) Rates, by Family Life-Cycle
Stage and Sex, 1970 and 1980

Life-Cycle Stage	Males		Females	
	1970	1980	1970	1980
Never married				
<30	10.3	20.4	12.0	22.5
30–44	37.8	50.6	36.5	56.5
45–49	48.3	56.0	46.6	55.0
Formerly married with children under age 18 Youngest child's age				
<6	83.2	83.7	74.5	79.5
6–11	88.0	89.8	90.2	89.8
12–17	92.4	93.6	93.3	95.4
Formerly married, no children under age 18				
<30	26.2	38.9	27.8	35.7
30–44	47.1	58.8	52.8	62.0
45–59	54.0	68.0	75.1	80.9
Elderly				
Never married	55.4	59.3	52.4	58.1
Formerly married	65.1	68.3	67.7	74.1

During the 1970s, householder rates increased for virtually every sub-group. The householder rate of young singles increased from about 10 percent to about 20 percent. There was an even larger increase for never-married persons aged 30–44. Also experiencing large increases were formerly married persons with no children. The householder rates of formerly married persons with children were very high in 1970 and became only slightly higher by 1980. Householder rates of formerly married elderly persons, especially those of women, also increased.[13]

13. For discussions of the changing living arrangements of young unmarried adults, formerly married persons, and the elderly, see Sweet and Bumpass, 1987:chapters 3, 6, and 8, respectively. The process of leaving the parental household has been the subject of much recent study. See Young, 1977b; Goldscheider and DaVanzo, 1985; Goldscheider and Goldscheider, 1987; Goldscheider and Waite, 1987; Heer, Hodge, and Felson, 1985; and Glick and Lin, 1986. See also Sweet and Bumpass, 1987:90–93, for a contrasting view of the trend. Studies of the living arrangements of the elderly include Schwartz, Danziger, and Smolensky, 1983; Wolf, 1984; and Sweet and Bumpass, 1987:chapter 8. Studies of the growth of female-headed families include Garfinkel and McLanahan, 1986; and Smith and Cutright, 1985. An example of demographic decomposition of the increase in the number and change in the composition of households is Sweet, 1984.

Family Life-Cycle Stage and Type of Housing

We have reviewed recent trends in the distribution of the population by family life-cycle stage and the demographic trends underlying these changes. We then examined changes in the living arrangements of the major life-cycle groups. Now we examine the relationship between family life-cycle stage and demand for different types of housing. In this section the unit of analysis shifts from the individual to the household.

Households are classified by the life-cycle stage of the householder. The housing-type classification involves tenure (owner versus renter) and number of units in the structure. The detailed housing classification has 14 categories (shown in Table 2.7, below). In most analyses, we combine some of the categories and work with a simpler six-category classification.

We will consider three related questions: What types of housing do households in different family life-cycle stages choose? How did the housing-type distributions of life-cycle categories change between 1970 and 1980? To what extent was the demand for various types of housing affected by the changes in the life-cycle distribution of the population?

Housing Choices of Households by Life-Cycle Stage

Not surprisingly, households at different family life-cycle stages have rather different housing distributions. In this section I will summarize the housing-type distributions for some of the life-cycle categories (see Table 2.5).

Never-Married Householders

Young single persons are greatly underrepresented among homeowners—only 12 percent are homeowners compared with 61 percent of all households. They are heavily overrepresented in rental housing in structures with five or more units (47 versus 15 percent of all households). They are also overrepresented in rental housing in structures with two to four units (20 versus 8 percent).

Older never-married persons have similar housing patterns, but the proportion in owned housing increases with increasing age. For those aged 45 and over, nearly half of never-married householders are homeowners.

Married Couples with No Children

Married couples with no children under age 18 are divided into four groups by age of the husband—under 30, 30–44, 45–59, and 60 and

Table 2.5. Percentage Distribution of Housing Types, by Life-Cycle Stage of Householder, 1980

| Family Life-Cycle Stage | Owned Housing[a] | Rented Housing | | | | Mobile Homes | Total |
		Single-Family	2–4 Units	5–19 Units	20+ Units		
Never married							
<30	11.6	16.6	20.4	25.8	21.2	4.4	100.0
30–44	30.1	12.6	15.5	19.3	19.4	3.2	100.0
45–59	44.7	10.3	11.8	12.8	16.5	3.8	100.0
Married couple with children under age 18							
Youngest child's age							
0–5	62.5	15.0	7.3	5.1	3.3	6.8	100.0
6–11	78.3	10.1	3.6	2.3	1.7	4.1	100.0
12–17	85.0	6.9	2.4	1.5	1.4	2.8	100.0
Married couple, no children under age 18							
Husband's age							
<30	42.2	15.3	12.8	12.3	9.0	8.4	100.0
30–44	72.5	8.0	5.0	4.7	4.8	5.0	100.0
45–59	84.1	4.9	2.7	1.9	2.4	4.0	100.0
Formerly married with children under age 18							
Youngest child's age							
0–5	25.0	24.6	19.3	15.0	9.6	6.6	100.0
6–11	40.9	20.2	15.3	11.3	7.2	5.0	100.0
12–17	53.8	15.8	10.8	8.7	6.5	4.5	100.0
Formerly married, no children under age 18							
<30	21.3	16.9	17.6	20.8	16.0	7.5	100.0
30–44	34.2	13.0	13.5	17.6	16.0	5.6	100.0
45–59	51.5	10.3	10.4	10.8	11.0	6.0	100.0
Elderly							
Never married	47.6	8.7	11.5	11.2	17.8	3.1	100.0
Married	79.8	5.1	3.3	2.6	4.1	5.0	100.0
Formerly married	57.5	9.0	8.8	7.5	12.3	4.9	100.0
Total	60.9	10.7	8.1	7.7	7.6	5.0	100.0

[a]Excluding mobile homes.

older. The youngest group consists primarily of recently married couples who have not yet had children. Those with husbands aged 30–44 are a combination of couples who have recently married at an older-than-average age, those who have been married for a while and will remain childless, and a few at the older end of the age interval who have had children, all of whom have already reached age 18 or left home. Those with husbands aged 45 and older are composed primarily of couples who have raised children and now have an empty nest (or have only children aged 18 or older in the household).

Only about 40 percent of the youngest group of childless married-couple households are homeowners. Eight percent live in mobile homes, the highest proportion of any life-cycle stage. Young childless couples are overrepresented in rented single-family homes (15 percent) and also in rental housing in structures with two to four units (13 percent).

A very high proportion of older married couples without children under 18 in the household are homeowners, reflecting the fact that because they are older, they have more income and savings and have already raised their families. Those who are not homeowners are scattered over the remaining housing categories.

Married Couples with Children under Age 18

A very high fraction of married couples with children in the household are homeowners. The proportion increases with age of the youngest child. Over three-fifths of married couples with children of preschool age are homeowners. The proportion rises to 78 percent for couples with the youngest child aged 6–11, and to 85 percent for those with the youngest child aged 12–17. The largest fraction of those couples who are not homeowners live in rented single-family housing. Mobile home and rental units in small buildings (of two to four units) are also relatively frequent choices of married couples who have children at home but who are not homeowners. Very few live in larger apartment buildings.

One-Parent Families

Homeownership is much less common for households of formerly married persons than for married couples. This undoubtedly reflects the effects of several factors: Marital disruption tends to occur early in marriage, prior to homeownership. Marital disruption is selective of economically disadvantaged persons, and remarriage is selective of those who are economically better off. (Homeownership, itself, may increase a person's remarriage probability.) Most formerly married persons with children are women, who tend to earn less than men and are less likely to be able to purchase and maintain homes. Also, it is likely that many separating couples who own homes while married sell the homes at the time of divorce.

Homeownership increases with the age of the youngest child for one-parent families as it does for married couples. About a quarter of those with preschool-age children are homeowners. The fraction increases to about two-fifths for those with the youngest child aged 6–11, and to somewhat more than half for those with the youngest child aged 12–17. Significant proportions of one-parent families are living in rented single-family homes—nearly a quarter of those with preschool-age children. Large fractions are also found in rental housing of two to four units. About a quarter of the formerly married persons with preschool children rent in buildings with more than four units. This fraction decreases with increasing age of the youngest child. One-parent families also disproportionately live in mobile homes.

Households of Formerly Married Persons with No Children under Age 18

The proportion of formerly married persons with no children under 18 who are homeowners increases with increasing age. Those who are not homeowners are spread widely over the remaining housing types. They seem to make housing choices that are very similar to those made by never-married persons, with significant proportions in large apartment buildings. A relatively large number live in mobile homes.

Households of Elderly Persons

Four-fifths of elderly married couples are homeowners, and the great majority of them live in single-family housing. Only 5 percent live in mobile homes, and very few live in apartment buildings with five or more units.

Nearly three-fifths of widows (most of the formerly married elderly are widows) are homeowners. Widows (and the small number of never-married elderly), however, are found in significant proportions in large apartment buildings—one in five lives in a building with five or more units. Fewer than 1 in 20 lives in a mobile home.

Changes in Housing Choices: 1970–1980

Next we consider how the housing-type distributions of various life-cycle stages changed during the 1970s. Table 2.6 shows the 1970–80 change in

Table 2.6   Percentage-Point Change[a] in the Distribution of Housing Type, by Life-Cycle Stage of Householder, 1970–80

| Family Life-Cycle Stage | Owned Housing[b] | Rented Housing | | | | Mobile Homes |
		Single-Family	2–4 Units	5–19 Units	20+ Units	
Never married						
<30	+4.6	+1.0	−1.0	−3.0	−2.9	+1.3
30–44	+5.2	−1.2	−0.9	−1.2	−2.1	+0.5
45–59	+2.9	−1.0	−2.6	−1.7	−0.7	+1.6
Married couple with children under age 18 Youngest child's age						
0–5	+5.7	−5.0	−3.2	−0.2	+0.2	+2.5
6–11	+2.2	−3.2	−1.2	+0.2	0.0	+2.2
12–17	+4.2	−3.0	−1.6	−0.4	−0.6	+1.4
Married couple, no children under age 18 Husband's age						
<30	+21.3	−4.7	−8.4	−5.0	−3.2	0.0
30–44	+9.5	−4.0	−3.9	−1.7	−1.1	+1.2
45–59	+7.7	−3.3	−2.7	−1.3	−1.6	+1.2
Formerly married with children under age 18 Youngest child's age						
0–5	−1.5	−3.6	−0.9	+1.2	+2.1	+2.7
6–11	−1.5	−5.3	+0.1	+1.8	+1.4	+1.7
12–17	+2.2	−3.0	−2.4	+0.6	+0.7	+2.1
Formerly married, no children under age 18						
<30	+5.9	−0.8	−2.6	−1.9	−1.9	+0.6
30–44	+8.2	−2.9	−3.9	−0.9	−1.9	+1.4
45–59	+5.3	−3.1	−4.3	−0.5	+1.5	+2.2
Elderly						
Never married	+3.3	−1.9	−1.7	−1.7	+0.9	+0.9
Married	+4.7	−2.2	−2.2	−0.9	−1.3	+2.0
Formerly married	+1.8	−2.1	−2.7	−1.3	+2.5	+1.7
Total	+1.4	−2.9	−1.7	+0.5	+1.0	+1.7

[a]Difference between 1980 and 1970 percentages in the housing types.
[b]Except mobile homes.

the percentage of households living in a given type of housing. For example, the 4.6 in the upper left cell of the table is the difference between the percentage of young single householders who owned their homes in 1980 (11.6 percent) and the percentage who owned their homes in 1970 (7.0 percent). Thus the percent who were homeowners increased by 4.6 percentage points over the course of that decade.

During the 1970s homeownership increased for households at every life-cycle stage, with the exception of formerly-married persons with children under the age of 12 years. The most dramatic increase occurred among households of childless married couples with husbands under age 30, whose homeownership rate doubled from 21 to 42 percent. Some of this increase was the result of the shift in the age structure of this group toward older ages. (See Sweet and Bumpass, 1987, for a discussion of changing homeownership patterns of married couples in relation to age, marriage duration, and the presence of children. Chevan [1989] analyzes intercohort change in homeownership between 1940 and 1980.) Although it is only a small increase in absolute terms, the fraction of households headed by single persons under age 30 who were homeowners increased from 7 to 12 percent. Again, some of this increase was due to change in the age structure toward older ages as age at first marriage increased. Other groups with substantial increases in homeownership during the 1970s include formerly married householders (of all ages) with no children under age 18 and married couples with the husband age 30 and older with no children under age 18.

Rental of single-family homes decreased among all but one life-cycle group. For example, the proportion of young married couples, both with and without children, in rented single-family homes decreased from about 20 to 15 percent. Similarly, the proportion of households who were renting apartments in buildings of two to four units also declined for all but one life-cycle stage during the 1970s. Especially notable were the declines for young married couples. The proportion of those with no children who were living in this type of housing declined from 21 to 13 percent, and that of couples with preschool-age children declined from 11 to 7 percent.

Although the modal housing choice of young singles continues to be large apartment buildings, they were somewhat less likely to be living in this type of housing in 1980 than in 1970. The declines were: in buildings of 5–19 units, from 29 to 26 percent, and in buildings of 20 or more units, from 24 to 21 percent. There was also a decrease in the proportion of young, childless married couples living in large apartment buildings, and a modest decrease in the proportion of young, childless formerly married households living in this housing type. Households of formerly married persons with children and households of elderly formerly married persons (widows) were slightly more likely to be living in larger apartment buildings in 1980 than a decade earlier. No life-cycle group has a very large proportion living in mobile homes. (The highest fraction is 8 percent for households of formerly married persons with preschool-age children.) However, during the 1970s the fraction increased for every group.

The Effect of Changing Distribution of Households by Life-Cycle Stage on Demand for Different Housing Types

In this final section we examine the effect of changes in the life-cycle stage distribution of households on demand for the various types of housing. The logic of the analysis is this: using direct standardization, we ask, "Supposing there had been no change between 1970 and 1980 in life-cycle-specific housing choices (and all that had changed was the life-cycle stage distribution of households), what would the distribution of households by housing type have looked like?" This is what we refer to as the standardized distribution of households by housing type in 1980. Thus, the standardized distribution has the same "rates" as the 1970 actual distribution. (It has the same life-cycle distribution as the 1980 actual distribution.) Therefore, the difference between the actual 1970 and standardized 1980 housing-type distribution reflects the effect of changes in the distribution of households by life-cycle stage.

The proportion of households in single-family detached homes changed very little during the 1970s: 54.1 percent in 1970 and 53.6 in 1980 (see Table 2.7). However, if the life-cycle stage-specific housing distributions had not shifted, only 50.4 percent of the households would have been in this category. Thus the change in the life-cycle stage distribution resulted in an expected decline of 3.7 percent in the proportion of households in single-family detached housing. The actual drop was much smaller (0.5 percent), because the life-cycle stage-specific probabilities of living in owned, single-family housing increased.

In 1970, 13.7 percent of households were in rental units in structures with five or more units. This proportion rose to 15.3 percent in 1980. The change in the life-cycle stage distribution was favorable to demand for this type of housing. If the life-cycle-specific fractions living in this type of housing had remained at 1970 levels, the change in the distribution of households by life-cycle stage would have resulted in an increase in the proportion in rental units in multiunit structures from 13.7 percent to 16.8 percent. The actual fraction did not grow this much because, for many life-cycle stages, this became a relatively less-frequent housing choice.

Table 2.7.   Percentage Distribution of Households by Housing Type, 1970 and 1980

	Actual 1970	Actual 1980	Standardized[a] 1980	1970–80 Change Actual	1970–80 Change Standardized
Owner					
Single unit, detached	54.1	53.6	50.4	−0.5	−3.7
Single unit, attached	1.7	2.3	1.6	+0.6	−0.1
2 units	2.7	2.2	2.6	−0.5	−0.1
3 or more units	1.0	2.8	1.0	+1.8	0.0
Mobile homes	2.8	4.1	2.7	+1.3	−0.1
Renter					
Single unit, detached	12.3	8.9	12.2	−3.4	−0.1
Single unit, attached	1.3	1.8	1.4	+0.5	+0.1
2 units	5.4	4.1	5.7	−1.3	+0.3
3 or 4 units	4.5	4.0	5.0	−0.5	+0.5
5–9 units	3.7	3.7	4.4	0.0	+0.7
10–19 units	3.5	4.0	4.4	+0.5	+0.9
20–50 units	3.0	3.0	3.8	0.0	+0.8
50 or more units	3.5	4.6	4.2	+0.9	+0.7
Mobile homes	0.5	1.0	0.6	+0.5	+0.1
Total	100.0	100.0	100.0		

[a]Holding constant the life-cycle stage-specific housing choices at their 1970 levels, but allowing for the actual change in the life-cycle distribution of households from 1970 to 1980.

The proportion of households in rental units in structures with two to four units decreased from 9.9 to 8.1 percent. If, however, the life-cycle stage-specific propensity to live in housing of this sort had not decreased, the fraction of households renting in buildings of two to four units would have risen from 9.9 to 10.7 percent.

In 1970, 3.3 percent of households lived in mobile homes; this fraction increased to 5.1 percent in 1980. If the rates had remained constant, and only the life-cycle distribution had changed, the percentage of households living in mobile homes would have remained at 3.3. Thus, all the increase in mobile home residence was due to increased life-cycle stage-specific propensities to select this kind of housing.

Conclusion

In this chapter I have shown how demographic processes affect housing demand through their effects on the family life-cycle distribution of the population. I have described some of the demographic changes that have occurred during the past two decades. I have also shown how the structure of housing demand of the various life-cycle groups has changed.

During the 1960s and 1970s, there were many demographic changes affecting housing demand: The number of young adults, who are responsible for much of net household formation, increased very rapidly during each decade. Marriage ages and rates of marital disruption rose to unprecedentately high levels. Fertility fell to very low levels, and births were delayed within marriage. Unmarried persons, of all ages, with and without children, were more likely to maintain their own households.

These demographic changes have resulted in a rapid growth in the proportion of young single households and households of formerly married persons, and a decline in the proportion of households composed of married couples with children. Interacting with these changes in the life-cycle distributions of households has been a change in the housing-type choices of households in particular life-cycle stages.

What will happen in the future? The absolute number of young adults will continue to decrease in the 1990s. Age at first marriage has continued to rise through the 1980s, but whether it will increase much more is difficult to predict. It seems unlikely, however, that marriage ages will decline very much. The rise in levels of cohabitation, however, offsets the trend toward increasing age at first marriage, at least from the point of view of household formation. Whether the housing choices (e.g., homeownership) of cohabitors and young marrieds are similar or not is unknown. The rate of marital disruption may have ceased increasing, but there is no sign of any impending decline. Remarriage rates, which have been quite high, have been declining. It is possible that they will fall further, with many persons never remarrying following marital disruption, and many others spending an extended period between marriages. Rising levels of cohabitation, however, confuse the picture, because the prevalence of cohabitation appears to be highest among those groups with the greatest drop in remarriage rates.

Householder rates have been increasing for some time and are now quite high for most life-cycle stages. Formerly married persons with children are virtually all householders, as are older formerly married persons with no children. Seven in 10 elderly widowed persons maintain their own households, and a large proportion of those who do not, have health problems which make it impossible for them to manage on their own. Had it not been for the aging of the elderly population (a larger proportion are very old), the householder rate of elderly widows would have risen much more than it did.

The only groups for which there is much potential for further increase in the householder rate are young singles and young formerly married persons. (These are groups with high levels of cohabitation, which is not adequately dealt with in the life-cycle stage classification which I or others have used.) The future householder rate of young, unmarried persons is likely to be affected by whether they can afford to maintain their own households. In the past two decades, the economic position of young adults has not been very good. We do not know the extent to which this is the result of the very large number of young persons entering the labor market (keeping wage rates low and increasing the competition for entry-level jobs) or the result of fundamental changes in the economy (causing a long-term increase in the proportion of jobs that are unskilled, dead-end, and low-paid). There have been several studies that suggest that the householder rates of young adults may have declined in the 1980s.

I have shown that during the 1970s there was change in life-cycle-specific housing choices, with households in all life-cycle stages being more likely to be homeowners at the end of the decade than at the beginning. I have also shown that change in the population's distribution by life-cycle stage which has resulted from the demographic changes summarized in this chapter has affected the aggregate demand for housing of different types. In particular, these changes have put downward pressure on the demand for owned housing, particularly single detached units, and have increased the demand for rental housing, particularly in structures with more than five units. Thus in the 1970s, changes in the life-cycle distribution of the population tended to offset changes in life-cycle-specific housing choices.

There is a great variation in housing choice by life-cycle stage, and it appears that a fairly detailed life-cycle classification such as the one used here is necessary to capture this variation. Furthermore, not only is there variation in homeownership among life-cycle categories, but there is also variation in the type of rental housing. It would be possible and desirable to undertake similar analyses using other characteristics of both rental and owned housing, such as number of rooms, value or rent paid, or locational characteristics. My analysis has been national in scope. It would also be interesting to undertake similar analyses within specific housing markets.

Acknowledgments

The research was supported by the Center for Population Research, National Institute of Child Health, and Human Development of NIH (HD 15227). The work was undertaken at the Center for Demography and Ecology of the University of Wisconsin–Madison, whose research facilities are also funded by the Center for Population Research (HD 05876).

References

Balakrishnan, T., K. Rao, E. Lapierre-Adamcyk, and K. Krotki. 1987. A hazard model analysis of the covariates of marriage dissolution in Canada. *Demography* 24:395–406.

Bennett, N., A. Blanc, and D. Bloom. 1986. Commitment and the modern union. *American Sociological Review* 53(1):127–138.

Bloom, D. 1982. What's happening to the age at first birth in the United States? A study of recent cohorts. *Demography* 19:351–370.

Bloom, D., and A. Pebley. 1982. Voluntary childlessness: A review of the evidence and implications. *Population Research and Policy Review* 1:203–224.

Bloom, D., and J. Trussell. 1984. What are the determinants of delayed childbearing and permanent childlessness in the United States? *Demography* 21:591–612.

Bourgeois-Pichet, J. 1987. The unprecedented shortage of births in Europe. Pp. 3–25 in K. Davis, M. Bernstam, and R. Ricardo-Campbell (eds.), *Below Replacement Fertility: Causes, Consequences, Policies*. New York: The Population Council.

Bumpass, L. 1984. Children and marital disruption: A replication and update. *Demography* 21(4):71–82.

Bumpass, L., and J. Sweet. 1972. Differentials in marital instability: 1970. *American Sociological Review* 37:754–766.

Bumpass, L., and J. Sweet. 1989. National estimates of cohabitation: Cohort levels and union stability. *Demography* 26(4):615–625.

Bumpass, L., J. Sweet, and T. Castro Martin. Forthcoming. Changing patterns of remarriage in the United States. *Journal of Marriage and the Family*.

Bumpass, L., J. Sweet, and A. Cherlin. 1989. *The Role of Cohabitation in Declining Rates of Marriage*. NSFH Working Paper No. 5. Madison: University of Wisconsin, Center for Demography and Ecology.

Castro Martin, T., and L. Bumpass. 1989. Recent trends in marital disruption. *Demography* 26(1):37–51.

Cherlin, A. 1980. Postponing marriage: The influence of young women's work expectations. *Journal of Marriage and the Family* 42:355–365.

Cherlin, A. 1981. *Marriage, Divorce, Remarriage*. Cambridge, Mass.: Harvard University Press.

Chevan, A. 1989. The growth of home ownership: 1940–1980. *Demography* 26(2):249–266.

Cuisenier, J., and M. Segalen (eds.). 1977. *The Family Life Cycle in European Societies*. The Hague: Mouton.

Davis, K. (ed.) 1985. *Marriage: Comparative Perspectives on a Changing Institution*. New York: Russell Sage Foundation.

Espenshade, T. 1985. Marriage trends in America: Estimates, implications, and underlying causes. *Population and Development Review* 11:193–245.

Festy, P. 1980. On the new context of marriage in Western Europe. *Population and Development Review* 6(2):311–315.

Garfinkel, I., and S. McLanahan. 1986. *Female Headed Families and Public Policy: A New American Dilemma?* Washington, D.C.: The Urban Institute.

Glick, P. 1947. The family cycle. *American Sociological Review* 12:164–174.

Glick, P. 1980. Remarriage: Some recent changes and variations. *Journal of Family Issues* 1:455–478.

Glick, P., and S. Lin. 1986. More young adults are living with their parents: Who are they? *Journal of Marriage and the Family* 48:107–112.

Glick, P., and R. Parke. 1965. New approaches in studying the life cycle of the family. *Demography* 2:187–202.

Goldman, N., C. Westoff, and C. Hammerslough. 1984. Demography of the marriage market in the United States. *Population Index* 50:5–25.

Goldscheider, F., and J. DaVanzo. 1985. Living arrangements and the transition to adulthood. *Demography* 22:545–563.

Goldscheider, C., and F. Goldscheider. 1987. Moving out and marriage: What do young adults expect? *American Sociological Review* 52:278–285.

Goldscheider, F., and L. Waite. 1987. Nest-leaving patterns and the transition to marriage for young men and women. *Journal of Marriage and the Family* 49:507–516.

Heer, D., R. Hodge, and M. Felson. 1985. The cluttered nest. *Sociology and Social Research* 49:3.

Hoffman, S., and J. Holmes. 1976. Husbands, wives, and divorces. Pp. 23–76 in G. Duncan and J. Morgan (eds.), *Five Thousand American Families: Patterns of Economic Progress,* Vol. 4. Ann Arbor: University of Michigan, Institute for Social Research.

Klein, D., and J. Aldous. 1979. Three blind mice: Misleading criticisms of the family life cycle concept. *Journal of Marriage and the Family* 41:689–691.

Lansing, J., and L. Kish. 1957. Family life cycle as an independent variable. *American Sociological Review* 22:512–519.

McLeod, P., and J. Ellis. 1983. Alternative approaches to the family life cycle in the analysis of housing consumption. *Journal of Marriage and the Family* 43:699–708.

Morgan, P., and R. Rindfuss. 1985. Marital disruption: Structural and temporal dimensions. *American Journal of Sociology* 90:1055–1077.

Mott, F., and S. Moore. 1979. The causes of marital disruption among young American women: Interdisciplinary perspectives. *Journal of Marriage and the Family* 41:355–365.

Mott, F., and S. Moore. 1983. The tempo of remarriage among young American women. *Journal of Marriage and the Family* 45:427–436.

Murphy, P., and W. Staples. 1979. A modernized family life cycle. *Journal of Consumer Research* 6:12–22.

Nock, S. 1979. The family life cycle: Empirical or conceptual tool. *Journal of Marriage and the Family* 41:15–26.

Norton, A. 1983. Family life cycle, 1980. *Journal of Marriage and the Family* 45:267–275.

Pratt, W. 1984. Understanding U.S. fertility: Findings from the National Survey of Family Growth. Population Reference Bureau, *Population Bulletin,* 39:5.

Preston, S., and J. McDonald. 1979. The incidence of divorce within cohorts of American marriages contracted since the Civil War. *Demography* 16:1–26.

Rodgers, R. H. 1977. The family life cycle concept: Past, present, and future. Pp. 39–57 in J. Cuisenier and M. Segalen (eds.), *The Family Life Cycle in European Societies.* The Hague: Mouton.

Rodgers, W., and A. Thornton. 1985. Changing patterns of first marriage in the United States. *Demography* 22:265–279.

Ryder, N. 1986. Observations on the history of cohort fertility in the United States. *Population and Development Review* 12:617–643.

Schoen, R., W. Urton, K. Woodrow, and J. Baj. 1985. Marriage and divorce in 20th-century American cohorts. *Demography* 22:101–114.

Schwartz, S., S. Danziger, and E. Smolensky. 1983. *The Choice of Living Arrangements by the Elderly.* Washington, D.C.: Brookings Institution.

Smith, H., and P. Cutright. 1985. Components of change in the number of female-headed family heads aged 15–44, an update and reanalysis: United States, 1940–1983. *Social Science Research* 14:226–250.

Spanier, G. 1983. Marriage and unmarried cohabitation in the United States. *Journal of Marriage and the Family* 45:277–288.

Spanier, G., and P. Glick. 1980. The life cycle of American families: An expanded analysis. *Journal of Family History* 5(1):98–112.

Spanier, G., W. Sauer, and R. Larzelere. 1979. An empirical evaluation of the family life cycle. *Journal of Marriage and the Family* 41:27–38.

Spencer, G. 1984. *Projections of the Population of the United States by Age, Sex, and Race: 1983–2080.* U.S. Bureau of the Census, Current Population Reports, Population Estimates and Projections, Series P-25, No. 952, Washington, D.C.: U.S. Government Printing Office.

Sweet, J. 1977. Demography and the family. *Annual Review of Sociology* 3:363–405.

Sweet, J. 1984. Components of change in the number of households, 1970–1980. *Demography* 21(2):129–140.

Sweet, J., and L. Bumpass. 1987. *American Families and Households.* New York: Russell Sage Foundation.

Taeuber, K., and J. Sweet. 1976. Family and work: The social life cycle of women. Pp. 31–60 in J. Kreps (ed.), *Women in the American Economy: A Look to the 1980s.* Englewood Cliffs, N.J.: Prentice-Hall.

Tanfer, K. 1987. Patterns of premarital cohabitation among never-married women in the United States. *Journal of Marriage and the Family* 49:483–497.

Thornton, A. 1988. Cohabitation and marriage in the 1980s. *Demography* 25:497–508.

Thornton, A., and D. Freedman. 1982. Changing attitudes toward marriage and single life. *Family Planning Perspectives* 14:297–303.

Thornton, A., and D. Freedman. 1983. The changing American family. Population Reference Bureau, *Population Bulletin* 38(3).

Trost, J. 1977. The family life cycle: A problematic concept. Pp. 467–481 in J. Cuisenier and M. Segalen (eds.), *The Family Life Cycle in European Societies.* The Hague: Mouton.

Waite, L., and G. Spitze. 1981. Young women's transition to marriage. *Demography* 18:681–694.

Weed, J. 1980. *National Estimates of Marriage Dissolution and Survivorship.* Vital and Health Statistics, Ser. 3 (Analytical Studies), No. 19 IV, U.S. Department of Health and Human Services Pub. No. (PHS)81-1403.

Westoff, C. 1987. Perspective on nuptiality and fertility. Pp. 155–170 in K. Davis, M. Bernstam, and R. Ricardo-Campbell (eds.), *Below Replacement Fertility: Causes, Consequences, Policies.* New York: The Population Council.

Winsborough, H. 1978. Statistical histories of the life cycle of birth cohorts: The transition from school boy to adult male. Pp. 231–260 in K. Taeuber, L. Bumpass, and J. Sweet (eds.), *Social Demography.* New York: Academic Press.

Wolf, D. 1984. Kin availability and the living arrangements of older women. *Social Science Research* 13:72–89.

Young, C. 1977a. *The Family Life Cycle.* Australian Family Formation Project, Monograph #6. Canberra City: Australian National University Press.

Young, C. 1977b. Factors associated with the timing and duration of the leaving-home stage of the family life cycle. *Population Studies* 29:61–73.

3 *Kenneth S. Y. Chew*

Urban Industry and Young Nonfamily Households

The passage from youth to adulthood is a tangle of ever-changing contingencies. Yet precisely the fluidity in this life stage, because it involves a marginal position in the housing market, makes young adults' living arrangements a sensitive window onto population-housing processes.

Young adults reside disproportionately in transitional and nontraditional living arrangements. The reason for this is plain, for in the decade following high school graduation, young adults transform themselves from a group that resides, overwhelmingly, with parents, to a group in which fewer than 1 in 10 do so (Sweet and Bumpass, 1987). The changeover produces a high demand for transitional living arrangements, including many that are nonfamilial or nontraditional. Cumulatively a quarter to a third of Americans have spent some time living in dormitories or barracks by the time they reach 24 (Goldscheider and DaVanzo, 1986); in each of the several years preceding that age, roughly a quarter can be found living either alone or in an independent household shared only with roommates (Goldscheider and DaVanzo, 1985: figure 1).

This chapter concerns nonfamily household living (residence alone or in a household shared only with nonrelatives). In the 30 years preceding the 1980 census, the number of nonfamily households more than tripled, outstripping the general household growth rate by a factor of four (U.S.

Kenneth S. Y. Chew is Assistant Professor in the Program in Social Ecology, University of California–Irvine, Irvine, California 92717.

Bureau of the Census, 1981:table 60). Along with changes in living patterns among the elderly, trends among young adults were the main factor underlying this growth.

At least since the nineteenth century, American home-leaving has usually involved some form of premarital, semi-autonomous living (Modell, Furstenberg, and Hershberg, 1976). Through the 1930s, this experience often meant boarding with another family (Laslett, 1973); still later it has implied a sojourn in group institutional quarters. But until the 1960s, living in a household consisting entirely of single residents was uncommon, and only in the 1980s has such experience approached the status of a normative expectation (Goldscheider and Goldscheider, 1987a,b). Moreover, nonfamily households include not only those with same-sex roommates but also others with unmarried heterosexual couples, an arrangement still viewed with some disapproval. Compared then with better-established expectations about dormitory or barracks life, expectations concerning nonfamily household living are less traditional; put another way, nonfamily household residence is a more marginal option. The distribution of nonfamily households is therefore a particularly sensitive indicator for analyzing housing processes. In this chapter I focus specifically on variation in young-adult nonfamily household rates across U.S. metropolitan areas. At the last census, these rates varied more than 10-fold (Table 3.1). Because metropolitan areas correspond more closely than any other geographical unit to housing and job markets, and to other factors that shape population-housing processes, this analysis should yield new understanding of those processes.

The central argument in this chapter is that an area's employment base, by shaping its migration pattern and its income and educational composition, underlies its nonfamily household rate. Young adults are most likely to live in nonfamily households in areas whose economies are "knowledge-intensive" rather than "smokestack"-based. A gross comparison based on Noyelle's (1983) classification of metropolitan areas indicates that mean nonfamily rates in service centers as a whole exceed those in manufacturing centers by 10–20 percent (Figure 3.1). This difference more than doubles if only "government-educational centers" are used to represent the knowledge-intensive economies. Service centers are dominated by professional rather than blue-collar employment, resulting in high rates of growth through in-migration, and in highly educated, high-income populations. Migration, high education, and high income all raise the disposition to live in nonfamily households. Offsetting these factors in the high-growth areas is the high cost of housing, which constrains the formation of nonfamily households.

To reach these conclusions, I have used information from the two

Table 3.1.   1980 Metropolitan Areas with Lowest and Highest Percentages of 20–24-
Year-Olds Living in Nonfamily Households (ranked in ascending order of
male percentages)

			Percentage in Nonfamily Households	
	Rank 1980	Rank 1970	Males	Females
McAllen, Tex.	1	—	3.4	2.5
Nassau, N.Y.	2	—	4.5	3.2
Johnstown, Pa.	3	1	5.2	5.1
Paterson, N.J.	4	4	6.7	5.1
NE Pennsylvania	5	2	6.8	5.6
Chattanooga, Tenn.	6	5	7.6	6.6
Charleston, W.Va.	7	19	7.8	7.7
El Paso, Tex.	8	17	7.9	4.4
Trenton, N.J.	9	57	8.6	7.8
Bridgeport, Conn.	10	31	9.2	5.8
Newark, N.J.	11	22	9.2	6.9
Long Branch, N.J.	12	—	9.4	6.6
Johnson City, Tenn.	13	—	9.5	7.4
Youngstown, Ohio	14	10	9.7	6.4
Newburgh, N.Y.	15	—	9.9	7.9
Augusta, Ga.	16	36	10.1	7.1
Jersey City, N.J.	17	9	10.1	6.6
Huntington, W.Va.	18	25	10.2	7.5
New York, N.Y.	19	45	10.4	9.6
Baltimore, Md.	20	43	10.5	8.6
	. . .			
	. . .			
San Diego, Calif.	128	114	20.8	14.0
Colorado Springs, Colo.	129	—	21.0	14.9
Lansing, Mich.	130	122	21.3	18.6
Houston, Tex.	131	83	21.3	12.4
Des Moines, Iowa	132	110	21.4	16.7
Las Vegas, Nev.	133	108	21.4	11.8
Daytona Beach, Fla.	134	—	21.5	12.4
Columbus, Ohio	135	117	21.6	16.7
Wichita, Kans.	136	89	21.6	13.6
Kalamazoo, Mich.	137	—	22.1	17.4
Sacramento, Calif.	138	116	22.2	16.6
Raleigh, N.C.	139	—	22.2	20.4
Tucson, Ariz.	140	115	22.6	11.7
Portland, Oreg.	141	102	22.7	16.5
Spokane, Wash.	142	104	23.7	18.2
Santa Barbara, Calif.	143	123	23.9	16.9
Seattle, Wash.	144	118	24.0	18.7
Denver, Colo.	145	120	24.9	16.6

(continued on following page)

Table 3.1. *(continued)*

	Rank 1980	Rank 1970	Percentage in Nonfamily Households	
			Males	Females
Ann Arbor, Mich.	146	—	28.5	25.9
Madison, Wis.	147	125	29.2	26.4
Austin, Tex.	148	124	31.8	23.9
Mean =			15.7	11.1
SD =			3.7	3.2
CV =			.24	.29

In 1970, 125 SMSAs and, in 1980, 148 SMSAs qualified for inclusion by having populations 250,000 or larger. A dash in the 1970 rankings indicates that the city did not exceed the 250,000 threshold that year.

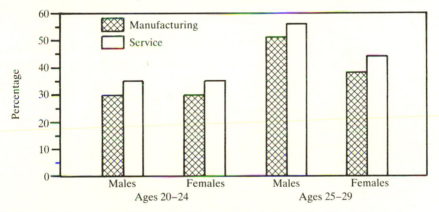

Figure 3.1 Percentage of Unmarried Young Adults in Nonfamily Households in Service and Manufacturing SMSAs in 1980

most recent censuses to describe the characteristics of large U.S. standard metropolitan statistical areas (SMSAs) with unusually high or low proportions of 20–29-year-olds living in nonfamily households. First, I review prior research to help specify the connections between nonfamily household patterns and other metropolitan characteristics. Next, I discuss data and procedures of the study. Findings are presented and discussed in the final sections of the chapter.

Literature and Hypotheses

Research on nonfamily households is fragmented, for three reasons. First, "nonfamily household" is a catchall category that includes both solo and partner households. Some studies have looked exclusively at the former, and others have looked at both. Yet others have examined "nonfamily living" even more generally by combining households with institutional arrangements, such as dormitories and barracks. Consistency across studies in the definition of nonfamily living cannot be taken for granted.

Second and related to the foregoing, the various nonfamily living statuses have no precise labels. In popular speech, for instance, we have no accepted word for describing a couple whose relationship falls somewhere between housemates and married partners. U.S. government data including the census and the Current Population Surveys have suffered from similar ambiguities (Goldscheider and DaVanzo, 1986:189). As a result, data on nonfamily households are imprecise and inconsistent across time compared with data on more traditional living arrangements.

Third and finally, young adults and the elderly, the two age groups accounting overwhelmingly for the increase in nonfamily households, are usually studied within separate areas of family relations: young families and gerontology. Few links have been made to draw these extreme phases of the life course together so that the overall nonfamily household formation process might be clarified.

In short, ambiguous data and a shifting definition of the dependent variable from study to study impede our understanding of nonfamily households. Nonetheless, three competing explanations for change in nonfamily household patterns can be identified. The first (and simplest) implicates variation in kin availability. The second implicates variation in the means to acquire household independence. The third focuses on variation in preference for household independence. In the ensuing sections, I describe each one and pit them collectively against the evidence.

Migrants and Kin Availability—
The Simplest Explanation?

People may be disposed to live without relatives for the simple reason that they lack relatives who want to share housing. This underlies Kobrin's (1976) explanation for the historic rise in nonfamily household residence among elderly women. She argues that declining fertility has demographically constricted the number of "daughters" available to take aged mothers in, contributing to the increase in elderly women who live alone.

Limited availability of kin should constrain young adults through another mechanism, migration. Migrants are less likely than established residents to have local kin with whom to share quarters; moreover, those with few or perhaps less-than-intimate family ties are most likely to move in the first place. Migrants should be more disposed than nonmigrants, therefore, to live in nonfamily households. Correspondingly, localities with high proportions of migrants should have high nonfamily household rates. Concord (1982) applies this argument in an examination of interregional differences in nonfamily household rates. She concludes that such differences are produced by the disproportion of unattached young workers drawn to economically expanding regions.

But what is it about an area that draws migrants? And might these characteristics influence the living arrangements of established residents as well as those of migrants? Differential migration may produce a significant portion, but certainly not all the variation in household composition. The literature suggests a number of other factors independent of migration that should be considered. These can be summarized within a preference-means framework.

A Preference-Means Framework

Living arrangements, especially those of young adults, are usually the result of a compromise between a preference, or taste, for some alternative and the means to achieve it. The nature of this compromise is debated in research explaining the post-1950 increase in nonfamily households, which variously emphasizes the importance of changes in living arrangement preference (Kobrin, 1976; Pampel, 1983) versus changes in income and housing affordability (means) (Michael, Fuchs, and Scott, 1980). The debate suggests a preference-means framework in which *spatial* differences in preference or means factors produce cross-areal differences in the level of nonfamily households.

Five factors to be reviewed include housing market conditions, income, and metropolitan population size as means factors, and education and occupation as preference factors. Racial composition will be discussed as a controlling factor.

Means

Housing market conditions and income. The first step in forming an independent household is to locate an affordable dwelling unit. Thus at the outset, household formation depends on housing affordability (which is determined by income level and housing price) and on the vacancy rate. Affordability and vacancy together indicate the availability of "means" for achieving and maintaining residential autonomy.

Housing that is affordable or in abundant supply eases the formation of all households, whether family or nonfamily (Chudacoff, 1979; Miron, 1980; Harrison, 1981; Smith et al., 1984). In Leppel's (1986) comparison of residents in 12 metropolitan areas, an increase in housing cost lowers the probability of living alone. Studies of solo households, both elderly and young, suggest that those most disposed to living alone are those who can best afford it (Beresford and Rivlin, 1966; Carliner, 1975; Michael, Fuchs, and Scott, 1980; Ermisch, 1981; Harrison, 1981). In short, places with adequate supplies of especially affordable housing should have higher-than-average nonfamily household rates.

Nonetheless, including income as a component of housing affordability introduces a complication. If higher income increases the means to fulfill preferences for residential autonomy (including nonfamily households), then young adults will be more disposed to live in nonfamily households in areas where income is above average. But increased income also makes young men (though not women) more marriageable and so possibly *less* likely to live in nonfamily households (Michael, Fuchs, and Scott, 1980). This implies an inverse correlation between income and the propensity to live in nonfamily households. The male outcome for income will reflect, then, a net effect of opposing influences and a possible difference in the direction of influence for males and females.

Population size. Larger populations are more likely than smaller ones to have the mass necessary for supporting the variety in dwelling types and lifestyle services that facilitate nonfamily household living (Fischer, 1976). Large places, then, should have a greater number of and variety in their restaurants, domestic services, and social or cultural resources aimed at singles—and correspondingly a higher proportion of nonfamily households—than smaller places.

Preference

That children leave home when they enter adulthood is universally preferred; nearly all leave home in the decade following high school. Events such as marriage, college enrollment, or entry into military service can precipitate home-leaving, but in a large proportion of cases, increasing age by itself is justification (Goldscheider and DaVanzo, 1986). Home-leaving leads to living arrangements that range from highly traditional (married-couple households, military barracks) to nontraditional (nonfamily households). What disposes home-leavers to choose less traditional over more traditional living arrangements? I begin with education, then proceed to a related factor that might be called occupational culture.

Education. Education increases cultural tolerance and general taste for the nontraditional (Hyman and Wright, 1979; Davis, 1982); attending college makes students more liberal regarding lifestyle issues (Jennings and Markus, 1986). The highly educated, then, should view nonfamily households more favorably than the less educated. In fact, earlier studies note (unfortunately without elaboration) that the highly educated are more likely than the less educated to live alone (Duncan,

1976; Chevan and Korson, 1972, 1975; Michael, Fuchs, and Scott, 1980). What specific aspect of education disposes young adults to choose nontraditional living arrangements? Two studies of cohorts coming of age during the 1970s make plain that both formal and informal aspects of college education are involved (Goldscheider and DaVanzo, 1986; Waite, Goldscheider, and Witsberger, 1986).

In a study that traces older adolescents through their middle to late 20s, Waite, Goldscheider, and Witsberger (1986) examine the impact of nonfamily living on work plans, expected family size, attitudes toward mothers' employment, and traditional sex roles in the family. Nonfamily living (group as well as household) has striking impact in these areas, in each case pushing young women (and to a smaller extent men) toward the nontraditional end of the spectrum (lowering expected family size, for example). Educational attainment itself erodes traditional family orientations, and living away from home while a student "reinforces the lessons learned at college" (p. 550).

In a related study that traces the living arrangements of high school seniors for eight years following their graduation, Goldscheider and DaVanzo (1986) examine the impact of group-quarters residence (mainly in dormitories and barracks) on later residential independence. They find that young adults are more likely to leave home and establish their own residence if they have group-quarters experience to serve as a stepping stone. Among the various group situations, living in a dormitory is more likely than living in barracks to lead to later independence, because college forges new community ties that military service does not.

In short, education promotes taste for nonfamily household residence as a byproduct not only of formal instruction but also of ideas, skills, and social relationships acquired outside the classroom, "away from parental control and influence" (Waite, Goldscheider, and Witsberger, 1986:550). That away-from-home college, much more than military service, increases taste for residential independence (Goldscheider and DaVanzo, 1986) leads to consideration of a wider circumstance that shapes living arrangement preferences.

Occupational culture. Personal characteristics and life course events are interdependent. By ignoring this interdependence, a simple preference-means model might imply that persons with, say, similar income should be similarly disposed to living in nonfamily households. Yet within the same income level, money can either be saved for marriage (implying a longer stay in the parental home) or can go toward maintaining separate quarters. The choice may depend less on absolute level of income and more on the totality of one's life plans. Different occupations and their associated earning patterns and life styles imply different spending strategies across the life cycle (Oppenheimer, 1982). The clearest difference appears between young adults entering blue-collar and those entering professional occupations.

Blue-collar men marry young, especially compared with men in the professions (Oppenheimer, 1982:123–162); blue-collar culture permits or even rewards early marriage to the extent that a period of independent bachelorhood preceding marriage should be unattractive. By contrast, delayed marriage and some period of independence are instrumental for establishing professional careers. Moreover, although a large proportion of all young adults experience some form of semi-autonomous or independent living before marriage, for the blue-collar population this experience comes disproportionately in the form of military service, whereas for their white-collar counterparts it comes disproportionately in the form of college—with the divergent effects on living preferences described earlier.

In short, occupational culture is an additional influence that may shape living arrangement preferences independently of cross-sectionally measured income or educational achievement. How can the pervasiveness of blue-collar or professional cultures be estimated across metropolitan areas? One indicator might be an area's occupational composition. All else being equal, places whose occupational, or employment, base is primarily blue-collar should have lower-than-average nonfamily household rates, whereas those whose base is dominated by the professions should have higher-than-average rates.

Race (A Control Variable)
Beyond educational and occupational composition, a final characteristic that should influence a locality's household composition is its racial composition, specifically its proportion of black residents. Black families diverge significantly from those of nonblacks in household and family formation patterns and in nonnuclear kin relations (Hofferth, 1985; Cherlin, 1981). It is difficult to anticipate whether the proportion of blacks will affect nonfamily household rates positively or negatively, because evidence points in both directions. On one hand, blacks have low marriage rates and could be overrepresented among nonfamily household residents because they spend disproportionate amounts of time in unmarried statuses. On the other hand, high rates of nonmarital childbearing and more malleable kin relations imply that, even when unmarried, blacks may be less inclined toward nonfamily household residence than is average for the population at large. In any case, racial composition must be used as a control variable.

Data and Method

The data are taken from census tabulations for all 1970 and 1980 metro-politan areas exceeding 250,000, the population threshold above which detailed characteristics are published. This amounts to samples of 125 metropolitan areas for 1970 and 148 for 1980 (U.S. Bureau of the Census, 1973, 1983). Ordinary least squares regression equations, con-structed separately for each sample, predict sex-specific proportions of nonfamily household residents among 20–24-year-olds.

I focus on 20–24-year-olds because living arrangements for this age group are more variable than for any other five-year group in the census. This variability reflects exodus from youth roles and the assumption of adult status. For example, a third of 20–24-year-olds are students at the start of the age interval, but the proportion declines to a tenth by the end of it; the proportion married goes from a plain minority to a clear majority (Goldscheider and DaVanzo, 1985:548–551).

Because many young adults still live in nonfamily households after age 24, I also analyze data for 25–29-year-olds. This older group is much less likely to be living in dorms or barracks, and provides the contrast of a period in the life cycle where group-quarters residence is infrequent.

Separate equations are constructed for solo residents. This is done for 1980 but not for the earlier census, because the earlier tabulations can-not be decomposed in the necessary manner.

The 1970 and 1980 data include identical variables, though with some differences in measures. Definitions and decriptive statistics for the vari-ous measures are shown in Tables 3.2 and 3.3. The problematic imple-mentations are discussed below.

Measurement of the Dependent Variable

The dependent variable is the age- and sex-specific proportion in each metropolitan area that resides in nonfamily households. To control for local differences in marriage, military service, or dorm-living propensity, the institutional population and residents of married-couple households are excluded from the denominator of this ratio. The resulting measure has less intuitive appeal than the more straightforward one used in Table 3.1, where localities are ranked by nonfamily proportion without taking marital composition into account, but it is conceptually more precise. Whatever the case, the two versions correlate highly ($r = .8$, $p < .001$ or better, for all age-sex groups).

Table 3.2. Dependent Variable Means and
Standard Deviations for Metropolitan
Areas (SMSAs) over 250,000, 1970 and
1980

Dependent Variable	Mean	Standard Deviation
Percentage in nonfamily households, 1970[a]		
Males		
20–24	24.5	11.1
25–29	39.1	13.2
Females		
20–24	23.0	10.1
25–29	25.3	8.7
Percentage in nonfamily households, 1980[a]		
Males		
20–24	33.7	11.8
25–29	54.6	11.6
Females		
20–24	33.3	12.1
25–29	42.3	10.3
Percentage living alone, 1980[b]		
Males		
20–24	12.6	3.7
25–29	29.2	5.8
Females		
20–24	11.4	3.4
25–29	22.0	4.7

[a]Percentage of unmarried persons residing in households. This differs from the measure set forth in Table 3.1, which does not control for marital status. See discussion in the "Data and Method" section of the text.

[b]Solo residents are a subset of nonfamily household residents. Separate data for solo residents are not available for 1970.

Measurement of the Independent Variables

Migration is measured as the ratio of men or women in each 5-year age group to the corresponding number in the age group 10 years younger at the preceding decennial census (i.e., 20–24-year-olds in 1980 are divided by the 10–14-year-olds in 1970). This expression of net migration is an

Table 3.3. Definitions, Means, and Standard Deviations for Independent Variables

	1970		1980	
	Mean	Standard Deviation	Mean	Standard Deviation
Median (gross) monthly rent[a] in dollars	108	19	240	32
Rental vacancy rate, %	7.0	2.7		
Home vacancy rate, %			1.8	0.7
Income (median $)[a]				
Annual income, ages 20–24				
Females	2,724	454		
Males	3,916	782		
Weekly earnings, ages 18–24				
Females			173	16
Males			218	28
Average education, % college graduates in population aged 25 and older	11.5	3.2	17.3	5.1
College enrollment, % 22–24-year-olds in school	14.7	5.4	17.8	6.0
Craft employment,[b] % labor force in crafts	21.9	2.6	20.9	2.9
Migrational growth[c]				
20–24-year-olds in 1970	1.1	0.3		
10–14-year-olds in 1960				
20–24-year-olds in 1980			1.2	0.4
10–14-year-olds in 1970				
Percentage black				
Ages 20–24				
Females	11.3	10.4		
Males	10.1	7.9		
Total blacks			11.2	9.3
SMSA total population size[a] (in thousands)	986	1,291	980	1,284

[a]Transformed to log base 10 in regressions.

[b]Adjusted for intercensal reclassification of some occupations.

[c]Adjusted for intercensal boundary changes.

indirect indicator of kin availability, for which direct measures are unavailable. When growth through migration is high, the availability of kin is low.

Housing markets are compared by using median gross monthly rental rates to gauge housing cost, and rental or owner vacancy rates to gauge housing availability.

Because of intercensal differences in tabulation, measures of income differ most among all independent variables. In 1980, the weekly individual wage rate is used, whereas in 1970 total individual annual income is used. Nonetheless, all measures are age and sex specific, and different measures within each cross-section (whether total income or wage rate) correlate highly (on the order of r = .75 or better).

Average education is represented in each locality by the proportion of residents aged 25 or over who have graduated from college. A measure of local college enrollment is used to control for "college town" effects.

Differences in occupational culture can be estimated in only the roughest form. The percentage of each area's labor force that constitutes "crafts" (1970) or "precision production" (1980) occupations is treated as a reflection of the area's blue-collar orientation. The higher the percentage of workers in crafts occupations (the workers most clearly "blue-collar" in their income and marriage patterns [Oppenheimer, 1982:123–162:table 3.3]), the more blue-collar the occupational culture. At the complementary end of the occupational spectrum, I explored the use of percentage of professionals as an alternative indicator of occupational culture, but did not retain it when it proved collinear with education.

Results: Metropolitan Correlates of Nonfamily Households

In which metropolitan areas are young adults most likely to live in nonfamily households? Unequivocally, the areas are most likely those whose residents are highly educated and whose populations are rapidly growing. Somewhat less clearly (because effects vary across time, age, sex, and specific living arrangement), nonfamily living is more common in areas with favorable housing markets, high average income, and a low proportion of blacks. Finally, the size of an area's population seems unrelated to its nonfamily household rate. Although labor-force composition appears similarly unrelated, I argue that it is a master variable operating through other more proximal factors.

In setting forth details, I discuss 1970 and 1980 results together, and present independent variables in order of strongest to weakest. Equations for 20–24-year-olds are set forth in Tables 3.4–3.6; numerical results for 25–29-year-olds are omitted to save space.

Table 3.4. Regressions Estimating Percentages of 1970 Metropolitan Residents Aged 20–24 Who Lived in Nonfamily Households

Variable	Raw Coefficient	Standard Error	Standardized β	p Value of t
		Females		
Rent, median	10.4	9.4	.071	<.500
Rental vacancy rate	0.8	0.25	.206	<.001
Income	2.6	12.1	.017	<.500
Average education	1.3	0.32	.374	<.001
College enrollment	0.3	0.18	.129	<.050
Craft employment	−0.7	0.29	−.155	<.025
Migrational growth	8.8	2.2	.280	<.001
Black, %	−0.2	0.06	−.155	<.005
SMSA size	1.8	2.2	.057	<.500

Intercept = −30.2
R^2 = .67

Variable	Raw Coefficient	Standard Error	Standardized β	p Value of t
		Males		
Rent, median	3.0	7.9	.020	<.800
Rental vacancy rate	0.9	0.19	.228	<.001
Income	14.6	7.2	.112	<.025
Average education	1.0	0.25	.284	<.001
College enrollment	0.7	0.12	.356	<.001
Craft employment	0.3	0.23	−.060	<.250
Migrational growth	13.4	1.9	.418	<.001
Black, %	−0.2	0.07	−.143	<.003
SMSA size	−0.4	1.5	−.116	<.005

Intercept = −59.6
R^2 = .80

Strong Correlates

Education and College Enrollment

Average education is positively related to nonfamily household rates and produces the single greatest standardized coefficient in almost every equation, irrespective of year, age-sex group, or specific living arrangement. This effect persists after controlling for college enrollment level. The coefficient for education is at its weakest for 20–24-year-old men in 1970, (β = .284 with p < .001); the effect is somewhat weaker than that of enrollment or migration but somewhat stronger than that of income or housing availability (Table 3.4). More typically

Table 3.5.   Regressions Estimating Percentages of 1980 Metropolitan Residents Aged
20–24 Who Lived in Nonfamily Households

Variable	Raw Coefficient	Standard Error	Standardized β	p Value of t
	Females			
Migrational growth	5.7	1.7	.202	<.001
Rent, median	−48.5	15.3	−.224	<.005
Home vacancy rate	3.9	1.0	.215	<.001
Income	3.7	20.4	.012	<.900
Average education	1.1	0.11	.625	<.001
College enrollment	0.6	0.13	.320	<.001
Craft employment	0.2	0.24	.054	<.750
Black, %	−0.2	0.06	−.126	<.025
SMSA size	−2.6	1.9	−.076	<.750
Intercept = 48.9				
R^2 = .72				
	Males			
Migrational growth	6.8	1.8	.248	<.001
Rent, median	−30.7	13.8	−.145	<.050
Home vacancy rate	5.0	1.0	.281	<.001
Income	35.6	11.2	.167	<.025
Average education	1.0	0.11	.556	<.001
College enrollment	0.5	0.13	.261	<.001
Craft employment	0.2	0.24	.060	<.500
Black, %	−0.1	0.06	−.074	<.250
SMSA size	−5.3	1.9	−.160	<.050
Intercept = −58.1				
R^2 = .71				

(20–24-year-old men in 1980), the coefficient for education is twice as great as for the next most important factor (β = .556 with p < .001, Table 3.5).

Enrollment level itself boosts the nonfamily household rates for 20–24-year-olds in both 1970 and 1980 (for example, β = .356 with p < .001, and β = .261 with p < .001, for male 20–24-year-olds in 1970 and 1980, respectively), but the effect falls off for 25–29-year-olds, consistent with the falloff in college attendance at those ages. The connection between enrollment level and the 1980 living-alone component of the nonfamily household rate is inconsistent if not indiscernible.

Table 3.6.   Regressions Estimating Percentages of 1980 Metropolitan Residents Aged
                   20–24 Who Lived Alone

Variable	Raw Coefficient	Standard Error	Standardized β	p Value of t
		Females		
Migrational growth	2.6	0.61	.327	<.001
Rent, median	−43.6	5.4	−.707	<.001
Home vacancy rate	1.5	0.36	.298	<.001
Income	17.0	7.2	.195	<.050
Average education	0.4	0.04	.829	<.001
College enrollment	−0.1	0.05	−.104	<.250
Craft employment	0.1	0.09	.089	<.250
Black, %	0.0	0.02	.015	<.900
SMSA size	0.3	0.70	.027	<.800

Intercept   =   42.5
R^2 =   .58

Variable	Raw Coefficient	Standard Error	Standardized β	p Value of t
		Males		
Migrational growth	2.6	0.70	.303	<.001
Rent	−31.9	5.3	−.477	<.001
Home vacancy rate	2.1	0.37	.381	<.001
Income	26.4	4.4	.392	<.001
Average education	0.3	0.04	.614	<.001
College enrollment	−0.1	0.05	−.143	<.100
Craft employment	0.2	0.10	.131	<.100
Black, %	0.0	0.02	.027	<.900
SMSA size	−1.0	0.70	−.096	<.750

Intercept   =   −2.5
R^2 =   .60

Note: Residents living alone are a subset of nonfamily household residents.

Migration

In both 1970 and 1980 equations, migrational growth produces a strong positive coefficient for all age and sex groups. At minimum, the coefficient is fifth strongest but still highly significant (β = .202, p < .001) for nonfamily women in 1980 (Table 3.5); in general its magnitude is less than that of education or enrollment and comparable to those for housing. The coefficient remains uniformly strong and positive for both the 1980 nonfamily household rate and its component living-alone rate.

Correlates That Vary

Income

The influence of income presents a mixed picture. Where discernible, its influence is positive, as expected, and affects men more than women, 20–24-year-olds more than 25–29-year-olds, and solo residents more than housemates.

In 1970 regressions, income is unrelated to the nonfamily household rate for any group except for 20–24-year-old men, for whom the coefficient is modestly positive (β = .112, p < .025, Table 3.4).

In 1980 regressions, a rise in average income implies a modest rise in the nonfamily household rate for 20–24-year-old males but not females (β = .167, p < .025 for men versus β = .012, p < .900 for women, Table 3.5). Nonetheless, when only solo households are considered there is a clearly positive income effect for both sexes (β = .195 with p < .05 for women, β = .392 with p < .001 for men, Table 3.6). The greater salience of income for those living alone suggests high setup and maintenance costs relative to partner households, a difference that emerges again when considering housing market conditions.

Housing

Housing market conditions constrain nonfamily households as expected, but they do so unevenly. In general, the housing market becomes a stronger factor in going from partner to solo households and from 1970 to 1980.

To begin with an unexpected result, nonfamily household rates in 1970 are *positively* correlated with rental cost ($\beta \cong$ .200 with p < .001 for both male and female 20–24-year-olds, Table 3.4). That young adults are more likely to be living in nonfamily households in high-rent SMSAs suggests that some third unaccounted factor pushes both rent level and the number of nonfamily households upward. Whatever that factor may be, by 1980 rental cost becomes negatively correlated with partner-household rates (β = −.145 with p < .05 for younger men, and is slightly stronger for younger women, Table 3.5), although the effect diminishes in going from 20–24 to 25–29-year-olds.

At both censuses, the positive correlation between housing vacancy rates and nonfamily household rates confirms that young adults are more likely to achieve residential independence in places where housing is comparatively plentiful.

Housing coefficients for the solo component of the 1980 nonfamily household rate conform to those for partner households, although high rental costs seem a stronger constraint. Unlike housemates, solo residents are unable to pool resources or to divide up living expenses. For both male and female solo residents, the negative coefficients for rental cost are larger and more discernible than the corresponding numbers for partner residents: $\beta = -.707$ for women and $\beta = -.477$ for men, both with $p < .001$ (Table 3.6). However, the effect of rental cost in these equations is still exceeded by that of education.

Although housing market conditions work generally as hypothesized, their impact in total context is moderate at best. This can be understood if one considers that new in-migrants contribute disproportionately to an area's nonfamily household population. An unfavorable housing market may deter potential in-migrants from moving to an area in the first place, but once having arrived, newcomers usually lack alternatives to paying sellers' prices for housing. In localities with substantial in-migration, the impact can be sizable. Moreover, where the in-migrant stream is persistent, demand for housing is continuously replenished and becomes relatively insensitive to normal housing market price mechanisms.

Racial Composition
Areas with higher-than-average proportions of blacks have somewhat lower-than-average nonfamily household rates. This holds for both sexes, both age groups, and at both censuses. In contrast, the relative size of black subpopulations is unrelated to the living-alone rate. A similar result has been reported by Leppel (1986) but left unexplained; I also lack an explanation. Regressions not shown fail to support explanations involving regional differences or differences in racial patterns of metropolitan and nonmetropolitan migration.

Weak or Indiscernible Correlates

Population Size
The disposition of young adults to live in nonfamily households is modestly but inconsistently related to metropolitan population size. In 1970, 25–29-year-old residents of areas with larger populations (especially females) were more likely to be living in nonfamily households than their counterparts in areas with smaller populations. This is as expected, but contrasts with 20–24-year-olds, of whom males in areas with larger populations are somewhat *less* likely to live in nonfamily households. (For the younger females, size makes no difference.) In 1980, any effect of population size is indiscernible.

Once other metropolitan attributes are taken into account, size has no clear connection to the nonfamily household rate. If any critical mass effects exist, they seem to have fallen below the 250,000 threshold delimiting my samples.

Occupational Composition

Analysis of occupational composition, first with the present regressions, then with supplemental equations (not shown), yields two levels of results.

At one level of analysis, Tables 3.4–3.6 imply that ties between the makeup of an area's labor force and its household composition are modest at best. In 1970, women were somewhat less likely to live in nonfamily households in areas where blue-collar employment predominates. Men in 1970 and men and women in 1980 showed not even minor changes in living arrangements with variation in local level of craft employment.

At another level, alternative regressions (not shown) imply that occupational composition is in actuality a central influence on nonfamily household rates. Consistent with original expectation, when blue-collar employment is regressed in a simpler equation with only housing market measures (but not education, enrollment, or migration) as co-predictors, it generates a substantial negative effect on nonfamily household rates, both female and male. Only when average education, college enrollment, and migrational growth are added in the more comprehensive models shown is the influence of occupational base diminished. This suggests that education, enrollment, and migration act at least partly as components of occupational base. Indeed, as I argue in the following section, occupational base is a concept that unifies the various discrete relationships that have been described.

Summary and Discussion

The determinants of high nonfamily household rates are highly educated residents, high college-age school enrollment, high levels of migrational growth, high average income, a work force dominated by professional rather than blue-collar occupations, a low proportion of blacks, and affordable housing. With the exception of affordable housing, these match the defining attributes of "information processing" centers, metropolitan areas whose employment is concentrated in government, commerce, and services (Abbott, 1981; Noyelle, 1983). Throughout the 1960s and 1970s, such places enjoyed robust economic health that fed in part on the growth of highly educated professional labor forces, and in turn fueled that growth. Thus metropolitan areas with high proportions of nonfamily households disproportionately comprise state capitals, centers of higher education, and places that otherwise attract young in-migrants through generation of job opportunities for professionals (Austin, Madison, and Ann Arbor are conspicuous examples; see Table 3.1 and Figure 3.2).

By comparison, information-processing cities are rare among areas with low nonfamily household rates, which instead occur disproportionately in places engaged in manufacturing, resource extraction, or related activities. Such smokestack centers (Abbott, 1981) experienced flat or declining economic fortunes in the 1960s and 1970s, with a key lack of growth through migration. New York City, a national hub of commerce and finance, is an apparent anomaly in this low-rates group (Table 3.1). If one considers New York's costly housing, however, as well as its large black subpopulation and its loss of population and economic vitality during the 1970s, then the area's ranking becomes less than surprising.

The Varying Effect of Preference and Means

Knowledge-intensive economies, then, provide conditions generally conducive to nonfamily household residence. The conditions that most specifically affect young adults nonetheless vary with age, sex, and specific living arrangement. Because high average education is uniformly associated with high nonfamily household rates, the focus here is on the differences in the complementary roles of income and housing cost.

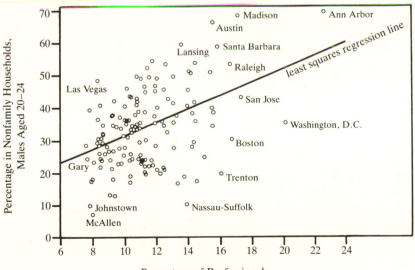

Figure 3.2 Professional Employment and Nonfamily Household Rates Rise Together (1980 SMSAs over 250,000)

Age

The living arrangements of 20–24-year-olds are more sensitive to variation in income and in rental cost than are those of their older, 25–29-year-old counterparts. This is partly a statistical artifact (the younger group has wider variance in income), but one that relates to the general observation that the household behavior of the youngest (and least well-established) age groups is most vulnerable to economic constraints (Goodman, 1986:11).

Sex

High average income goes with high levels of nonfamily household residence among men, but much less so among women, for whom the income effect ranges downward from modestly positive to zero. I find no adequate explanation for this difference (the variance in income is no wider for males than females, for instance); further exploration is warranted.

Solo Versus Partners

Finally, housing market and income constraints are stronger for solo than for partner households, because partners enjoy certain economies of scale.

The upshot is that neither means nor preference factors alone can adequately explain variation in nonfamily household patterns for all young adults. A more satisfactory explanation might involve some form of dynamic interplay. At least that is the implication when results are examined across time, as in the following section.

Decline in the Role of Preference Factors
from 1970 to 1980

From 1970 to 1980, the U.S. proportion of nonfamily households rose from 19 to 26 percent of all households (U.S. Bureau of the Census, 1985:table 54), with a corresponding increase for young adults (Table 3.2). Despite these changes in absolute level, metropolitan areas retained their relative positions: SMSA rankings for 1970 closely resemble those for 1980 (Table 3.1), with high intercensal correlation between measures of household composition ($r = .8$ or higher). Taking the evidence as a whole, similar if not identical processes appear to shape living arrangement composition in both years. Nonetheless, at least one important difference remains.

The constraint of housing cost and income—minor across metropolitan areas in 1970—became significantly stronger by 1980. This rising salience of means relative to preference factors may stem from shifts in real income or the housing market, but may also result from a decline in the influence of education. Because nonfamily living arrangements were still unconventional in the late 1960s, highly educated trendsetters were more likely to be found in them than were the less educated. But as these arrangements have become conventional and preference for them has spread, their connection with education has diminished, and the role of means factors has accordingly expanded.

This chapter has examined the characteristics of metropolitan areas with unusually high or low proportions of young adults living in nonfamily households. Young adults are most likely to live in nonfamily households in areas whose employment is predominantly knowledge-intensive rather than smokestack-based. The link between employment and household composition is mediated primarily by education; the labor forces of information-processing centers include high proportions of the highly educated, and highly educated young adults are more disposed to live in nonfamily households than are the less educated, even after controlling for income. The positive effect of education is offset by the high cost of housing in these areas, a factor that assumed increasing salience across the 10 years studied. Hence, of three competing explanations for the variation in young-adult household composition—kin availability, housing preference, and economic means—only the effects of preference and means proved discernible, with preferences making a greater impact in 1970 but means rising in importance by 1980.

References

Abbott, C. 1981. *The New Urban America: Growth and Politics in Sunbelt Cities.* Chapel Hill: University of North Carolina Press.

Beresford, J., and A. Rivlin. 1966. Privacy, poverty, and old age. *Demography* 3:247–258.

Carliner, G. 1975. Determinants of household headship. *Journal of Marriage and the Family* 37(February):28–38.

Cherlin, A. 1981. *Marriage, Divorce, Remarriage.* Cambridge, Mass.: Harvard University Press.

Chevan, A., and J. H. Korson. 1972. The widowed who live alone: An examination of social and demographic factors. *Social Forces* 51(September):45–53.

Chevan, A., and J. H. Korson. 1975. Living arrangements of widows in the United States and Israel, 1960 and 1961. *Demography* 12(August):505–517.

Chudacoff, H. 1979. New branches on the tree: Household structure in the early stages of the family life cycle in Worcester, 1860–1880. *Proceedings of the American Antiquarian Society* 86:303–320.

Concord, C. 1982. Spatial distribution of primary individuals. *Professional Geographer* 34:167–177.

Davis, J. 1982. Achievement variables and class cultures: Family, schooling, job, and forty-nine dependent variables in the cumulative GSS. *American Sociological Review* 47(October):569–586.

Duncan, G. 1976. Unmarried heads of household and marriage. Pp. 77–115 in James Morgan (ed.), *Five Thousand Families—Patterns of Economic Progress,* Vol. 4, *Analyses of the First Seven Years of the Panel Study on Income Dynamics.* Ann Arbor: University of Michigan, Survey Research Center.

Ermisch, J. 1981. An economic theory of household formation. *Scottish Journal of Political Economy* 28(February):1–19.

Fischer, C. S. 1976. *The Urban Experience.* New York: Harcourt-Brace-Jovanovich.

Goldscheider, F. K., and J. DaVanzo. 1985. Living arrangements and the transition to adulthood. *Demography* 22:545–564.

Goldscheider, F. K., and J. DaVanzo. 1986. Semiautonomy and leaving home in early adulthood. *Social Forces* 65(1):187–201.

Goldscheider, C., and F. K. Goldscheider. 1987a. Ethnic Continuity and Leaving Home: The Structural and Cultural Bases of Traditional Family Values. Paper presented at the annual meeting of the American Sociological Association, Chicago.

Goldscheider, C., and F. K. Goldscheider. 1987b. Moving out and marriage: What do young adults expect? *American Sociological Review* 52:278–285.

Goodman, J. L. 1986. *Economic Determinants of Household Formations and Living Arrangements.* Working Paper 66. Economic Activity Section, Division of Research and Statistics, Federal Reserve System, Washington, D.C.

Harrison, B. 1981. *Living Alone in Canada: Demographic and Economic Perspectives, 1951–1976.* Publication No. 98-811. Ottawa: Statistics Canada.

Hofferth, S. L. 1985. Children's life course: Family structure and living arrangements in cohort perspective. Pp. 75–112 in G. H. Elder (ed.), *Life Course Dynamics: Trajectories and Transitions, 1968–1980.* Ithaca: Cornell University Press.

Hyman, H., and C. Wright. 1979. *Education's Lasting Influence on Values.* Chicago: University of Chicago Press.

Jennings, M. K., and G. B. Markus. 1986. Yuppie politics. *Institute for Social Research Newsletter* (Ann Arbor), Spring/Summer:5–7.

Kobrin, F. 1976. The fall in household size and the rise of the primary individual. *Demography* 13(February):127–138.

Laslett, B. 1973. The family as a public and private institution: An historical perspective. *Journal of Marriage and the Family* 35:480–492.

Leppel, K. 1986. A trinomial logit analysis of household composition. *AREUA Journal* 14(4):537–556.

Michael, R., V. Fuchs, and S. Scott. 1980. Changes in the propensity to live alone: 1950–1976. *Demography* 20(February):39–56.

Miron, J. 1980. *The Rise of the One-Person Household: The Ontario Experience, 1951–1976.* Paper No. 16. Toronto: Centre for Urban and Community Research.

Modell, J., F. F. Furstenberg, Jr., and T. Hershberg. 1976. Social change and transitions to adulthood in historical perspective. *Journal of Family History* 1:7–32.

Noyelle, T. J. 1983. The rise of advanced services: some implications for economic development in U.S. cities. *APA Journal* 49(3):280–290.

Oppenheimer, V. K. 1982. *Work and the Family: A Study in Social Demography.* New York: Academic Press.

Pampel, F. C. 1983. Changes in the propensity to live alone: Evidence from consecutive cross-sectional surveys, 1960–1976. *Demography* 20(November):433–448.

Smith, L. B., K. T. Rosen, A. Markandya, and P.-A. Ullmo. 1984. The demand for housing, household headship rates and household formation: An international analysis. *Urban Studies* 21:407–414.

Sweet, J. A., and L. Bumpass. 1987. *American Families and Households.* New York: Russell Sage Foundation.

U.S. Bureau of the Census. 1973. *1970 Census of Population: 1970,* Vol. 1, *Characteristics of Population.* Washington, D.C.: U.S. Government Printing Office.

U.S. Bureau of the Census. 1981. *Statistical Abstract of the United States, 1981* (101st ed.). Washington, D.C.: U.S. Government Printing Office.

U.S. Bureau of the Census. 1983. *1980 Census of Population,* Vol. 2, *Detailed Characteristics of the Population.* Washington, D.C.: U.S. Government Printing Office.

Waite, L., F. K. Goldscheider, and C. Witsberger. 1986. Nonfamily living and the erosion of traditional family orientations among young adults. *American Sociological Review* 51:541–554.

4 *Daphne Spain*

Housing Quality and Affordability among Female Householders

One of the basic changes in household composition over the past several decades has been the growth in the number of single householders—male and female—and the concomitant decline in married-couple households (as described in the chapter by James A. Sweet in this volume). This shift in the sex and marital status of householders has important implications for housing demography. Single persons or single parents and their children have different housing needs from those of married-couple families. Demands for size, type, location, and affordability of units will vary by household composition, and may in turn eventually affect the housing supply (see Hayden, 1984).

Of all household changes, the growth in the number of families maintained by women has gained the greatest public attention (Birch, 1985; Garfinkel and McLanahan, 1986; Weitzman, 1985). The situation of female householders is relevant to housing demography for several reasons. First, their increasing numbers have influenced the overall decline in household size and thus the demand for smaller housing units. Second, female householders typically have fewer economic resources than either married couples or male householders, limiting their ability to compete in the housing market. Third, female householders are disproportionately located in central cities. Thus, their hous-

---

Daphne Spain is Assistant Professor in Urban and Environmental Planning, University of Virginia, Charlottesville, Virginia 22903.

ing choices are often limited to older, more deteriorated units. Finally, female householders have higher than average residential mobility rates, which means they are engaged in housing searches more often than other households.

This chapter focuses on the quality and affordability of housing by household type, with special attention to female householders in regard to numbers, economic status, location, and residential mobility. Whether residential mobility acts equally to improve housing quality for all household types will also be examined in an attempt to link household composition, housing quality, and the process of adjustment between households and housing. The work reported here is primarily descriptive and is meant to explore: if sex of householder has an effect on housing quality and affordability independent of other household characteristics; and if residential mobility operates differently by household type as a housing adjustment mechanism.

Whether changing demographic trends are creating the "unsheltered woman" (Birch, 1985) is a topic of relevance to housing demographers in assessing future housing needs. If female householders are poorly housed relative to other households, public policy may need to focus on housing issues independently of welfare and other support services. Thus the issue of women and housing connects the concerns of urban planners, sociologists, demographers, and policy analysts.

Changing Demographics

The Growth in the Number of Female Householders

The type of household for which most post–World War II housing was built—a nuclear family of husband, wife, and children—constituted only 30 percent of all American households by 1980. A combination of falling fertility and an aging population has reduced the proportion of households including children, and the growth in the number of single householders has reduced the share of all households maintained by married couples.

The proportion of all households maintained by women rose from 15 to 28 percent between 1950 and 1985, those maintained by men rose from 8 to 14 percent, and the proportion of married-couple households fell from 77 to 58 percent. In 1985, there were approximately 24 million female householders, 12 million male householders, and 50 million married-couple households (Bianchi and Spain, 1986; U.S. Bureau of the Census, 1986a:table A). A later age at marriage, the rising rate of out-of-wedlock births, growth in the size of the elderly population, and a steady increase in the divorce rate have all contributed to the growth in the number of female householders.

Three subgroups of female householders face particular problems in the housing market: blacks, the elderly, and single mothers (see Birch, 1985). Black women are more likely than white women to maintain their own households. In 1980, 39 percent of adult black women were family householders or lived alone compared with 24 percent of adult white women (Bianchi and Spain, 1986:table 3.2). That is, more than one out of three black women were responsible for their own households compared with fewer than one out of four white women.

Elderly women are more likely to maintain their own households than elderly men. In 1980, among persons aged 65 and over, 77 percent of women compared with 67 percent of men maintained their own households. The percentages, however, downplay the magnitude of the numbers involved in the difference by sex. Seven million elderly women maintained their own households in 1980 compared with only 1.8 million men (Bianchi and Spain, 1986:95). This imbalance of unmarried persons at the older ages results partly from women's longer life expectancy and partly from men's higher remarriage rates.

Female householders with children are of particular interest because their numbers more than doubled between 1960 and 1980, and the majority of single mothers are now never married, divorced, or separated rather than widowed. That means they are younger and more likely than widows to be in a transitional phase, both in terms of marital status and housing (Ross and Sawhill, 1975). In 1960, 1 of every 12 children lived in a single-mother family; by 1983 this had changed to more than 1 of every 5 children (Garfinkel and McLanahan, 1986). This group of women and children in female-maintained families is of special interest because they are disproportionately likely to be living in poverty.

The growth in the number of female householders and the variety within the group have implications for the current housing market. Whether the female householder lives alone, with children, or is elderly, there are numerous size, supply, and design issues that differ from the housing issues facing married couples (Hayden, 1984). If the female householder lives alone, there will be less demand for large units than when married couples account for a larger share of the market. If the female-maintained household includes children, as a quarter do, there may be as much need for space as among married couples, but at a much lower price. Elderly female householders (a third of the total) may need units with special built-in features such as lowered cabinets and safety railings enabling them to continue living alone (U.S. Bureau of the Census, 1986a:table A).

Household Differences in Poverty

Families maintained by women have higher poverty rates than any other family type, and their economic position relative to such groups as the elderly and disabled has declined over time. Approximately 1 out of 2 mother-only families is poor and dependent on welfare compared with 1 in 10 two-parent families (Garfinkel and McLanahan, 1986).

The poverty level in 1983 was $10,178 for a family of four (U.S. Bureau of Census, 1985a:1). In that same year, the median income of female family householders was $11,835 compared with $21,925 for male family householders and $27,378 for married couples (U.S. Bureau of the Census, 1986b:table A). Thus the typical female family householder lives much closer to the poverty threshold than other types of families.

There are several reasons for higher poverty rates among female householders. One is the gap between men's and women's average earnings: even women who are employed full time are not able to achieve the same standard of living as men (U.S. Bureau of Census, 1986b:table 26). Second, the lack of adequate and affordable child care prevents many mothers from working or from working full time (O'Connell and Rogers, 1983:16). Third, fewer than half of all mothers awarded child support receive the full amount due from absent fathers (U.S. Bureau of Census, 1985b:table A). And finally, federal public-assistance programs provide inadequate benefits for the needs of mother-only families (Garfinkel and McLanahan, 1986).

The primary effect female householders' reduced economic resources have on the housing market is in the increased demand for inexpensive rental and owner-occupied units. Unfortunately, just when the demand for such low-cost housing is expanding because of the growth of female householders, the supply is shrinking because of rising construction costs and federal cutbacks in housing subsidies. Because of their greater poverty—in both money and time—female householders have not been a vocal group with the ability to exert political pressure regarding housing needs.

Location of Female Householders

Because of the extremely different financial circumstances under which the typical married couple and the typical female householder operate, it is not surprising that they exhibit different residential distributions within the metropolitan area. Much of this residential pattern is determined by economic necessity. Of female householders living in poverty in 1980, 65 percent lived in central cities (U.S. Bureau of Census, 1983b:tables 111 and 119).

Female householders tend to be residentially concentrated in central cities, and female householders with children are considerably more likely than married-couples with children to live in central cities. Approximately a quarter of married-couple families live in central cities compared with about 44 percent of female family householders (U.S. Bureau of Census, 1983b:table 111).

Why are female householders disproportionately concentrated in central cities? The availability of affordable housing is at least part of the explanation. Female householders, because of their lower average incomes, are concentrated in central-city neighborhoods with the oldest, most deteriorated housing and the lowest rents (Cook and Rudd, 1984). Indeed, female householders have so few resources in the housing market that their succession into certain "neighborhoods of last resort" is a precursor of the eventual abandonment of this housing (Wolpert and Seley, 1985).

Women may also be more likely to live in central cities for access to public transit. Numerous studies have shown that, in relation to men, women use public transit more often (they are about twice as likely to use public transportation for work trips) and private cars less often (Fox, 1983; Michelson, 1985).

Race operates as a third factor influencing the residential distribution of female householders. Because black women are more likely than white women to maintain their own households and blacks are disproportionately located in central cities, there is a race and sex interaction resulting in greater central-city representation among female householders.

Uneven metropolitan distribution means greater demand for housing in central cities among female householders. Whether by economic necessity or by choice, female householders will be looking for urban housing, which may be of the poorest quality in the metropolitan area.

Residential Mobility and Housing

A common assumption underlying residential mobility theory is that people move to improve their housing quality. Housing conditions have repeatedly emerged as an important predictor of mobility (Goodman, 1976; Newman and Duncan, 1979; Rossi, 1955), and people seldom make a local move unless there is a positive housing adjustment, given the expenses involved in moving. The typical move is to a place that is slightly larger and more expensive than the previous unit, so that a process of "upward mobility" through the housing stock characterizes most moves (Goodman, 1978a; Myers, 1983).

One of the most thoroughly tested theories of residential mobility is the decision-making model developed by Speare, Goldstein, and Frey (1975). This theory proposes that people stay in their current residence only as long as they are satisfied with it. Once dissatisfaction occurs (because of overcrowding or a desire to own, for example), the household will decide whether a move would increase satisfaction and, if so, a move occurs.

Yet the economic constraints associated with sex of the householder have become increasingly important issues since Speare's theory was proposed. The preference–decision-making model was formulated during a period in which married-couple households were a more predominant family type, and the increased number of female householders may have reduced the suitability of these models.

Speare's model may not be as applicable to female householders as it is to married couples, because marital disruptions often leave women with few economic resources and the necessity of moving (Weitzman, 1985). Thus many women's moves are not the result of a rational decision-making process of maximizing satisfaction, but are necessitated by a change in marital status. Residential mobility is very high for women immediately following divorce: approximately 38 percent of divorced mothers and their children move during the first year after a divorce, with subsequent annual rates dropping off but still remaining higher than those for married couples (McLanahan, 1983; see also Long, 1972). In 1983, the mobility rate for all female householders was 20 percent compared with 13 percent for married couples (U.S. Bureau of the Census, 1984:table 13).

In terms of housing demography, the higher residential mobility rates of female householders mean they are engaged in housing searches more often than other households. It may be that single mothers have little time for lengthy housing searches to fill all their needs, or their needs may change fairly quickly with fluctuations in employment and income (Anderson-Khleif, 1981; Weiss, 1980). Another problem for single mothers is the practice of excluding families with children from rental units. Although now illegal, landlords who may still discriminate against women with children recognize that single mothers have few resources with which to pursue legal redress.

The passage of no-fault divorce laws also may have contributed to women's higher mobility. Before 1970, under the old laws, wives were typically awarded the house after a divorce. But today homes are being sold to settle joint-property agreements. The number of divorce cases in which there was a court order to sell the house rose from 1 in 10 in 1968 to 1 in 3 by 1977 (Weitzman, 1985:31). Whereas in the past newly divorced women may have been "overhoused" relative to other female householders, divorcees are now less likely to benefit from their history of married-couple housing consumption.

This introduction has provided a summary of the main reasons why female householders warrant a special interest among housing demographers. Their numbers are growing, their economic resources are meager, they are disproportionately located in central cities, and they have higher than average residential mobility. The remainder of this chapter will examine the issues of housing quality and affordability while incorporating these four topics.

Data and Methods[1]

The study of female householders and their housing presents several methodological difficulties. The first concerns the diversity of the category. Women who maintain their own households may have never married, or they may be separated, divorced, or widowed. Children might be included in the household, and so might other adults. There is also a wide age range: from young adults who are keeping apartments to the elderly living in single-family detached units. Variables will be introduced in the analysis to control for such differences.

A second drawback is the lack of information regarding the length of time a woman has maintained her own household. Traditionally, female householders were in a relatively brief "time of transition" between marital disruption and remarriage (Ross and Sawhill, 1975). Yet, more recent data indicate that the time spent between divorce or widowhood and remarriage has lengthened considerably, and never-married mothers have increased as a proportion of all female householders (Garfinkel and McLanahan, 1986). Finally, sex of householder is not a permanent classification; a change in marital status and/or a new household formation may also involve a shift in who is recorded as the householder, which in turn would involve a shift in gender. Unfortunately, the data used in the current analysis do not allow for an examination of recent moves that involve changes in householder status (and the corresponding shifts from one sex to the other). The American Housing Survey

---

1. The data used in this chapter were made available through the Inter-University Consortium for Political and Social Research. Data for the 1983 American Housing Survey (formerly the Annual Housing Survey) were collected by the U.S. Bureau of the Census (U.S. Bureau of the Census, 1983a).

(AHS) records information about recent moves only for households with the same head before and after the move. Thus household composition changes that occur as a result of marital disruptions are not captured as accurately for women as for men.

Because of these data limitations, it is necessary to perform a cross-sectional analysis of a basically longitudinal phenomenon. The 1983 national American Housing Survey is used to examine housing quality and affordability by household type. A total of six indicators of housing quality are examined: homeownership, age of housing, value of owned housing, gross monthly rent, the crowding ratio (number of persons per room), and government subsidy status (whether the rented unit is subsidized by a government agency). The three measures of housing affordability include housing costs as a percentage of income for owners, rent as a percentage of income for renters, and selected monthly housing costs for owners.

The national AHS contains information on approximately 60,000 households. The current analysis is based on a subset of approximately 26,000 metropolitan households which can be identified by location—central-city or outside central-city. Households are classified into three categories in this research: married couples, female householders with no spouse present, and male householders with no spouse present.

The AHS is unique in providing information about the previous and current housing units for households which have moved into the sample in the 12 months preceding the survey. It is therefore possible to compare housing quality before and after a move; information on affordability is not available for both previous and current units. Movers are defined as householders who have moved into their current units from elsewhere within the same metropolitan area. (As already noted, only those persons who maintained both their previous and current units were asked for information about the previous units.) Because most short-distance moves (local mobility) are made for family, housing, or neighborhood reasons whereas most long-distance moves (migration) are made for employment reasons (Long and DeAre, 1980; Zimmer, 1973), the current analysis is restricted to local moves.

Five indicators are used to measure the effects of residential mobility on housing quality. The first measure is *tenure,* or whether the dwelling is owned or rented. There are many rental units which are in better physical condition than owner-occupied units, and there are a few people who might prefer renting to owning a home, but homeownership is an integral part of the "American dream." Thus a shift from renter to owner status is defined as an improvement in housing quality, and a shift from owning to renting is considered a decline (see Myers, 1983).

Housing *value* and gross monthly *rent* are compared for previous and current units to assess whether quality has improved for the householder. Gross rent includes the monthly contract rent and the cost of fuel and utilities; it is a recode computed by the U.S. Census Bureau to standardize reported housing costs among renters. Any move from a lower to a higher value or rent is considered an improvement in housing quality. Although higher rent and higher value do not necessarily insure better living conditions, there is generally a positive correlation between housing costs and quality (Goodman, 1978b).

The *crowding* ratio, or number of persons per room, is measured for the previous and current units, with a decline in crowding defined as an improvement in quality. If the household receives a rental subsidy, it is labeled *government subsidy* and applies to only a small proportion of all households. Moving out of subsidized housing and into a nonsubsidized unit is generally considered an improvement in housing quality, given the stigma attached to public housing in the United States.

After descriptive statistics are used to compare housing quality and affordability by household type, ordinary least squares regression equations are run on each indicator to determine the effects of a variety of independent variables on quality and affordability. With the exception of tenure, all dependent variables are interval-ratio. (Value of owned units and age of householder are recoded to the midpoints of their ordinal scale to create interval-ratio scales). In the case of tenure (0 = rent; 1 = own), an ordinary least squares regression equation will yield reliable statistical results when the dichotomous dependent variable is not seriously skewed (Cleary and Angel, 1984). Homeownership meets the criterion of approximately a 60–40 percent split in the population.

Analysis

Descriptive Indicators of Quality

Table 4.1 summarizes some of the ways in which housing quality varies by household type. On nearly every measure of quality, female householders rank lower than married couples; they rank lower than male householders on half the indicators. All differences by household type are statistically significant.

Female householders are far less likely to own their own homes than married couples (44 versus 74 percent), although they are slightly more likely to own than male householders (38 percent). This advantage over male householders may reflect a greater tendency for ex-wives than ex-

Table 4.1. Variations in Housing Quality, by Household Type, 1983

| Housing Quality Indicators | Type of Household | | | |
	All Households (N = 25,961)	Married Couple (N = 15,067)	Female Householder (N = 7,124)	Male Householder (N = 3,770)
Homeowners, %	60.5	73.9	44.2	37.8
Mean value of owned units ($)	83,411	88,206	68,210	76,393
Mean gross monthly rent ($)	350	386	316	346
Renters with government subsidy, %	4.4	2.4	7.5	2.7
Mean crowding ratio	0.54	0.61	0.44	0.42
Households in units built 1939 or earlier, %	28.4	23.5	35.5	35.0

Source: 1983 national American Housing Survey (U.S. Bureau of the Census, 1983a).
Note: For all indicators, F-test differences by household type are significant at $p \leq .01$.

husbands to receive title to the house after a divorce settlement, but it is more likely due to widows' inheritance of their houses. Approximately half of all women who own their own homes are 65 or older, suggesting titles pass to them after the death of spouses (Shalala and McGeorge, 1981).

Among households owning their own homes, those owned by women have the lowest value. There is approximately a $20,000 difference between houses owned by married couples and those owned by female householders, and about an $8,000 difference between those owned by female and those by male householders. A similar picture is reflected by rent. Female householders pay the lowest rent of any household type: $316 per month compared with $386 for married couples and $346 for male householders. Lower rent implies lower-quality housing, often located in central cities.

Among renters, female householders are over twice as likely as other households to be living in subsidized units. Some analysts have proposed thay we have two housing markets in this country: a private owner-occupied market consisting of married couples and a public renter-occupied market dominated by female householders (Shalala and McGeorge, 1981).

Crowding is considerably lower among unmarried than married householders, with males and females about evenly matched. Unmarried householders are also more likely than married couples to live in older housing. This difference in age of housing may reflect the greater propensity of single householders to live in central cities where the housing stock is oldest.

Descriptive Indicators of Affordability

Table 4.2 reveals that female householders experience a greater housing-cost burden than other households. Although their absolute housing costs are the lowest of all owners ($306 monthly compared with $500 for married couples and $390 for male householders), their median family incomes are so much lower than other households that they are least able to afford the housing they occupy.

Married couples who own homes pay about a fifth of their incomes for housing expenses, and male householders pay about a quarter. Female householders, however, spend nearly a third of their incomes on housing-related expenses. This suggests that a woman who keeps a house after divorce or in widowhood is financially strapped without the husband's income and may eventually have to give up the house.

The situation is worse for renters, who pay proportionately more for their housing, on average, than owners. Married couples spend almost a third of their incomes on rent, male householders slightly over a third, and female householders spend close to half (45 percent). When shelter consumes nearly half of all economic resources, there is little left for the other necessities of life, such as food and clothing, and even less left for the niceties of life.

Having established a profile of housing quality by household type, it is possible to explore whether residential mobility affects housing quality comparably for all households.

Table 4.2.   Housing Affordability, by Household Type, 1983

| Affordability Indicators | Type of Household | | | |
	All Households (N = 25,961)	Married Couple (N = 15,067)	Female Householder (N = 7,124)	Male Householder (N = 3,770)
Mean monthly housing costs (owners) ($)	455	500	306	390
Mean costs of owned units, % of income	22.5	20.3	30.2	24.7
Mean rent, % of income	37.0	30.1	44.8	35.3

Source: 1983 national American Housing Survey (U.S. Bureau of the Census, 1983a).
Note: For all indicators, F-test differences by household type are significant at p ≤ .01.

Residential Mobility and Housing Quality

Table 4.3 was created by comparing characteristics of the previous housing unit with characteristics of the current unit for households that have made a recent local move. A matrix of previous by current characteristics was constructed for each variable.[2] Cell frequencies above the diagonal were counted as housing improvements, and frequencies below the diagonal were counted as declines in quality; frequencies on the diagonal were categorized as no change.

According to Table 4.3, the only criterion on which movers clearly improve their housing quality is housing value. Sixty percent of movers left a unit of lower value for one of higher value, but that is the only indicator of quality for which a majority of movers improved their status. The most typical outcome is for movers to experience no change in quality. For example, the majority of movers experienced no change in tenure (74 percent) and no change in government subsidy status (94 percent). Renters of both the previous and current units are almost equally likely to pay the same or less in rents for their new units, and households are about equally as likely to experience no change in the crowding ratio as they are an improvement in crowding.

But taken from another perspective, the figures suggest that *if* there is a change in housing quality, it is more often an improvement than not. Households are more likely to move from renter to owner (14 percent) than from owner to renter status (12 percent); are more likely to pay higher rent in the new unit than in the old (38 versus 29 percent); and are more likely to move to a less crowded unit (40 percent) than a more crowded unit (21 percent). But it is also more likely that a household will move from a nonsubsidized to a subsidized unit than vice versa. Thus it is difficult to conclude that residential mobility operates consistently to improve housing quality.

Given the mixed evidence of housing improvements for all movers, we can turn next to whether the effects of residential mobility on housing quality differ by household type. The assumption is that married

2. The crowding ratio was recoded into the following categories: fewer than 0.21 persons per room; 0.21–0.40; 0.41–0.60; 0.61–0.80; 0.81–1.00; 1.01–1.20; 1.21–1.40; 1.41 and more persons per room.

Gross monthly rent was recoded into the following categories: less than $100; $100–$199; $200–$299; $300–$399; $400–$499; $500–$599; $600–$699; $700–$799; $800–$899; $900–$999; $1,000 or more per month.

Housing value was recoded into the following categories: less than $10,000; $10,000–$19,999; $20,000–$29,999; $30,000–$49,999; $50,000–$69,999; $70,000–$99,999; $100,000–$199,999; $200,000 or more.

Table 4.3   Percentage of Change among Local Movers, by Selected Indicators of
Housing Quality and Household Type, 1983

| Indicator | Type of Household | | | |
	All Mover Households (N = 4,718)	Married Couple (N = 2,105)	Female Householder (N = 1,426)	Male Householder (N = 1,187)
Tenure				
Moved from renter to owner	14	20	8	10
Moved from owner to renter	12	8	13	16
No change in tenure	74	71	79	74
Value (owners only)				
Moved from lower to higher value	60	64	38	44
Moved from higher to lower value	14	8	38	36
No change in value	27	28	25	20
Rent (renters only)				
Moved from lower to higher rent	38	43	36	33
Moved from higher to lower rent	29	25	30	34
No change in rent	33	32	34	32
Crowding				
Moved from greater to lesser crowding	40	38	40	44
Moved from lesser to greater crowding	21	23	19	19
No change in crowd-ing ratio	39	39	41	37
Government subsidy				
Moved from subsi-dized to nonsubsidized	1	1	2	1
Moved from nonsubsidized to subsidized	4	2	8	3
No change in subsidy status	94	96	90	96

Note: For all indicators, chi-square differences between household types are significant at $p \leq .01$.

Source: U.S. Bureau of the Census, 1983a.

couples, with more resources in the housing market, are most able to follow the decision-making model of mobility and are therefore more likely to improve their housing quality after a move.

On all measures except crowding, married couples are more likely than average to improve their housing quality, whereas female householders are less likely than average to improve their housing quality. Male householders typically fall somewhere between the other two household types on indicators of quality, although they are least likely to have moved from a less costly to more costly rental unit and are most likely to have reduced crowding by making a move. The outcome on crowding can perhaps be attributed to the larger size of married-couple households, and female-maintained households are more likely to include children than male-maintained households. These differences in typical size and presence of children might explain the lack of improvement in crowding ratios for married couples and the greatest improvement for male householders.

Female householders are four times as likely as married couples to move from a nonsubsidized to a subsidized unit. They are also considerably less likely to move from renting to owning a unit, and they are the least likely of any household type to increase the value of their owned housing through a move. Female householders are as likely to move to owned units of lower value as to those of higher value, whereas male householders and married couples are more likely to "trade up" to higher-priced units. Female householders are thus more likely to experience horizontal or downward mobility than upward mobility after a move.

The data in Table 4.3 suggest that residential mobility may not work as the positive adjustment mechanism for housing quality that has been assumed, but that it is more likely to work positively for married couples than for either female or male householders.

Such descriptive statistics are informative, but tell us little about the effects of income or presence of children on quality and affordability by household type. The final section examines a series of variables to explore whether household composition has an effect on quality and affordability independent of other influences.

Multivariate Analyses

Two indicators of housing quality reported in Table 4.1 were omitted from the next two analyses. Government-subsidy status was eliminated because it applies to so few households (4 percent) that there is little variance to explain. Preliminary analysis of age of housing revealed only

3 percent of variance explained by the model and thus is not reported. Table 4.4 represents the results of equations for the four measures of quality for which meaningful multivariate analysis is possible.

Sex of the householder has a significant effect on two of the four indicators of housing quality. Because men in this sample can be either married or unmarried but female householders can be only unmarried, marital status was included in the equations to control for both aspects of household composition.

Marital status has a significant but weak effect on homeownership independent of income or age (the strongest predictors). Being married, white, older, having children, and a higher income increase the likelihood that a household will own its home. Recent mobility and central-city residence decrease the likelihood of homeownership. Table 4.3 leads to the assumption that residential mobility is not a significant variable in homeownership, because the majority of households (74 percent) experi-

Table 4.4.   Results of Ordinary Least Squares Regression Equations for Selected Indicators of Housing Quality, 1983

Independent Variables	Home-ownership (1 = own)		Value of Owned Units		Gross Monthly Rent		Crowding Ratio	
	b	β	b	β	b	β	b	β
Sex of householder (1 = male)	−.010	−.009	−3,515	−.025	−11.85*	−.033	.031*	.048
Marital status (1 = married)	.169*	.173	−1,478	−.012	5.94	.016	.120*	.205
Race of householder (1 = white)	.056*	.039	19,852*	.104	42.41*	.095	−.064*	−.074
Age of Householder	.007*	.257	398*	.112	−0.75*	−.077	−.002*	−.116
Presence of children (1 = one or more)	.078*	.076	6,580*	.059	19.17*	.050	.245*	.404
Total family income	.000008*	.253	1.50*	.416	0.01*	.444	−.0003*	−.157
Recent Mobility (1 = recent move)	−.259*	−.193	4,544	.018	39.30*	.101	.025*	.032
Metropolitan location (1 = central city)	−.133*	−.134	−6,500*	−.054	−21.02*	−.059	.046*	.078
Mean response	.616		$81,369		$360		.523	
Adjusted R²	.319*		.182*		.264*		.317*	
N	24,824		10,935		9,033		23,824	

*Significant at p ≤ .01

Source: 1983 national American Housing Survey (U.S. Bureau of the Census, 1983a).

ence no change of tenure with a move. The sign of the coefficient in this equation probably reflects the higher mobility rates of renters and hence the negative effect of residential mobility on homeownership.

Both sex and marital status drop out as predictors of housing value, as does residential mobility (despite suggestions in Table 4.3 that value clearly rises after a move). Total family income is the major influence on housing value, with each dollar of family income adding $1.50 to housing value. Being white adds approximately $20,000 to value, each year of age adds $398, the presence of children adds about $6,500, and central-city location subtracts $6,500 from value. More children no doubt imply larger houses, accounting for the positive relationship between children and housing value, and the older housing in less desirable neighborhoods may account for the negative influence of central-city location. The effect of race independent of income substantiates earlier research on racial differences in housing value (Berry, 1976; Lake, 1981).

Just as multivariate analysis reduced the effect of sex and marital status on housing value anticipated from Table 4.1, it also presents a different picture for gross rent. Being male actually *reduces* the rent paid after other factors are controlled. Controlling for income (the strongest coefficient) and other household characteristics reverses the effect of sex of householder. Thus, all other things being equal, male householders (married or unmarried) pay less for rental housing than female householders. This may reflect discrimination in the rental market, because it clearly does not reflect women's greater ability to pay higher rents. Whites pay more for rental units than blacks (an effect similar to that of race on value), and those which children pay more than those without (probably for more space). Movers pay higher rents than nonmovers, a result which supports evidence in Table 4.3 that renters tend to pay more in rent, rather than less, after a move. The elderly and those living in central cities pay less rent.

The final measure of quality, crowding, is influenced by householders' sex and marital status. Male householders and married couples are the most crowded, as are those with children and those living in central cities. One would expect presence of children to be most important in predicting crowding: compared with one- or two-person adult households, those including children tend to be more crowded. Given differences in the age of the housing stock and intensity of land use, urban units tend to be smaller than suburban units. Whites and the elderly are least crowded, and higher income buys more space to reduce crowding. The results regarding the effects of residential mobility are puzzling given the data reported in Table 4.3 showing that movers are more likely to experience a decrease than an increase in crowding. Controlling for other factors shows a very slight (0.02 percentage points) increase in crowding after a move.

On the assumption that sex might interact with one or more of the independent variables to create different effects on housing quality, interaction terms were calculated for sex and each of the other seven independent variables. It was hypothesized, for example, that race and sex or race and presence of children might have an effect on homeownership independent of sex or race alone. However, running stepwise regression equations with the interaction terms added in the second block increases the amount of variance explained by no more than 0.02 percentage points for any of the four equations. Those results are therefore not reported.

Analyses of the measures of affordability are reported in Table 4.5. Sex of the householder is a significant variable for both types of housing cost burdens, as suggested by Table 4.2 Total family income has the strongest effect on all measures of affordability. Among homeowners, housing costs as a proportion of income are greatest for female householders, blacks, younger householders, those with low incomes, and those living in the suburbs. Younger householders may be carrying mortgages at higher interest rates than older householders, which may combine with lower average earnings to give young householders a greater cost burden. Higher average housing prices in the suburbs than in central cities help explain the effect of suburban location on housing cost burdens.

Just as male homeowners carry a lower housing cost burden, they pay a lower proportion of their incomes for rent than women. The difference is reduced to about 3 percentage points after other factors are controlled. Whites carry a greater rental burden than blacks, a finding which fuels the debate about which race pays more for comparable housing (see Follain and Malpezzi, 1981; King and Mieszkowski, 1973; Marullo, 1983; Yinger, 1978). It may be that whites are paying for better units in better neighborhoods than blacks and thus have relatively higher costs which are not offset by higher median incomes. As among homeowners, older householders and those with the highest incomes carry the lowest rental burden. Presence of children adds about 2 percentage points to the proportion of income spent on rent, and recent mobility adds almost 5 percentage points. The results regarding the effects of mobility on affordability are consistent with earlier results showing increased rental expenses after a move (Tables 4.3 and 4.4).

Actual monthly housing costs among homeowners are affected most clearly by age and income: housing costs rise with income and decline with age. The presence of children adds to costs, as do recent mobility

Table 4.5   Results of Ordinary Least Square Regression Equations for Selected Indicators of Housing Affordability, 1983

Independent Variables	Dependent Variables					
	Costs of Owned Units as Percentage of Income		Rent as Percentage of Income		Monthly Housing Costs (Owners)	
	b	β	b	β	b	β
Sex of householder (1 = male)	−1.92*	−.040	−2.79*	−.054	1.94	.002
Marital status (1 = married)	0.17	.004	−0.30	−.006	−12.23	−.015
Race of householder (1 = white)	−2.27*	−.034	2.10*	.033	19.51	.015
Age of householder	−0.30*	−.244	−0.05*	−.039	−5.23*	−.219
Presence of children (1 = one or more)	1.67*	.044	2.09*	.038	67.68*	.090
Total family income	−0.0008*	−.618	−0.001*	−.644	0.01*	.298
Recent mobility (1 = recent move)	6.72*	.080	4.82*	.088	260.18*	.158
Metropolitan location (1 = central city)	−1.49*	−.036	−0.38	−.007	−39.49*	−.049
Mean response	22.6%		36.9%		$463	
Adjusted R²	.379*		.442*		.272*	
N	10,935		9,033		10,935	

*Significant at p ≤ .01
Source: 1983 national American Housing Survey (U.S. Bureau of the Census, 1983a).

and suburban residence. The four variables which consistently affect every measure of affordability are age of householder, presence of children, total family income, and mobility. Their precedence over sex and marital status suggests that household type is not as important in assessing affordability as age, children, income, and mobility. Contrary to popular images of the house-poor elderly, older householders do not carry the greatest housing cost burdens. Rather, it would appear that lifetime assets or earnings peaks, combined with paid-up mortgages or possibly rent-control subsidies, have operated to reduce affordability problems as householders age.

As with the equations for housing quality, interaction effects were computed for sex and the other independent variables and entered into the second block of a stepwise regression for all three equations. In no case was there more than a 0.02 percentage point increase in the amount of variance explained.

Summary

This chapter began by listing the reasons for examining housing quality and affordability by household type and for concentrating on female householders. The number of female householders is growing, they have the fewest economic resources, they are concentrated disproportionately in central cities, and their residential mobility rates are higher than those of married couples. These factors set the stage for anticipating lower housing quality and greater cost burdens among female householders.

Descriptive statistics uphold many of these expectations. Female householders are less likely than married couples to own their own homes, but have higher ownership rates than male householders (possibly because of inheritance in widowhood). The average value of female householders' homes is lower than other householders', as is the rent they pay. Single householders (male and female) are more likely than married couples to live in older housing, but they also experience less crowding. Female householders are far more likely than other householders to be receiving rent subsidies from the government.

Female householders pay a higher proportion of their incomes for housing costs than other householders. Among homeowners, women pay almost a third of their incomes for housing, and among renters, women pay nearly half their incomes for shelter. Although actual housing costs are lowest for female householders, their lower average incomes result in the highest cost burdens.

Data for recent movers suggest that residential mobility acts as a positive adjustment mechanism between households and their housing, but that it works more effectively for married couples and male householders than for female householders. Female householders are the least likely to move from renting to owning their units, are least likely to "trade up" in housing value, and are the most likely to move from nonsubsidized to subsidized housing.

Multivariate analyses bear out the importance of sex of householder for rent, crowding, and two measures of affordability. Men (married or unmarried) actually pay less rent than female householders when other factors are controlled, and men experience slightly more crowding than female householders. The positive coefficients for marital status and presence of children in the crowding equation help explain the discrepancy between these and the descriptive findings that female householders pay lower rents and have higher crowding ratios than male house-holders. Multivariate analyses substantiate the descriptive statistics on female householders' higher housing costs. Unmarried women pay pro-portionately more of their incomes for housing than married or unmar-ried men.

What implications do these findings have for housing demography? First, unmarried householders—male and female—are most likely to be renters. Because this is the fastest growing group of households, demand on the rental market can be expected to increase. Marital status is more important than sex of householder in predicting homeownership, al-though age and income are the strongest factors. The great discrepancy between rates of homeownership for married and unmarried household-ers might be addressed with income subsidies rather than housing subsi-dies, which are currently targeted primarily at renters and primarily at female householders.

Second, housing affordability is clearly linked to sex of the household-ers independently of income. Female householders pay more for owned and rented units than other householders despite comparable incomes. This means that female householders will remain relegated to the least expensive housing, and moving repeatedly in an attempt to reduce hous-ing costs will not solve the problem because housing costs typically rise with a move and affordability declines. Householders living in central cities have the lowest cost-to-income ratios partly because of lower rents and lower housing values in central cities. To the extent that female householders continue to concentrate in central cities for housing rea-sons, central cities will bear proportionately more of the metropolitan dependency burden as these resource-deficit households grow.

Third, race, age, presence of children, income, and metropolitan loca-tion are consistently more important than sex or marital status in predict-ing housing quality. Race and central-city residence have negative ef-fects on quality, whereas age, children, and income have positive effects. Although planners and policy-makers can do nothing about a person's race and perhaps little about his or her location, they may be able to influence ways in which these characteristics are treated in the housing market. Proper enforcement of Fair Housing legislation, for example, or increased urban ownership opportunities through homesteading pro-grams, might reduce the negative effects of race and urban residence on housing quality.

Finally, actual income subsidies may be of little use for rent or af-fordability problems. Factors other than income are operating to pro-duce rent reductions for men and greater cost burdens for women. A range of unmeasured variables could account for this outcome. If one of those factors is discrimination against families maintained by women, Fair Housing legislation needs to be expanded to incorporate protection for women and their children.

This chapter has explored several reasons for the importance of changing household demographics to the housing field. Analysis has shown that recent shifts in the sex and marital status of householders may have important implications for housing demography.

References

Anderson-Khleif, S. 1981. Housing needs of single-parent mothers. pp. 21–38 in Suzanne Keller (ed.), *Building for Women*. Lexington, Mass.: D. C. Heath and Co.

Berry, B. 1976. Ghetto expansion and single-family housing prices: Chicago, 1968–72. *Journal of Urban Economics* 3:397–423.

Bianchi, S. M., and D. Spain. 1986. *American Women in Transition*. New York: Russell Sage Foundation.

Birch, E. L. (ed.). 1985. *The Unsheltered Woman*. Rutgers, N.J.: Center for Urban Policy Research.

Cleary, P., and R. Angel. 1984. The analysis of relationships involving dichotomous dependent variables. *Journal of Health and Social Behavior* 27:1–14.

Cook, C. C., and N. M. Rudd. 1984. Factors influencing the residential location of female householders. *Urban Affairs Quarterly* 20(September):78–96.

Follain, J. R., and S. Malpezzi. 1981. Another look at racial differences in housing prices *Urban Studies:* 18:195–203.

Fox, M. B. 1983. Working women and travel. *Journal of the American Planning Association* 49(Spring):156–170.

Garfinkel, I., and S. McLanahan. 1986. *Single Mothers and Their Children: A New American Dilemma*. Washington, D.C.: The Urban Institute Press.

Goodman, J. L. 1976. Housing consumption disequilibrium and local residential mobility. *Environment and Planning*. A 8:855–874.

Goodman, J. L. 1978a. *Urban Residential Mobility: Places, People, and Policy*. Washington, D.C.: The Urban Institute Press.

Goodman, J. L. 1978b. Causes and indicators of housing quality. *Social Indicators Research* 5:195–210.

Hayden, D. 1984. *Redesigning the American Dream*. New York: W. W. Norton and Co.

King, A. T., and P. Mieszkowski. 1973. Racial discrimination, segregation, and the price of housing. *Journal of Political Economy* 81:590–606.

Lake, R. W. 1981. The Fair Housing Act in a discriminatory market. *Journal of the American Planning Association* 47:48–58.

Long, L. H. 1972. The influence of number and ages of children on residential mobility. *Demography* 9(August):371–382.

Long, L., and D. DeAre. 1980. *Migration to Nonmetropolitan Areas: Appraising the Trend and Reasons for Moving.* Special Demographic Analyses CDS-80-2. Washington, D.C.: U.S. Bureau of the Census.

McLanahan, S. 1983. Family structure and stress: A longitudinal comparison of two-parent and female-headed families. *Journal of Marriage and the Family* 45(May):347–357.

Marullo, S. 1983. Racial differences in housing consumption and filtering. Pp. 229–253 in J. Pipkin, M. LaGory, and J. Blau (eds.), *Remaking the City.* Albany, N.Y.: State University of New York Press.

Michelson, W. 1985. *From Sun to Sun.* New Jersey: Rowman and Allenheld.

Myers, D. 1983. Upward mobility and the filtering process. *Journal of Planning Education and Research* 2:101–112.

Newman, S. J., and G. J. Duncan. 1979. Residential problems, dissatisfaction, and mobility. *Journal of the American Planning Association* 45(April):154–165.

O'Connell, M., and C. Rogers. 1983. *Child Care Arrangements of Working Mothers: June 1982.* Current Population Reports, Special Studies, Ser. P-23, No. 129, U.S. Bureau of the Census. Washington, D.C.: U.S. Government Printing Office.

Ross, H. L., and I. V. Sawhill. 1975. *Time of Transition: The Growth of Families Headed by Women.* Washington, D.C.: The Urban Institute Press.

Rossi, Peter H. 1955. *Why Families Move.* Glencoe, Ill.: The Free Press.

Shalala, D. E., and J. McGeorge. 1981. The Women and Mortgage Credit Project: A government response to the housing problems of women. Pp. 39–46 in Suzanne Keller (ed.), *Building for Women.* Lexington, Mass.: D. C. Heath and Co.

Speare, A., S. Goldstein, and W. Frey. 1975. *Residential Mobility, Migration, and Urban Change.* Cambridge, Mass.: Ballinger Publishing Co.

U.S. Bureau of the Census. 1983a. *American Housing Survey, 1983.* National File (MRDF). Washington, D.C.: U.S. Bureau of the Census (producer); Ann Arbor, Mich.: Inter-University Consortium for Political and Social Research (distributor).

U.S. Bureau of the Census. 1983b. General social and economic characteristics. Pp. 1–90 in *1980 Census of Population,* Part 1, United States Summary, PC80-1-C1, Chapter C. Washington, D.C.: U.S. Government Printing Office.

U.S. Bureau of the Census. 1984. *Geographical Mobility: March 1982 to March 1983.* Current Population Reports, Ser. P-20, No. 393. Washington, D.C.: U.S. Government Printing Office.

U.S. Bureau of the Census. 1985a. *Characteristics of the Population below the Poverty Level: 1983.* Current Population Reports, Ser. P-60, No. 147. Washington, D.C.: U.S. Government Printing Office.

U.S. Bureau of the Census. 1985b. *Child Support and Alimony: 1983.* Current Population Reports, Special Studies, Ser. P-23, No. 141. Washington, D.C.: U.S. Government Printing Office.

U.S. Bureau of the Census. 1986a. *Household and Family Characteristics: March 1985.* Current Population Reports, Ser. P-20, No. 411. Washington, D.C.: U.S. Government Printing Office.

U.S. Bureau of the Census. 1986b. *Money Income of Households, Families, and Persons in the United States: 1984.* Current Population Reports, Ser. P-60, No. 151. Washington, D.C.: U.S. Government Printing Office.

Weiss, R. S. 1980. Housing for single parents. Pp. 67–76 in Robert Montgomery and D. R. Marshall (eds.), *Housing Policy in the 1980's.* Lexington, Mass.: D. C. Heath and Co.

Weitzman, L. 1985. *The Divorce Revolution.* New York: The Free Press.

Wolpert, J., and J. E. Seley. 1985. Why Urban Triage Cannot Work. Paper presented at the Annual Meeting of the Association of Collegiate Schools of Planning, Atlanta, October.

Yinger, J. 1978. The black-white price differential in housing: Some further evidence. *Land Economics* 54(May):187–206.

Zimmer, B. 1973. Residential mobility and housing. *Land Economics* 49(August):344–350.

5 *Dowell Myers and Alan Doyle*

Age-Specific Population-per-Household Ratios: Linking Population Age Structure with Housing Characteristics

The interface between population and housing remains a relatively unexplored frontier for research. The vast majority of the population resides in households sheltered by units of various sizes and structure types. These physical dwelling characteristics have differential appeal to households with varying compositions. Economists typically stress the fit between incomes and housing costs, but demographers more often stress the fit between household size or composition and dwelling type. Of course, both factors are important.

Primarily it is in the housing unit method of local population estimation where demographers have addressed the link between household size and dwelling characteristics. Yet this applied method is relatively disconnected from mainstream currents of demography and the urban social sciences. In particular, closer integration with the subfield of household demography promises greater insights into the processes of changing household size. At the same time, urban planners and geographers can contribute additional knowledge about the growth and structure of the physical housing stock and how this interacts with changing neighborhood social composition.

This chapter explores the population-housing interface from a housing-unit base. We examine how the age composition of persons per

Alan Doyle is Research Analyst at Market Data Company, 1111 Fawcett Ave, Tacoma, Washington 98402

household varies in relation to housing stock characteristics. Of particular interest in housing demography are the key temporal dimensions: age of occupants, housing vintage (year built, defining a housing cohort), and duration of occupancy. Within this temporal context, major housing stock characteristics—structure type (single-family, multifamily, or mobile home) and size (number of bedrooms)—exhibit differential attraction for households with different age members.

In this chapter we outline a methodology of value to both applied and theoretical demographers. Tying population characteristics of households to characteristics of their dwellings is shown to be a more functional model than relating population age groups only to total population. The chapter also demonstrates how the housing unit method can be integrated with other perspectives, to the benefit of the emerging multidisciplinary field of housing demography. Of practical note, we illustrate two major extensions to the housing unit method. On the population side, we show how household size can be usefully disaggregated into age-specific population per household. And on the housing unit side, we show how the housing unit base can be disaggregated to reflect not only structure type differences but also vintage of construction, size of unit, and duration of occupancy.

Household Size and Local Populations

Average household size (total residential population divided by total households) is a fundamental concept in social demographic and urban population analysis. The twentieth-century fall in household size has been construed to reflect changes in fertility, mortality, marital status, and the propensity to set up one's own household (Kobrin, 1976; Sweet, 1984). Not only is average household size an indicator of broad demographic changes, it also is the key measure linking population and housing. Average household size varies markedly across subareas of cities, and the changing household size in these subareas reflects both national trends and particular local differences.

This simple measure has many practical applications. For example, urban planners and market researchers often estimate the need for future housing construction by dividing a projected future population size by the current or expected average household size. Conversely, local population size can be estimated by multiplying the numbers of newly constructed units by the average household size (population per unit), as in the housing unit method. More accurate applications require a firmer understanding of how and why household size differs between places and changes over time.

The Housing Unit Method

Demographers' most explicit attention to housing variables has been through the housing unit method of local population estimation (Starsinic and Zitter, 1968; Smith and Lewis, 1980, 1983). Given that different types of housing units attract different types of households and that the housing stock remains fixed in space and generally invariant in characteristics over time, housing variables provide an essential substructure for small-area demography (Myers, 1987a). Although this perspective has little value for research of national-level demographic patterns and trends, it is essential for understanding intraurban population distributions.

The basic equation in the housing unit method is an identity where the population in a local area is equal to the product of the number of households and the average population per household (household size), plus the population living in group quarters. The number of households equals the number of occupied housing units, which are estimated by applying an estimated occupancy rate (1 minus the vacancy proportion) to the estimated stock of units. Evaluation of estimation errors from this method shows that the weakest link in the model is the estimated occupancy rate (Lowe, Myers, and Weisser, 1984). Administrative records are very weak with regard to vacancies in the stock, although utility disconnections are often of some use.

Smith and Lewis (1983) present clear evidence that estimates by this method are substantially improved if the changing mix of housing characteristics in the stock is accounted for. However, their housing classifications are limited only to structure type—single-family, multifamily, and mobile home—because this is most readily attainable from administrative records. Additional variables to be examined here—vintage of construction and size of structure—also may be observed fairly easily in many cities.

Beyond Average Household Size

Although appealing in their simplicity, analytical techniques based on average household size suffer the great weakness that persons of all ages are counted equally. Under conditions of rapidly shifting age distributions, standards developed in prior eras may yield misleading conclusions when applied to future households with different age compositions.

The obvious drawback concerns the importance of children relative to adults in the population per household ratio. Declining fertility has shrunk average household size, but it has not reduced the number of households being formed or the number of cars and houses being purchased. Only adults do those sorts of things. Conversely, school enrollment projections must be sensitive to the school-age component of average household size.

A second weakness of average household size is the lack of disaggregation in the housing unit base over which it is calculated. Different types and sizes of housing unit hold different-sized households. The importance for local-area analysis is that housing characteristics are distributed very unevenly across the urban landscape. At smaller geographic scales the housing stock is more homogeneous, with larger units (and larger household sizes) in some areas and smaller units (and smaller household sizes) in others.

In recognition of the need for greater disaggregation and more local specificity, a major extension to the housing unit method has been developed by urban planning researchers at Rutgers University. Burchell and Listokin (1978) extended the basic housing unit classification to include more detailed delineation of structure types (distinguishing between high-rise and garden apartments). More important, they introduced a further dimension: number of bedrooms in the unit. Tabulations of 1970 public-use sample data showed strong variation in household sizes across these housing characteristics; these tabulations were later repeated with 1980 data (see Table 5.1). In addition, Burchell and Listokin contributed the further innovation of segmenting household size into school-age and other components. Their purpose was to construct "demographic multipliers" local officials can apply to proposed new construction in order to estimate service needs of the resident population in local districts. As shown below, this general method can be extended by defining more detailed age groups and by disaggregating the housing unit base also by vintage of construction and duration of occupancy.

Table 5.1 Average Size of Households Occupying New Homes, by Structure Type and Number of Bedrooms

Structure Type	Number of Bedrooms				
	Studio	One	Two	Three	Four
Single-family	—	—	2.390	3.225	4.006
Mobile home	—	1.946	2.286	3.489	—
Townhouse	—	1.670	2.040	2.694	—
Garden apartment	—	1.409	2.138	3.262	—
Multifamily, 2–4 units	—	1.643	2.257	3.187	—
High rise	1.128	1.260	1.989	—	—

Source: Calculations from 1980 National Public Use Microdata, presented in Burchell, Listokin, and Dolphin, 1985: exhibit 12.

The Linkage to Household Demography

To date, research related to the housing unit method has been highly inductive, lacking guidance from an underlying theory of how household sizes change over time or how they differ between places. The literature in household demography can help with the understanding of changing household size. Local population changes reflect the changes occurring within individual households. We may view this linkage as a summing of individual household changes, or alternatively as the imprinting of broader demographic trends on individual households in specific locations. Little work has been carried out on these interactions in localities.

Greater understanding has been achieved of national-level changes in household demography. Kobrin (1976) has analyzed the long-run decline in average household size, attributing this to changes in fertility and (more recently) changes in the propensity of adults to head separate households. Masnick and Bane (1980) present detailed tables revealing trends in age-, sex-, and marital-specific headship rates. Rising headship and the declining proportion of married couples have increased the rate of household formation in the population and decreased the average household size.

The 1970s were unusual: the maturation of the baby-boom generation into adulthood spawned a surge in small-household formation at the same time as parents' household sizes also shrank from child launching. Sweet and Bumpass (1987:table 9.7) contrast the 1970–80 experience with previous decades, showing that the 11.6 percent decline in average household size was much greater than any other decade since 1850 or earlier. (Only the 1930s were similar in rate of decline.) Indeed, the great bulk of the 1970s decline in household size came in the number of household members under age 18 (Sweet and Bumpass, 1987:table 9.10).

The major household changes of the 1970s—smaller households, more young-adult households, fewer married couples, and fewer families with children—altered the previous pattern of housing demand, but the stock could not change so swiftly. Moreover, many of the households experiencing these changes were already in place, residing in homes chosen prior to 1970. A major question deserving research is the manner in which the changes of the 1970s were distributed across the housing stock. The chapter in this volume by Patricia Gober addresses the spatial patterns of distribution; the present chapter bears space in mind but uses a rich, national data set to address more detailed relationships between types of houses and households.

Impacts of Local Variation in the Housing Stock

At present, differences in household size between places fall outside the domain of house*hold* demography (but not *housing* demography). These spatial differences are more often explored by geographers and reflect underlying differences in the distribution of housing units of different types and sizes. In principle, adequate understanding of household size requires attention to both temporal change and spatial differentiation.

Gober's (1986a) study of Phoenix found that household sizes fell most sharply in the 1970s in close-in middle-aged suburbs, apparently because residents had aged to the point where children were leaving home. In subsequent work Gober (1986b) demonstrates how pervasive has been the impact of national demographic trends on local social geography. Changes in the family life cycle between 1970 and 1980 were imprinted on census tracts throughout 20 cities analyzed, but single-family neighborhoods experienced the greatest change, becoming much more diverse in their household composition. Newly built tracts especially reflected the dramatic changes of the period, both because of changes within single-family homes and because of an increase in apartment construction. Construction of apartments in outlying areas caused these new neighborhoods to have smaller household sizes. One lesson here is that housing age and household size (as well as other variables) should be computed separately for single-family and multifamily housing. A second lesson Gober prefers to stress is that we cannot assume that past correlations of family types and neighborhood age and location will persist. As she argues in her chapter in the present volume, a more detailed model is required that explains how national demographic changes are played out in the context of the rich variation of neighborhoods in every urban area.

Careful analysis is required to separate changes occurring within individual dwelling histories from broader demographic changes impacting the population at large. Better understanding of longitudinal processes of change within dwelling units of a given vintage is required before we can understand the manner in which national and regional demographic trends manifest themselves locally. The complex interplay of these temporal dynamics is a challenge for demographers interested in the changing internal distribution of populations.

The search for answers must begin at the housing unit level, because the housing stock provides the base for resident population. Following the lead of the geographer John Adams (1970), the foundation for analyzing the stock is the vintage layering of cities. Each vintage is built to meet the housing demands of the day, but then is carried into the future.

For example, in the United States each decade's construction after 1940 was built to larger and more elaborate specifications, reflecting the increasing numbers of families with growing baby-boom children and the rising economic standard of living (Myers, 1984). The durability and longevity of housing units cause the unique qualities of each period's construction to persist over many decades. Thus we can usefully view the residential structure of the city as composed of layers of vintages. These are added sequentially in time and also generally follow a sequential spatial pattern of concentric rings.

The layers of vintages contain households whose demographic characteristics are closely related to the age of their housing. In an early study of the correlation between housing age and population age, analysis of 1970 census tracts in the San Francisco Bay Area revealed a pattern of strong regularity (Myers, 1978). Tracts with high proportions of the housing stock in newer vintages held higher proportions of young children and young adults. Successively older vintages correlated with successively older population age groups. The 20–24 age group showed no significant correlation with any dwelling vintage, reflecting the dispersed behavior within this transitional age bracket.

This study of aging in census tracts identified occupancy duration as the critical intervening variable that causes older houses to contain older population. Given that approximately 60 percent of homeowners have occupied their units for at least 10 years, aging of households in place is typical of single-family neighborhoods. Upon eventual turnover, we might expect homes to return to a population age distribution resembling that of recent construction.

Ratios of Population per Household

Consider the two alternative bases for computing age composition. The traditional approach expresses each age group as a proportion of the total population. Yet this common method does not describe a functional relationship such as does the child-woman ratio, and it can yield misleading results. For example, the proportion in a given age group can fall—even when the absolute number holds constant—because other age groups are increasing more rapidly. No behavioral meaning can be ascribed to the proportion in a given age group.

As an alternative to the traditional, population-based age ratios, consider the advantages of housing-based age ratios. People reside in households and generally move as household groups that occupy housing units. The alternative of dividing age groups by number of occupied housing units expresses a more functional relation with regard to population change in small areas. Age-specific population-per-household ratios hold greater meaning for some purposes than age-group percentages of the total population. In particular, by expressing age compostion relative to occupied housing units (households) we open the opportunity for stratification by type of dwelling unit.

Data and Methods

To illustrate the usefulness of a more disaggregated household-size analysis, we will draw upon data compiled for a complete national sample of households in the Annual Housing Survey of the fall of 1974 (see Goering, 1979). As described more fully in the chapter by Moore and Clark in this volume, the Annual Housing Survey provides a very rich source of housing data, including detailed information about both dwelling characteristics and household composition. Households with missing data on any variables essential for our analysis were excluded from the sample, leaving some 62,000 valid cases.

The data were processed into a pair of linked, multidimensional arrays. The dwelling matrix tabulates the number of households occupying dwellings of given types (specified along six dimensions). The population matrix tabulates the number of persons within 16 five-year age groups, further classified by the same dwelling characteristics as the dwelling matrix. To calculate the age-specific population-per-household ratios, we simply divided the age-dwelling slice of the population matrix by the dwelling matrix. Through a REDUCER program (maintained at the Population Research Center of the University of Texas at Austin) the linked pair of matrices can be reduced (collapsed) along matched dimensions to permit calculation of ratios of population to housing for housing units specified by different combinations of characteristics.

The age composition of households is measured by computing the ratio of persons in each age group to the number of housing units of a given type they occupy. These *age-specific ratios* are arithmetically useful because they can be treated as demographic multipliers to estimate the number of persons of a given age who occupy 100 homes of a given type. The housing-based ratio approach is not only more practical than the traditional population-based ratios, it also has greater theoretical appeal: population resides in households that are distributed spatially through the occupancy of housing units of different types. Age-specific persons-per-household distributions provide a method of measuring age composition while emphasizing the essential link that households form between population and housing.

The aim of this chapter is to depict graphically the influence of differ-

ent housing characteristics upon the age profiles of household occupants. We can portray the strong systematic relationships revealed in our
data by graphing selected patterns of interest. We believe this simple
descriptive method is most valuable for introducing the disaggregated
perspective on household size. A number of interesting research questions are suggested through this data presentation, and subsequent researchers may wish to explore specific issues with more formal statistical
methods.

Housing Characteristics and Household-Age Composition

The pattern of variation in age-specific household size is explored in
three stages. We begin with the variation across a housing stock defined
on two dimensions: type of structure and number of bedrooms. Subsequently, we examine selected strata formed by adding a third dimension
to the housing unit classification: vintage of construction. Within the
multifamily stock we will study vintage differences among two-bedroom
units, and within the single-family stock we will study vintage differences
among both two- and four-bedroom units. Finally, in a third analysis
stage, we add a further dimension: duration of occupancy (or recency of
turnover). We will apply this final dimension to two- and four-bedroom
single-family units of pre-1950 vintage.

Number of Bedrooms and Type of Structure

Figures 5.1 and 5.2 present the age-specific household-size profiles of
housing units classified by number of bedrooms for multifamily and
single-family units. In general, the differences between the two structure
types are slight if we control for the number of bedrooms. In fact, in the
child ages, the multifamily units exhibit slightly higher ratios, but in the
adult ages, the single-family ratios are higher.

Examining each of the bedroom categories, the age-disaggregated
household size of one-bedroom homes is consistently lowest, and successively larger homes have higher sizes in almost every age group. By far
the greatest increase in household size in larger units is observed in the
child ages. In contrast, variations in the number of adults aged 20–29
and 60 or older are very slight.

Figure 5.2, representing single-family structures, is described in more
detail. The number of bedrooms has dramatic influence upon the number of teenage children: four-bedroom units have 136 children age 10–19
per 100 homes, three-bedroom units have 79 teenagers, and two-
bedroom units have only 29 teenagers. The larger units also contain

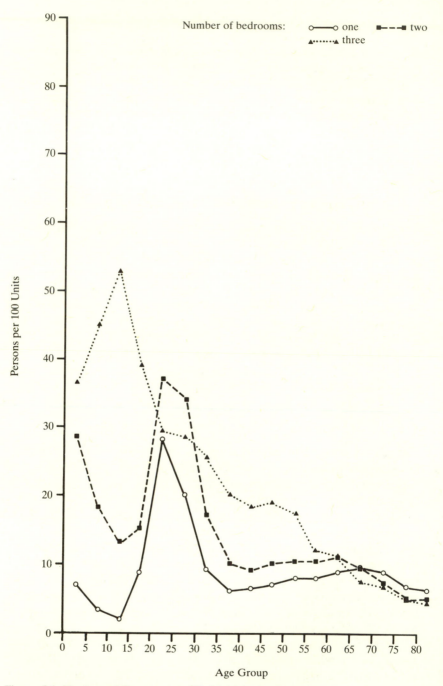

Figure 5.1 Number of Persons per 100 Multiple-Family Dwellings, by Number of Bedrooms (as observed in 1974)

118

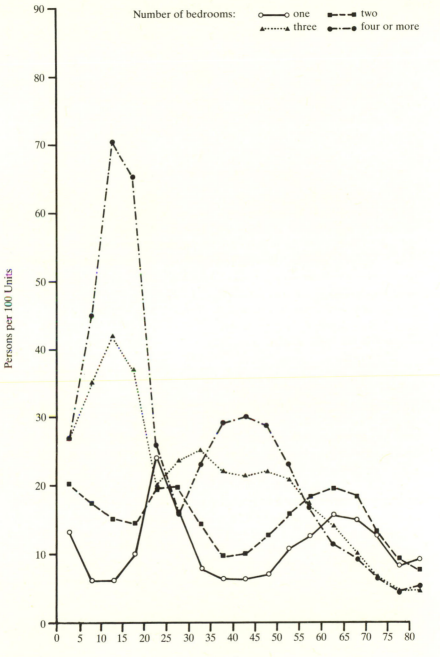

Figure 5.2 Number of Persons per 100 Single-Family Dwellings, by Number of Bedrooms (as observed in 1974)

many more adults aged 30–49. Above age 55 the age profiles of different size units merge together, and the numbers of elderly persons in one- and two-bedroom units actually surpass those in larger units. In fact, it is noteworthy that the concentration of older persons peaking at age 60–64 in one- and two-bedroom homes is double that of persons aged 35–39. One might speculate that elderly persons have moved to these smaller homes, but an alternative explanation is offered in a later section.

Impacts of Housing Vintage

A further significant characteristic of housing units is their vintage, or year built. Although this characteristic is often neglected in housing analysis, it has implicit appeal to demographers, who are accustomed to tracing cohorts over time. And we should note that the vintage distribution of housing units is recorded at all levels of census geography down to the census tract. Hence, there is no absence of data available for describing vintage of construction. An important drawback is that the vintage data are collected from the occupants of the dwellings, leading to a certain amount of respondent error as discussed in Appendix 1 to chapter 11 by William Baer.

Four vintages of homes are identified in the 1974 national sample: new homes built 1970–74; 1960s homes; 1950s homes; and older homes built before 1950. Our search for "pure" vintage differences in household-age composition is assisted by stratifying the sample by structure type and number of bedrooms, thereby controlling for these factors. Let us examine the vintage differences in household-age profiles for three housing types: two-bedroom multifamily, two-bedroom single-family, and four-bedroom single-family.

Figure 5.3 depicts the household-age profile of the two-bedroom multifamily units. The profiles for four different vintages are relatively similar: a large peak in the 20s with an associated upturn among the youngest children. However, two major differences among the vintages are worth noting. First, we observe successively higher concentrations of elderly in older apartments. A potential explanation is that these elderly are seeking older, more central locations. Another explanation is that they have aged in place (yet we see little evidence of successive aging at younger ages).

The second noteworthy feature is the higher concentration of young adults in newer apartments. Young adults could be seeking newer housing in more suburban locations; however, the fact that the number of children is not correspondingly greater in newer housing suggests that the 20–29-year-old concentrations might be lower in older housing be-

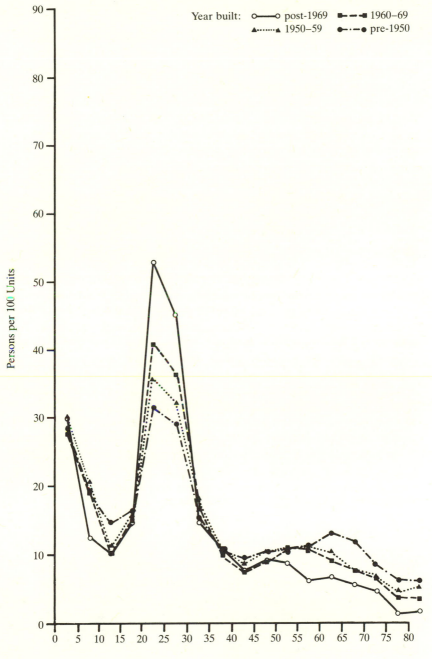

Figure 5.3 Number of Persons per 100 Two-Bedroom Multiple-Family Dwellings, by Vintage (as observed in 1974)

121

cause of greater occupancy by single-parents (households with only one adult in her 20s, but holding the same number of children). Alternatively, older housing may hold members of disadvantaged ethnic groups who have larger numbers of children present.

Turning to the two-bedroom single-family homes, their household-age profiles by vintage are depicted in Figure 5.4. Although these housing units have the same number of bedrooms as the multifamily units just examined, we note that their age profiles are much different. The two-bedroom single-family age profile is distinctly trimodal. Twin peaks of young adults and young children are counterbalanced by a very large concentration of late-middle-aged and elderly adults. Overall, the age profile of the two-bedroom single-family units is more evenly spread, with much less concentration in the 20s than is observed for the apartments. The only noteworthy vintage difference among the two-bedroom single-family units is that newer homes exhibit a distinctly greater concentration of young adults and children and exhibit lesser concentrations of older adults than do the older homes.

The household-age profiles of single-family homes with four or more bedrooms are dramatically different. Figure 5.5 depicts peak concentrations in the 10–19 year age range of children, with an extremely sharp drop off at ages 20–24. What is most notable is the successively ordered adult age peaks: 30–39 among homes less than five years old; 35–44 among 5–15-year-old homes; and 45–54 among 15–25-year-old homes. Remarkable regularity is observed also in the progressively greater concentrations of elderly adults in successively older housing units. Conversely, the newer homes show greater concentrations of young children, although teenagers predominate in every vintage save the oldest. Figure 5.5 likely reflects the imprint of households moving to large homes when their family sizes are fullest and their children are older, followed by aging in place with their housing units.

Impacts of Turnover

Turnover in the housing stock occurs as a result of residential mobility. Much research has fruitfully examined the housing choices of movers, such as that demonstrated in Chapter 9 by Moore and Clark, but less attention has been given to the impacts on the housing unit created by its vacation and reoccupancy through the mobility process. Our emphasis here is on how turnover serves to renew the resident population. When long-term occupants are eventually replaced, the aging clock is turned back. Of course, the nature of the in-movers will not necessarily replicate the characteristics exhibited by the prior occupants when they first

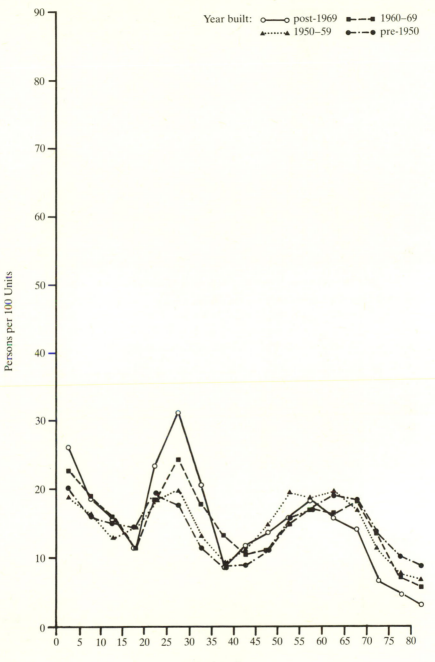

Figure 5.4 Number of Persons per Two-Bedroom Single-Family Dwellings, by Vintage (as observed in 1974)

123

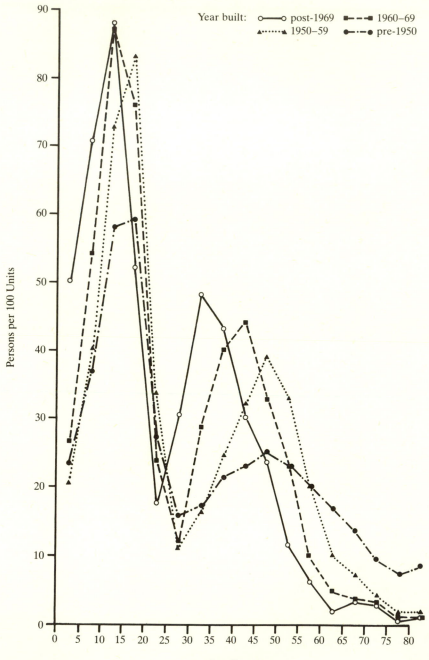

Figure 5.5 Number of Persons per 100 Single-Family Dwellings with Four or More Bedrooms, by Vintage (as observed in 1974)

moved in. At the very least, we know there are fewer large families seeking housing today than in the decade of the 1960s, which followed the cumulative impact of the baby boom. Despite the impact of these historical changes in fertility, we would expect incoming household heads, or householders, to be younger than those who had aged in place. Depending on the size of the housing unit we would also expect in-movers to bring varying numbers of children. Do recent occupants of older homes have household-age profiles resembling those who have recently occupied new construction?

Figures 5.6 and 5.7 represent the effect of occupancy duration in older-vintage dwellings, distinguishing the age profiles of households with successively longer-occupancy durations: in-movers within the preceding five years (after 1969), in-movers between 1965 and 1969, and those before 1965. It should be noted that occupancy pre-1965 includes even longer-time residents, because the stayers may date from the year in which the dwelling was built. The collapse of the number of children should be especially notable in houses built before 1950 and occupied for at least 10 years.

Given the importance of number of bedrooms and vintage in shaping household-age profiles, we must stratify our analysis by those variables. Figure 5.6 presents household-age profiles by occupancy duration for pre-1950 single-family houses with two bedrooms. The differences are extreme, with age profiles of longer-term occupants bunched above age 50 and with recent in-movers much younger. The most recent arrivals are concentrated in their 20s and in the young-child ages, reflecting the greater propensity of these age groups to be movers.

How closely do the age profiles of new arrivals in older homes correspond to the new arrivals in recently constructed homes? The age profiles of the recent movers to two-bedroom older houses are more concentrated in the 20–29 and 0–4 age range in Figure 5.6 than for the newest two-bedroom single-family houses depicted in Figure 5.4. In fact, the recent in-movers to older two-bedroom single-family homes resemble the occupants of two-bedroom apartments reported in Figure 5.3. The age concentration of recent arrivals in these older single-family houses also likely reflects a higher incidence of renting than in the newer houses. The newly constructed two-bedroom houses in Figure 5.4 simply attract more middle-aged and elderly occupants, more of whom could demand high-quality housing such as that built new.

Differences observed within larger, four-bedroom houses are also substantial, but reflect a different market from that of the smaller houses (Figure 5.7). Again, the age profiles of longer-term occupants are bunched above age 50, but a noticeable peak is also observed among

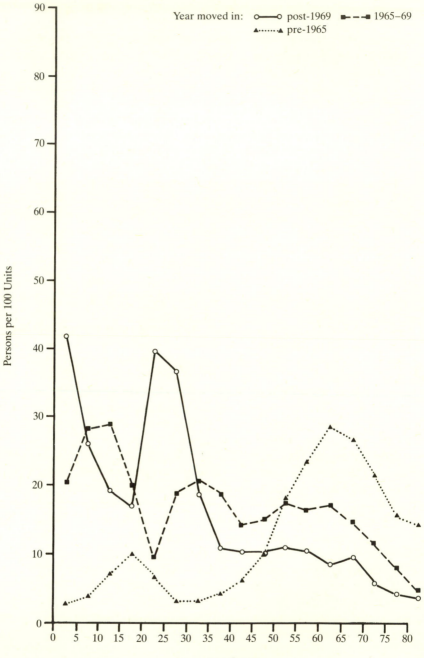

Figure 5.6 Number of Persons per 100 Two-Bedroom Single-Family Dwellings, Built Pre-1950, by Recency of Occupancy (as observed in 1974)

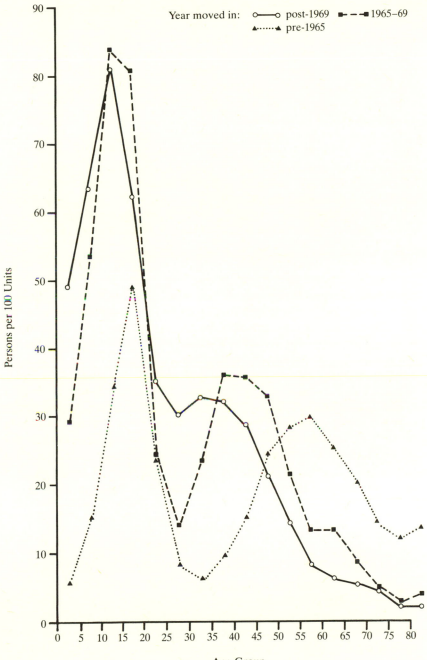

Figure 5.7 Number of Persons per 100 Four-Bedroom Single-Family Dwellings, Built Pre-1950, by Recency of Occupancy (as observed in 1974)

older children. These are likely the youngest children in the family, still remaining in the family home after the others have been launched. In contrast, occupants of 5–10 years duration have adults concentrated in the 35–50 age range and have many more children of all ages. And the most recent occupants are about 10 years younger in adult ages, with more young children and fewer teenagers.

Comparing this pattern to the newly built houses in Figure 5.5, we see only small differences between recent occupants of new homes and recent occupants of pre-1950 homes: both attract about the same number of young parents and children, although the older houses have slightly more 20–24-year-olds and fewer 30–39-year-olds. This reflects the somewhat greater likelihood of young renters or young owners with less income entering these older houses. However, the differences are fairly slight and are minor in view of the small fraction of older houses with recent arrivals. Given the much greater opportunity to accumulate long-term occupants in the older houses, we can see why the overall household-age profile for pre-1950 houses is so much older than for newer construction. The preponderance of longer-term occupants in the older houses heavily weights the overall age profile to resemble that observed for long-term occupants in Figure 5.7.

Summarizing the importance of turnover, we have focused on impacts created by turnover on the age compositions of households. Older homes have had time to accumulate long-term occupants who have aged in place, but turnover renews the number of children and young adults in the housing stock. Turnover does not turn back the aging clock to recreate exactly the household-age profile of an earlier period in the vintage's life cycle, nor does it generate the same age profile as found in new construction of the current period. Nevertheless, the broad impacts of turnover are a dominant factor in shaping household-age profiles.

Conclusion

Demographers can profit from extending their interests in household demography to include characteristics of the dwellings in which households reside. This chapter has explored a merger of household demography, the housing unit method, residential mobility research, and housing stock analysis. We have shown strong interrelationships among dwelling type, number of bedrooms, vintage, household-age composition, and turnover. Larger units attract households with more children, but this attraction in moderated in units that have not recently turned over. Aging in place is more common among single-family units, because they are owner-occupied, and therefore has a particularly strong impact upon household-age distributions as the dwellings grow older. It is clear that the analysis of housing characteristics can add much to the analysis of household composition.

Addressing housing characteristics holds special advantages for small-area demography. In subareas of our nation—counties, cities, suburbs, and neighborhoods—variations in the composition of the housing stock can have strong effects on the composition of the resident population. Most demographic models are designed for large regions where housing differences are averaged out and economic growth is the principal determinant of migration. But in small areas it is housing decisions that are the principal determinant of migration. Small-area demographers can benefit from knowledge of how the characteristics of the local housing stock help to shape the characteristics of the population.

The interaction of housing and population is attractive for theoretical reasons as well. There is a certain elegance to the interrelations of housing and population. Despite the apparent complexity of relationships, we have described systematic relationships linking larger dwelling units to larger households whose members are concentrated in particular age groups. We have shown how older homes hold progressively older populations because of occupancy duration, and we have shown how the event of turnover renews the age distributions of housing stocks. The process of dwelling turnover and selection and the subsequent joint aging of population and housing deserve to be modeled more comprehensively. Attention to housing can add further richness to demographic theories and models and also aid practical advances in small-area demography.

References

Adams, J. S. 1970. The residential structure of midwestern cities. *Annals of the Association of American Geographers* 60:37–62.

Burchell, R. W., and D. Listokin. 1978. *The Fiscal Impact Handbook.* New Brunswick, N.J.: Rutgers University, Center for Urban Policy Research.

Burchell, R. W., D. Listokin, and W. R. Dolphin. 1985. *The New Practitioner's Guide to Fiscal Impact Analysis.* New Brunswick, N.J.: Rutgers University, Center for Urban Policy Research.

Gober, P. 1986a. How and why Phoenix households changed: 1970–1980. *Annals of the Association of American Geographers* 76(4):536–549.

Gober, P. 1986b. Homogeneity versus heterogeneity in household structure: The recent experience of twenty U.S. cities. *Environment and Planning A* 18:715–727.

Goering, J. M. 1979. *Housing in America: The Characteristics and Uses of the Annual Housing Survey.* Annual Housing Survey Study No. 6. Washington, D.C.: U.S. Department of Housing and Urban Development.

Kobrin, F. E. 1976. The fall in household size and the rise of the primary individual. *Demography* 13:127–138.

Lowe, T. J., W. R. Myers, and L. M. Weisser. 1984. A Special Consideration in Improving Housing Unit Estimates: The Interaction Effect. Paper presented at the annual meeting of the Population Association of America, Minneapolis.

Masnick, G. S., and M. J. Bane. 1980. *The Nation's Families: 1960–1990.* Boston: Auburn House.

Myers, D. 1978. Aging of population and housing. A new perspective on planning for more balanced metropolitan growth. *Growth and Change* 9:8–13.

Myers, D. 1984. Turnover and filtering of postwar single-family houses. *Journal of the American Planning Association* 50:352–358.

Myers, D. 1987a. The Housing Substructure of Small-Area Demography. Paper presented at the annual meeting of the Population Association of America, Chicago.

Smith, S. K., and B. B. Lewis. 1980. Some new techniques for applying the housing unit method of local population estimation. *Demography* 17:323–340.

Smith, S. K., and B. B. Lewis. 1983. Some new techniques for applying the housing unit method of local population estimation: Further evidence. *Demography* 20:407–413.

Starsinic, D. E., and M. Zitter. 1968. Accuracy of the housing unit method in preparing population estimates for cities. *Demography* 5:475–484.

Sweet, J. A. 1984. Components of change in the number of households, 1970–1980. *Demography* 21:129–140.

Sweet, J. A., and L. Bumpass. 1987. *American Families and Households.* New York: Russell Sage Foundation.

PART 2
LIFE COURSE AND COHORT MODELS
OF HOUSING CHOICE

6 *Hal L. Kendig*

A Life Course Perspective on Housing Attainment

This chapter examines ways in which individuals over their life courses move through stocks of housing which also are changing. Understanding these housing "trajectories" requires an appreciation of the diverse histories and characteristics of households and dwellings in the context of broader economic, political, and social developments. The chapter thus attempts to present some conceptual and analytical linkages between the life courses of individuals and birth cohorts, societal change, and the operation of housing markets.

The idea of a "housing career"—the succession of dwellings occupied by individuals over their lives—provides the central concept in the chapter. Housing careers are parallel to and interwoven with family, employment, and other life "careers" which structure experiences over the life course. They, of course, are also shaped by prevailing market conditions, including the influence of public policies. In turn, the composition and occupancy of the housing stock are influenced by the adjustments being made by individuals already in the market and the continuing streams of individuals entering and leaving it.

The attainment of homeownership, if it is ever achieved, is taken as the most significant step along housing careers. Housing tenure arguably is the central divide in most housing markets, because it relates closely to the

Hal L. Kendig is Director of the Lincoln Gerontology Centre, La Trobe University, Melbourne, Australia.

costs and other features of housing, the impacts of policies, and the characteristics of the occupants. This is an oversimplification, however, because a full application of the life course approach to housing also would pay close attention to interrelationships between tenure and the costs, types, quality, and locations of housing (Bourne, 1981; Gober, this volume).

The impact of market and policy contexts on housing careers is suggested through illustrations from American, British, and Australian literatures. Most of the empirical examples are provided for Australia, which, in comparison to the United States, has had a slightly higher homeownership rate, a larger public-housing sector, a more urbanized population, and more substantial upgrading of inner-city housing (Kendig, 1984a; Kendig and Paris with Anderton, 1987). Both countries had rapid rises of housing quality and homeownership earlier in the postwar years, large-scale suburbanization for many decades, substantial apartment booms in the 1960s, and more recently sizable rises in the initial costs of buying homes. Britain provides a significant contrast with its generally older and poorer-quality housing, much larger public sector, and relatively low but rising homeownership rates.

The next section of the chapter examines conceptual approaches to changes of housing as individuals grow older and markets change over time. The discussion then turns to applications of the housing-careers perspective for understanding the operation of housing markets over relatively short periods of time. This line of reasoning is further developed by reviewing how housing careers vary as markets and policies change over the longer term. The chapter concludes with some implications of the life course approach for assessing the distributional effects of housing policies and possible directions for future research.

Life-Cycle and Life Course Approaches

The roots of a life course approach to housing studies can be traced back to Victorian England and the special concern for the accommodation of children and its effects on their life-long development. The literature reflects the development of housing-demand studies from a focus on the age of individuals and householders, to simple and static life-cycle classifications, and over recent years to the more dynamic and flexible life course approach.

Age

Chronological age remains as a central variable in many contemporary analyses of households and their housing, particularly those that deal

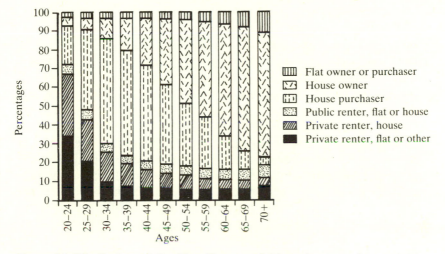

Figure 6.1 Distribution of Dwelling Tenure and Type, by Age of Householder, Australia, 1981

with aggregate data such as that provided by censuses. Figure 6.1, for example, shows the significant age differences in the housing tenure and type of Australian householders. Relatively more younger people live in rented flats (apartments); middle-aged people are more likely to live in owner-occupied houses; and those at later ages are more likely to have paid off their home mortgages or own and live in flats. Occupancy patterns, of course, vary depending on the composition and costs in particular housing stocks, but similar age-related tendencies would be found in most American as well as Australian markets (Sweet, this volume).

The strong association between householders' ages and their housing nevertheless has little direct explanatory power. First, age is important for housing primarily through its varying relationship with the family, employment, income, wealth, and other characteristics which directly affect housing demand. Second, cross-sectional differences in the housing of age groups confound possible accommodation changes, because people have grown older with the periods of history in which they entered housing markets. Rather than being used as a crude explanatory variable in itself, age is most appropriately viewed as a basis for charting the timing of key life events and (as will be explored later in the chapter) the period of history in which these events take place (Elder, 1975).

Life Cycle

The concept of the life cycle, as pioneered in housing analyses by Rossi (1955), represents a substantial advance over age alone in understanding housing demand. A number of life-cycle typologies have subsequently been devised to classify individuals into groups according to such variables as age, marital status, and presence and ages of children (for example, Lansing and Kish, 1957; Glick, 1977). The primary strength of these classifications in housing analyses is twofold: first, they examine *combinations* of characteristics which jointly influence housing demand; and second, the notion of "stages" recognizes that individuals are at a particular point along a series of changes which influence housing over a lifetime. The utility of life-cycle classifications is shown by their strong association with household formation, housing tenure, housing type, and location, as is shown by Sweet and other contributors in this book.

Life-cycle classifications relate most directly to needs and preferences for housing, but they also are associated with the financial means to secure it. Incomes and wealth generally rise with age as people advance in careers and accumulate savings (Kreps, 1971). Families can face a "life-cycle squeeze," however, if expenses of child rearing rise faster than increases of economic resources (Oppenheimer, 1982). Accordingly, couples which delay childbearing and continue with two earners can have considerable resources available for meeting the high entry costs of owner occupancy (Griffen-Wulff, 1982; Myers, 1985).

Studies which attempt to explain housing choices on the basis of life-cycle classifications alone face two substantial limitations. First, the capacity to pay for housing depends primarily on levels of income, which vary widely between occupational groups and other social categories at all stages of the life cycle. In Britain, for example, homeownership rates vary significantly by social class within life-cycle positions (Sullivan and Murphy, 1984). Similarly, among couples with dependents in Australia, 83 percent of those with higher incomes (above approximately 150 percent of average earnings) are owners as compared with 55 percent of those with lower earnings (below half of average earnings) (Kendig and Paris, with Anderton, 1987:34).

A second difficulty with life-cycle classifications is that static descriptions of peoples' present circumstances do not show very well the processes of individuals' life changes. Many housing studies make mechanical assumptions that all people pass through "the" uniform life-cycle stages, for example, by terming all young couples without children as prefamily or by excluding second marriages from analyses. Family and employment experiences, of course, can be highly variable, and there can be no presumption of any "normal" or necessary determinism (Stapleton, 1980; Watson, 1986). Moreover, present life-cycle positions do not show past circumstances when people may have gained access to their housing, nor do they show the aspirations and expectations which can influence future housing circumstances.

In summary, the complexity and processes of housing choices can be obscured by life-cycle analyses unless full account is taken of interrelationships with economic resources, diversity of life-cycle experiences, and the biographies through which people come to arrive at their present life-cycle and housing circumstances.

Life Course Approaches and Social Structure

The concept of life course development provides a flexible and dynamic basis for understanding housing choices. The basic idea is that individuals' life histories can be summarized in terms of different experiences of marriages and relationships, childbearing, employment, and other life careers (Hagestad and Neugarten, 1985; Riley, 1987). The approach examines divergence of experiences along life careers and their sequencing, combinations, and timing. Individuals are understood in terms of the ongoing effects of earlier life experiences as well as their current circumstances. The approach requires a broadening of the strictures of traditional life-cycle analyses to include topics such as divorce, remarriage, and migration (Hohn, 1987).

Conceptualizing housing choices as one stream among several interwoven life careers has major advantages. First, rather than examining matches between households and dwellings at one point in time, it examines change over time. Second, it shows the way in which housing decisions are influenced by a variety of changes of family or employment circumstances, albeit often with major "lag" or "lead" effects. Major life events such as leaving a parent's home, marriage, divorce, and moves between labor markets almost always require a change of housing (Clark and Onaka, 1983). Changes in family size or incomes can induce, if not directly cause, continuing households to adjust their housing (Goodman, 1976; Quigley and Weinberg, 1977).

There also can be two-way relationships between housing and other life careers. For example, decisions on buying homes can be made jointly with those for childbearing and married women's labor-force participation (Murphy and Sullivan, 1985; Kohlase, 1986). Some British couples who are unable to buy homes are reported to have the timing of childbearing influenced by rules to qualify for admission into public housing.

A central feature of the life course approach is the recognition of social structures in shaping the various careers of individuals. Individuals' life chances are heavily predisposed by their membership in particular social classes, racial groups, and other major "status divides" in a society (Maddox and Campbell, 1985; Riley, 1987).

British traditions of housing research have paid particularly close attention to the influence of social structure in constraining access to housing (Thorns, 1981). Rex and Moore's (1967) pioneering work on "housing classes" emphasized that housing "choice" is highly conditioned by markets and institutional rules. For example, public housing in England and Scotland in the past has rivaled homeownership as a tenure of "destination" in housing careers, and access has depended on eligibility rules such as having a child or a modest income (Payne and Payne, 1977; Sullivan and Murphy, 1984). An important line of British urban theory argues that inequalities in housing consumption and in wealth accumulation through housing can be so substantial as to rival the class inequalities derived from economic production (Saunders, 1984).

Social Change and Housing Markets

Related literatures from economics, human development, and demography provide powerful analytical tools for unraveling the dimensions of aggregate change in housing markets. Although terminology and techniques vary between disciplines, these approaches account for social change by iden ifying the separate influence of aging, period, and cohort effects. For understanding housing choices, aging effects basically are individuals' progression through family life and employment careers, as discussed above. Period effects are the social and economic conditions which affect all individuals in the market at particular points in history. Cohort effects are seen when the conditions in a particular period of history have an impact on specific age groups at the time of occurrence and have continuing consequences for them later in life (Ryder, 1965).

Period effects are of obvious importance in understanding overall changes in housing markets (Sternlieb and Hughes, 1986). Population growth puts pressure on the existing stock and stimulates new construction. Economic booms and busts have pervasive effects on housing demand through shifts in real wages and risks of unemployment. Changes in the real costs of building housing or borrowing money also affect, either directly or indirectly, anyone who wishes to enter the market or adjust his or her housing. Policy changes can have pervasive effects on both the supply of and demand for housing. Important questions thus arise concerning the leads and lags as different parts of housing markets adjust to social and economic change.

Cohort effects are most pronounced as causes of housing-market changes. The massive baby boom, for example, resulted in a "disordered cohort flow" (Waring, 1975) which contributed to the suburban expansion of the 1950s, the apartment boom of the 1960s, and probably will expand retirement housing early in the next century. The size of cohorts and economic conditions when they enter labor markets can have significant impacts on life-long employment and investment opportunities, which provide the means to buy housing (Easterlin, 1980). Changes in timing of marriage and childbearing (Uhlenberg, 1974; Nissel, 1987) and rising labor-force participation among married women (Roistacher and Young, 1979) also have cohort-specific impacts with far-reaching implications for housing. The replacement of earlier cohorts by new ones is a major mechanism for the social and economic changes which impact on housing markets.

Housing Careers and Market Operations

A career metaphor represents the distinct steps taken by individuals attempting to improve their housing over the life course. Each dwelling is a package of many goods which seldom can be purchased separately, and (especially for owner occupants) there are significant financial and practical barriers to moving. Michelson's (1977) "deficit compensation" model of mobility recognizes that households pass through a series of dwellings which increasingly meet their long-term housing aspirations. Myers (1982) reports that most Americans in the mid-1970s felt that their individual housing circumstances had improved over the last five years, and they expected circumstances to improve further over the next five years.

Housing-Tenure Progression

The use of housing tenure as the primary basis for defining housing careers would be appropriate in a number of countries. Homeownership—with the advantages of security, government subsidies, and possible capital gains—is the eventual goal of most individuals in the United States (Myers, 1982), Australia (Kendig, 1984b), and (to a lesser but increasing extent) Britain (Couper and Brindley, 1975). Myers (1981:109) reports that "single-family homeownership is a standard of housing sought by nine-tenths of Americans under age 45." Decisions about other features of housing adjustments are nearly always made according to a prior decision or constraint on tenure choice (Kendig, 1984b; Goodman, 1976). The time spent in a particular tenure—for example, while saving in a rented property or while an owned dwelling appreciates—can have a major influence on the financial ability to move on to other housing (Doling, 1976; Coupe and Morgan, 1981; and McLeod and Ellis, 1982).

A simplified picture of significant steps along housing careers and some family and employment influences on them is shown for Australian markets in Figure 6.2. The usual progression is "upward" from tenancies to outright owner occupation, although some intermediate steps often are bypassed. A minority of careers may involve a direct move to outright ownership, progression no further than private or public tenancy, or a move back from ownership to tenancy again. The same concepts of moves "upward," "sideways," or "downward" along housing careers can also be applied to changes in other features of housing—such as type, value, and location—either within tenure categories or along with changes of tenure (Kendig, 1981).

The most critical step along housing careers is the move—if it is ever

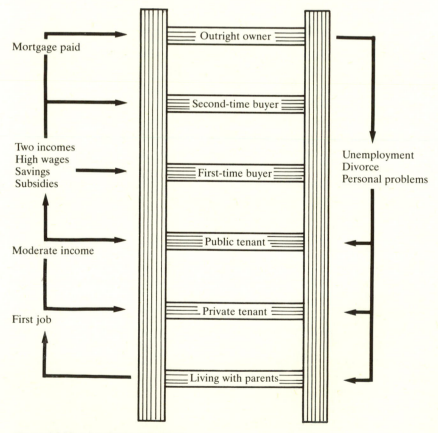

Figure 6.2 Housing-Career "Ladder"

made—from renting to buying. The early literature in the life-cycle tradition attributed first homeownership to the effects of marriage and childbearing on residential stability, strengthened preference for security, and demand for more space. Later analysts, in studies of a variety of markets, have explained initial home purchases with a much heavier emphasis on achieving the financial means to overcome the high entry costs of down payments and mortgage repayments (Boehm, 1982; Struyk, 1976; and Deurloo, Dieleman, and Clark, 1987). The interdependency between family situations and financial resources makes it difficult to sort out their independent influences.

A critical divide in housing careers is between people who eventually become owners and those who remain tenants for life. Inequalities of economic resources early in life can be accentuated over the life course, because permanent tenants' rents continue to rise with inflation whereas owners' mortgage payments fall in real terms and their property appreciates (Kendig, 1984b; Murie and Forest 1980; and Thorns, 1981). Further inequalities can be observed within the owner-occupied sector if people with limited economic resources have homes which do not appreciate as much as inflation (Edel, Sclar, and Luria, 1984; Karn, Kemeny, Williams, 1985) or if they buy much later in life. In Australia, Britain, and the United States, the divergent life chances of permanent tenants and eventual outright owners are most clearly seen among retired people near the end of housing careers (Kendig, 1984c, 1990).

Movers and Housing Careers: An Australian Case

A survey of movers in Adelaide analyzed some of the interconnections between life-cycle stage, life course transitions, and steps along housing careers (Kendig, 1981, 1984b). By examining only those who had moved during the previous year, the study explored processes of housing choice within a relatively fixed set of market conditions. Identifying past and expected changes in family and employment situations, as well as housing, facilitated analyses interrelating life careers. At the time of the survey in 1977, Adelaide was a city of 900,000 with a tenure pattern close to the Australian average shown in Figure 6.1. A substantial construction boom was coming to an end, average house prices amounted to 3.2 years of average male wages, average private rents were a low 13 percent of this wage, and interest rates on mortgages had risen to the then high level of 10 percent.

The Adelaide survey showed the close interrelationship between housing and other life careers. Fully a third of the movers were leaving their parents' homes (12 percent), marrying (9 percent), divorcing or separating (3 percent), or migrating to the city (15 percent). Another 11 percent of movers were pushed onto the market by evictions or forced sales. Relatively few of the 43 percent of movers experiencing household adjustments, migration, or forced moves were making major advances along housing careers. First-time buying and moves to more valuable housing within a tenure were restricted primarily to continuing households which chose to move within Adelaide.

Steps taken along housing careers followed an expected pattern across stages of the life cycle (Table 6.1). Most of the young singles were entering the private-rental sector or moving within it. Among the young couples, a third of whom moved while marrying or forming de facto relationships, there was a wide spread among entrants to the private-rental market, adjusters within it, and first-time buyers. Families with children generally were continuing households making voluntary housing moves within the private-rental sector, to first home purchases, or upward within owner occupancy. The relatively few households which moved at older ages were divided more clearly into continuing tenants or continuing owners.

These broad patterns mask the wide variation in housing careers (Kendig, 1981). "Fast track" entry to homeownership at a young age was associated with higher occupational status and delayed childbearing. Among families with children, continuing private tenants and new public tenants typically had one earner with a moderate wage; few of them expected to buy in the next five years. Steps "backward" from owning to renting often were short-term measures, as a result of migration or decisions to sell and rent before buying again, but others due to divorce appeared likely to be longer lasting. Moves upward within the owner-occupied market were most common among people who had bought early and had teenage children. They shared many similarities with other owners who were upgrading their housing by improving their existing home rather than moving (Seek, 1983).

Individuals' moves along housing careers formed interconnections within the housing market as shown in Table 6.2. Private-rental dwellings made up only 20 percent of the stock, but they received well over half of all movers: most of the entrants to the market, a few from owner occupancy, and a large number from other privately rented dwellings. Although most moves within this sector were between dwellings of the same type, shifts from flats to houses (which were generally rated as improvements by the movers) were more common than those from houses to flats. Many of the latter moves also were perceived as advances because the movers shifted from shared- to single-occupancy. The moves into private-rental housing by entrants to the market were balanced by a significant outward flow into owner occupancy.

Table 6.1. Percentage Distribution of Recent Movers in Adelaide, by Life-Cycle Stage and Tenure Change, 1977

Life-Cycle Stage	Tenure change (percentage of total movers)											Total Number of Cases
	Parents' Home to Private Tenant	Migrant to Private Tenant	Private Tenant to Private Tenant	Owner to Private Tenant	Owner to Public Tenant[a]	Parents' Home to Buyer	Migrant to Buyer	Private Tenant to Buyer	Public Tenant to Buyer	Owner to buyer	Total	
Single[b]	14	10	62	2	0	2	1	5	1	3	100	141
Couple[c]	19	8	29	1	1	6	5	26	1	5	100	199
Family[d]	2	8	22	6	7	1	9	17	3	25	100	291
Older household[e]	0	12	36	6	3	0	4	2	2	35	100	66
total	9	9	33	4	3	3	6	16	3	16	100	697

Source: Kendig, 1984b:276

Note: The rows may not add to the exact total of 100 because of rounding.

Chi-square significant at .01 level for the entire contingency table.

[a]Includes previous tenures of parents' home, migrant, private tenant, and owner.

[b]Childless, not married or living with a de facto spouse, and under age 45.

[c]Childless, married or living with a de facto spouse, and under age 45.

[d]Living with children, regardless of age or marital status.

[e]Childless and over age 44.

Table 6.2.   Percentage Distribution of Recent Movers in Adelaide, by
Current and Previous Housing, 1977

	Current Housing					
	Privately Rented		Publicly Rented	Owner-Occupied		Total
Previous Housing	Flat	House		House	Flat	
Entrants						
Migrants	3.6	4.8	0.5	5.4	0.4	14.7
From parents' home	6.5	2.4	0.2	2.1	0.5	11.6
Adjusters						
Other dwellings[a]	3.9	1.9	0.3	2.1	0.1	8.2
Privately let flats	9.1	4.8	1.0	7.0	1.1	23.0
Privately let houses	2.8	10.5	1.6	7.7	0.1	22.7
Publicly let dwellings	0.3	0.5	0	2.3	0.1	3.2
Owner-occupied houses	2.1	1.1	0	9.8	2.3	15.3
Owner-occupied flats	0.3	0	0	0.7	0.3	1.3
Total	28.5	26.0	3.6	37.1	4.9	100.0

Source: Kendig, 1984b:280
Note: All figures are the percentages of total cases (697). The survey excluded movers to publicly owned flats, nonprivate dwellings, and to locations
outside of Adelaide.
   Chi-square significant at .01 level for the entire contingency table.
   [a]Includes boarders, nonprivate dwellings, and mobile homes.

Being the last step of most housing careers, owner-occupied dwellings
(and to a lesser degree public housing) had relatively low rates of turnover. When people did leave these favored tenures, it was usually because the household disbanded or left the housing market. Table 6.2
shows that moves made by owner occupants within the stock were usually to other owner-occupied dwellings, predominantly between houses,
usually up to a much more valuable one. Some former owners moved to
less valuable dwellings, or from an owned house to an owned flat, usually in old age or after divorce.

Movers and Market Linkages

Household moves along housing careers are the most dynamic feature of
housing markets over the short term.[1] In Australian housing markets of
the early 1980s, only 3 percent of dwellings were newly built each year,
fewer than 0.5 percent were lost to demolition or conversion to nonresi-

1. The section "Movers and Market Linkages" and Tables 6.1 and 6.2 are reproduced
with the permission of *Urban Studies* from Kendig, 1984b.

dential use, and approximately 2 percent were substantially improved (Kendig, 1984b). The formation and dissolution of households, and changes of demand among stable households, were far more common. Over any given year the housing market is formed principally by the relatively large proportion of households (17 percent) which move around within the slowly changing stock of dwellings (5 percent).

Within the stock the linkages formed by movers suggest ways in which changes of demand, supply, or price can be transmitted through the market. For example, if rented houses were to become relatively expensive, the demand for them would probably spill over to rented flats, the main source of movers into rented houses, and perhaps to owner-occupied houses, the biggest receiver of movers from rented houses. The demand would be greatest for those tenanted flats and owner-occupied houses which, because of their costs and other features, are the closest substitutes for rented houses. Similarly, an increasing number of young adults leaving their parents would put most pressure on rented flats, with some overflow into other substitutes—shared rented houses and nonprivate dwellings. Conversely, an increase in the availability or affordability of owner-occupied houses would draw demand away from the private-rental sector and free housing opportunities within it.

The housing-career approach suggests, however, that there are a number of limitations and rigidities in how movers respond to fluctuations in the market. Firstly, the volume of movers is only partly a response to conditions in the market. As identified in the previous section, many moves are made for reasons largely unrelated to the cost or availability of housing. Among households in general, only the few already on the verge of moving would be likely to consider changing their housing consumption in response to developments in the market. This suggests that, over a relatively short period of time, the impact of changing market conditions may fall primarily on the dwelling selection of those who would be moving anyway.

Moves by private tenants would be expected to provide the principal mechanism for adjustment in the market. Most of them are at the beginning of their careers and their current housing is less likely to satisfy their long-term aspirations. They also are much more likely than households in other tenures to experience the household and personal changes that can thrust them onto the market. Finally, their housing outlays also are more sensitive to current market conditions, and moving for them is relatively inexpensive.

Especially within the private-rental market, transfers of demand probably are made disproportionately by particular groups which could more easily make the substitution. For example, if house rents increase, young singles on low incomes could well decide to share or move to flats, and couples on high incomes might buy sooner. Families with low incomes and young children, however, could be more likely to remain in privately rented houses and either trade off other features of housing or increase housing expenditure. A tightening or loosening in any one part of the market could result in marginal changes of moving patterns quite different from the average flows that indicate the underlying housing careers.

The housing-career perspective suggests that many of the interrelationships within the stock are predominantly one-way. For example, better opportunities in rented houses could be expected to attract some households out of rented flats, generally a housing improvement, but virtually none from owner-occupied houses. The paradox is that cheaper rents enable more tenants to save the down payment needed to move on to owner occupancy. Conversely, higher rents make homeownership more desirable but limit the savings necessary to achieve it. Thus, few households respond to market changes by moving unless they can improve their housing. As Goodman (1976:863) has observed, there is a "ratchet effect" in housing: "Households frequently take up opportunities to adjust their consumption upward but seldom reduce consumption. . . ." The concept of a housing career explains why households in different kinds of dwellings have widely varying responses to changes in incomes and housing prices (Boehm, 1982).

Acceleration or postponement of advancement along housing careers is a principal mechanism for short-term adjustments in the housing market. Although supply responses to price changes generally take a long time, households about to move are sensitive to relative prices and make choices at the margin between dwellings. In the middle term, providers of housing respond to price changes and provide more of the kinds of dwellings which are scarce and yield high returns. When it takes a long time for the supply responses, and when the kinds of housing in greater demand have few close substitutes, substantial relative price changes can occur between submarkets.

Longer-term changes in the market—as discussed in the next section—will determine the proportions of each new cohort which are able to make the critical steps toward their eventual housing goals. In these ways, the significant developments in the marketplace slowly change the overall allocation of households to dwellings.

Housing Careers and Market Change

The pathways which individuals and cohorts take through the housing stock are influenced by broader social change as well as life transitions and local housing markets. Understanding the processes and explanations of these changes arguably is the greatest potential for the developing field of housing demography.

Cohort effects are especially important for housing analyses, because the impact of market changes varies depending on peoples' positions along housing and other life careers at the time. For example, increases in housing costs relative to earnings can have a critical bearing on those on the verge of trying to buy their first homes. The consequences could include less expensive or delayed purchases. If the costs of buying remain high during a limited few years when couples may have two earners before childbearing, they conceivably could lose the chance to buy ever, even if the real costs of buying were to fall in the future.

Those who are already homeowners, however, are for the most part unaffected by rising prices, and they are less affected by rising interest rates. Indeed, sitting owners can benefit considerably from rising prices if they have fixed-mortgage payments with interest rates below the rate of inflation. Their ability to move up in the market is not limited by price rises, because the values of their current homes are rising too, and savings potential increases when repayments fall relative to earnings. Because sitting owners' equity in their homes increases disproportionately quickly during rapid inflation, their ability to move up in the housing market can actually increase as a result of escalating house prices.

The developing literature on housing demography is beginning to identify the interplay between life course development, social and economic change, and housing careers. Particularly important starts, including studies reported in other chapters in this book (by Masnick, Pitkin, and Brennan, and by Pitkin) have been made in applying demographic techniques to understand the tenure histories of successive cohorts. These and other research initiatives, as outlined below, have considerable promise for improving the comparative understanding of housing careers in different markets and policy environments.

British Fertility Surveys and Longitudinal Surveys

In Britain important advances have been achieved through comparing the housing histories identified in large fertility surveys in the 1960s and 1970s. Murphy (1984) and Murphy and Sullivan (1985) have examined the early housing careers of successive cohorts of young women over this period, when homeownership rates rose from 40 percent to 56 percent and the proportion of public tenants rose from 25 percent to 29 percent. These studies found that significantly greater proportions of couples in later cohorts were owners or became owners at the time of marriage. In explaining entry to homeownership or public tenancies after marriage, the most important factors for all cohorts were social class, number and timing of births, and age at marriage. Rising homeownership rates in Britain over these years could be explained largely by compositional and cohort changes of the population, for example, the baby-boom cohort's movement into the prime homebuying years and the passage of older protected tenants out of the housing market.

The gender dimension to early housing careers has been explored in Munroe and Smith's (1989) analyses of housing attainment among 23-year-olds in a 1982 round of the longitudinal National Child Development Survey. Rather than subsume women into analyses of households described primarily in terms of the characteristics of husbands, they compared the housing attainment of young men and women and the relationships between them. This study found that early housing careers of both sexes were significantly influenced by occupational status, financial assistance from family, and marital status. Men in skilled manual employment appeared to depend particularly heavily on working wives for buying homes. However, compared with the men, women's access to homeownership depended more heavily on being married and, if so, on their spouses' occupations. Analyses of a later round of this longitudinal survey, when respondents were 28 years of age in 1987, will shed further light on moves in the next steps in these peoples' housing careers.

U.S. Census and Annual Housing Survey Studies

A pioneering line of American research has examined the "housing progress" of young women over the postwar years (Myers, 1981). Aggregate census data identified the progress of cohorts in terms of both eventual tenure attainment and timing of entry into homeownership. The developmental trajectories of successive prewar birth cohorts showed substantial housing progress as they moved through their early housing careers during the 1950s and 1960s. For those born during or soon after the war, entry to homeownership was delayed compared with earlier cohorts, but homeownership rates achieved at older ages have continued to rise. Myers explains the later changes in terms of the "housing cost crisis" of the 1970s, which increased the financial incentive to buy but made the first purchase more difficult. For the most recent cohort, delayed childbearing (and presumably prolonged full-time employment) appeared to reduce homeownership rates in their early 20s but increased them by the time the women reached their 30s.

The 1970s were a watershed in American housing markets, and the Annual Housing Surveys (AHS) beginning in 1973 have provided an outstanding basis for exploring the impacts on housing careers. Drawing on the AHS data for the late 1970s, Myers (1985) provided further evidence that first-time buyers increasingly were households with young married women who delayed childbearing and continued full-time employment. The causal connection between change in these three variables has not been resolved in the literature, and could well vary significantly from person to person.

The impacts of rising costs of buying and fluctuations in construction cycles were examined in another Myers (1981) article based on the AHS. From 1973 to 1977, house prices relative to incomes rose steadily in the United States, mortgage rates jumped up sharply in one year and remained at the higher level, and construction rates turned downward until 1975 and then rose again until 1977. Former owners, many of whom had bought for the first time during the boom years of the late 1960s and early 1970s, were found to be forming an increasing share of movers over the mid-1970s. For both owners and tenants who moved during these years, the chances of buying the next home fell or rose parallel with the cycle of construction. However, former tenants' chances of buying rose less sharply along with the construction upturn, apparently because the continuing reductions of affordability affected them more than former owners. Explanations for the fluctuations of housing advances along with housing-market cycles are not well understood, and it is too early to know if they will eventually result in more permanent tenants.

The changing nexus between life cycle and homeownership over the 1970s has also been explored by Rudel (1987). Along with other commentators, he has pointed out that house price inflation and rising interest rates on new mortgages have two contradictory effects: they raise the entry costs to homeownership but also increase the incentive to buy as a hedge against inflation and indeed as a gain from it. Rudel's analysis of the AHS data confirmed that, as housing costs rose, moves from renting to owning had become more likely among young wealthy couples without children and less likely among less wealthy households with children. Financial status had been becoming relatively more important than increasing family size in explaining first-time buying. The market changes also explain why, over the 1970s, first-time buyers were getting less housing and paying more for it, whereas former owners were moving into increasingly valuable and better housing (Rudel and Neaigus, 1984).

Australian Life-History Studies

Retrospective surveys over long time periods can show the combined impact on housing careers of both individual life course variation and the broad sweep of history. A study of older people in Sydney in 1981 (Kendig, 1984c) found that approximately 85 percent of them had ever bought a home, much higher than the 73 percent who owned at the time of the survey. Those who had turned age 30 during the depression decade were twice as likely to have never bought a home as compared with those born 10 years later; the later cohorts were better placed to benefit from the increased housing opportunities in the early postwar years. Irrespective of birth cohort, the chances of remaining permanent tenants were relatively high for the working classes and even more so for never-married women. Access to public housing offset some of the class disadvantages but did little to redress the restricted housing access of earlier cohorts and never-married women.

Another Australian study is examining the housing careers of postwar entrants to the housing market (Kendig, 1987) as part of a national life-history survey (Bracher, 1987). These careers were being pursued while the overall homeownership rate rose from 50 to 70 percent from 1947 to 1961, and remained relatively stable thereafter; housing affordability, however, has been falling since the mid-1950s (Neutze and Kendig, forthcoming). Preliminary analyses found that homeownership trajectories have been similar for all cohorts, notwithstanding the massive postwar changes (Figure 6.3). A third of the women in every cohort had bought by age 25 and more than half by age 30; over 80 percent of those who had reached middle age by 1986–87 had bought or been buying a home.

Successive cohorts early in the postwar period show faster entry and higher eventual attainment of homeownership, as would be expected by the increasing housing opportunities, rising real household incomes, and pro-homeownership policies. People passing through their early 20s in the early 1960s showed a slower rate of early buying but more than caught up with their predecessors by age 30. The cohort which came of age at the tail of the postwar economic boom, in the late 1960s, appeared to be set on the most successful of any of the postwar housing trajectories. The two cohorts now in their 30s—who would have been in their prime homebuying years over the recent era of rising real costs of entry to homeownership—could be set on slightly slower rates and possibly lower eventual levels of attaining homeownership.

Later analyses of these data on women and parallel data on men (Neutze and Kendig, forthcoming) show substantial changes in the early adult life course experiences of successive cohorts. The average ages of leaving the parents' homes have been declining, whereas average ages have been rising for starting full-time work, marrying, and have a first child. The average ages of first-home purchases have been falling slightly, and women's work after marriage appears to have become a

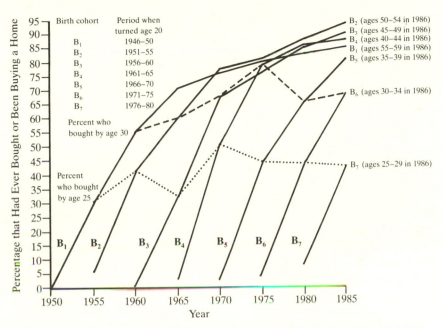

Figure 6.3 Proportions of Birth Cohorts of Australian-born Women Who Had Ever Owned or Been Buying Homes, by Specific Periods of Time

more important influence on the chances of buying a home. Migrants who arrived in Australia during their 20s or 30s generally have caught up quickly with the homeownership attainment of the Australian-born members of their cohorts.

Further analyses will explore the variety of mechanisms by which homeownership trajectories managed to stay so similar while Australian society and housing markets underwent fundamental change. The changing size and life course experience of cohorts also will be related to occupancy of the flats built during the 1960s and 1970s construction booms, widening differences of housing costs between spatial markets, and changes in the availability of public subsidies for homeownership and public housing.

Implications for Policy and Research

The life course perspective suggests a number of important policy issues which are not addressed very well by cross-sectional studies of age and income groups. Many inequities in housing policies can arise between the minority of people who probably will never buy and the majority who do become owners. Policies which are intended to increase access to homeownership—such as tax deductibility or mortgage interest rates in the United States and Britain, and sizable cash payments to first-time buyers in Australia—also can accentuate inequalities of wealth accumulation between social groups over the life course (Kendig and Paris, with Anderton, 1987; Kendig, 1990). Public housing in Britain and (to a lesser degree) in Australia provides secure and moderate-cost alternatives which are for all practical purposes unavailable for permanent tenants in the United States.

Social change can accentuate these inequalities and introduce new inequalities based on birth cohort as well as social class. Rapid increases in housing costs in the United States have added further to the tax and other advantages of established owners, while particularly disadvantaging blacks and others with low incomes who are unlikely ever to become owners (Rudel, 1987). If fewer people in current and future cohorts eventually become owners, it will add significantly to the demand for adequate income support for older people in the future (Kendig, 1990). When Australia and Britain cut back on their investment in public housing, they disadvantage low-income households for decades to come in order to benefit current taxpayers. The flow of wealth downward within family lineages, through assistance in home buying and inheritances, is becoming an increasingly significant issue given the substantial housing assets accumulated over the postwar years.

The existing housing literature has only begun to sketch the interplay between the life course experience of individuals and cohorts and broader changes of population structure, employment and housing markets, and public policies. Many important issues remained unexplored in the diverse pathways taken by individuals through the changing stock of housing. Topics for further exploration include the explanations and consequences of major moves upward, downward, and sideways in housing careers; subtle issues of timing and tradeoffs; and active strategies taken by individuals to pursue their chosen housing path. Tenure attainment may be the major divide in housing achievement, but it also needs to be related to changes of housing quality, value, and location.

The demand approach to housing emphasized in this chapter shows only one side of the market. The birth, change, and death of households (Richards et al., 1987, cited by Gober, this volume) can be related to comparable analyses of the histories of dwellings (Baer, this volume). The filtering literature, which examines the passage of households through dwellings (Grigsby, 1963; Lansing, Clifton, and Morgan, 1969), is a direct parallel to the housing-career literature on the succession of dwellings occupied by households. Integrated research interrelating housing supply and demand can show the dynamic processes by which streams of households and dwellings are brought together in the market.

The ability to pursue this substantial research agenda remains seriously constrained by the lack of adequate information. With relatively few exceptions, information relating housing to social and market change is available only for population aggregates (such as census data) and does not show diversity and interconnections in individuals' life transitions. Conversely, most information relating individuals' housing to their family and employment circumstances is cross-sectional or covers change over short periods of time. Bringing conceptual advances to full fruition in the understanding of housing careers will require substantial advances in the collection and analysis of data and their application to public policy (see Myers's introduction to this volume).

Acknowledgements

I am grateful for the helpful comments given me by Max Neutze, Susan Smith, Maryann Griffen-Wulff, and Dowell Myers on a draft of this chapter. The chapter was written while I served as a senior fellow in the Urban Research Unit at the Australian National University.

References

Boehm, T. P. 1982. A hierarchical model of housing choice. *Urban Studies* 20:47–57.

Bourne, L. S. 1981. *The Geography of Housing*. New York: John Wiley.

Bracher, M. 1987. The Australian Family Project. *Journal of the Australian Population Association* 4(2):106–122.

Clark, W. A. V., and J. Onaka. 1983. Life cycle and housing adjustments as explanations for residential mobility. *Urban Studies* 20:47–57.

Coupe, R. T., and B. S. Morgan. 1981. Towards a fuller understanding of residential mobility: A case study of Northhampton, England. *Environment and Planning A* 13:201–215.

Couper, M., and T. Brindley. 1975. Housing classes and housing values. *Sociological Review* 23:563–576.

Deurloo, M. C., F. M. Dieleman, and W. A. V. Clark. 1987. Tenure choice in the Dutch housing market. *Environment and Planning A* 19:763–781.

Doling, J. 1976. The family life cycle and housing choice. *Urban Studies* 13:55–58.

Easterlin, R. A. 1980. *Birth and Fortune: The Impact of Numbers on Personal Welfare*. New York: Basic Books.

Edel, M., E. D. Sclar, and D. Luria. 1984. *Shakey Palaces: Homeownership and Social Mobility in Boston's Suburbanization*. New York: Columbia University Press.

Elder, G. H., Jr., 1975. Age differentiation and the life course. Pp. 165–190 in A. Inkeles, J. Coleman, and N. Smelser (eds.), *Annual Review of Sociology,* 1. Palo Alto: Annual Reviews.

Glick, P. C. 1977. Updating the family life cycle. *Journal of Marriage and the Family* 39(February):5–13.

Goodman, J. L. 1976. Housing consumption disequilibrium and local residential mobility. *Environment and Planning A* 8:855–874.

Griffen-Wulff, M. 1982. The two-income household: Relative contribution of earners to housing costs. *Urban Studies* 19:343–350.

Grigsby, W. G. 1963. *Housing Markets and Public Policy.* Philadelphia: University of Pennsylvania Press.

Hagestad, G. O., and B. Neugarten. 1985. Age and the life course. Pp. 35–61 in R. Binstock and E. Shanas (eds.), *Handbook of Aging and the Social Sciences* (2d ed.). New York: Van Nostrand Reinhold.

Hohn, C. 1987. The family life cycle: Needed extensions of the concept. Pp. 65–80 in J. Borgaarts, T. Burch, and K. Wachler (eds.), *Family Demography: Methods and their Applications.* Oxford: Clarendon Press.

Karn, V., J. Kemeny, and P. Williams. 1985. *Salvation or Despair: Low Income Homeownership in the Inner City.* Aldershot, England: Gower.

Kendig, H. L. 1981. *Buying and Renting: Household Moves in Adelaide.* Canberra: Australian Institute of Urban Studies.

Kendig, H. 1984a. Gentrification in Australia. Pp. 235–253 in J. J. Palen and B. London (eds.), *Gentrification, Displacement, and Neighborhood Revitalization.* Albany: State University of New York Press.

Kendig, H. 1984b. Housing careers, life cycle, and residential mobility: Implications for the housing market. *Urban Studies* 21:271–283.

Kendig, H. 1984c. Housing tenure and generational equity. *Ageing and Society* 4:249.

Kendig, H. 1987. The Housing Attainment of Postwar Cohorts: Preliminary Plans for Analysing the 1986–87 Australian Family Project Survey. Unpublished working paper. Canberra: The Australian National University, Urban Research Unit.

Kendig, H. 1990. Comparative perspectives on housing, aging, and social structure. Pp. 288–306 in R. Binstock and L. George (eds.), *Handbook of Aging and the Social Sciences* (3d ed.). San Diego: Academic Press.

Kendig, H., and C. Paris, with N. Anderton. 1987. *Towards Fair Shares in Australian Housing.* Canberra: National Nongovernment Committee for the International Year for Shelter of the Homeless.

Kohlase, J. E. 1986. Labor supply and housing demand for one- and two-earner households. *Review of Economics and Statistics* 68(1):48–57.

Kreps, J. 1971. *The Allocation of Income over the Life Cycle.* Durham, N.C.: Duke University Press.

Lansing, J, and L. Kish. 1957. Family life cycle as an independent variable. *American Sociological Review* 22(October):512–519.

Lansing, G. B., C. W. Clifton, and J. N. Morgan. 1969. *New Homes for Poor*

People: A Study of Chains of Moves. Ann Arbor: University of Michigan Press.

McLeod, P. B., and J. R. Ellis. 1982. Housing consumption over the life cycle: An empirical analysis. *Urban Studies* 19:177–185.

Maddox, G., and R. T. Campbell. 1985. Scope, concepts, and methods in the study of aging. Pp. 3–31 in R. Binstock and E. Shanas (eds.), *Handbook of Aging and the Social Sciencies* (2d ed.). New York: Van Nostrand Reinhold.

Michelson, W. 1977. *Environmental Choice, Human Behaviour and Residential Satisfaction.* New York: Oxford University Press.

Munroe, M., and S. J. Smith. 1989. Gender and housing: Broadening the debate. *Housing Studies* 4:3–17.

Murie, A., and R. Forest. 1980. Wealth, inheritance, and housing policy. *Policy and Politics* 8:1–19.

Murphy, M. J. 1984. The influence of fertility, early housing-career, and socioeconomic factors on tenure determination in contemporary Britain. *Environment and Planning A* 16:1303–1318.

Murphy, M., and O. Sullivan. 1985. Housing tenure and family formation in contemporary Britain. *European Sociological Review* 1(December):230–243.

Myers, D. 1981. A cohort-based indicator of housing progress. *Population Research and Policy Review* 1:109–136.

Myers, D. 1982. Housing progress in the seventies: New indicators. *Social Indicators Research* 9:35–60.

Myers, D. 1985. Wives earnings and the rising costs of homeownership. *Social Science Quarterly* 66:319–379.

Neutze, M., and H. Kendig. forthcoming. Achievement of Homeownership among Post War Australian Cohorts. *Housing Studies.*

Nissel, M. 1987. Social change and the family cycle. Pp. 209–242 in G. Cohen (ed.), *Social Change and the Life Course.* London: Tavistock Publications.

Oppenheimer, V. K. 1982. *Work and the Family.* New York: Academic Press.

Payne, J., and G. Payne. 1977. Housing pathways and stratification: A study of life chances in the housing market. *Journal of Social Policy* 6:129–156.

Quigley, J. M., and D. M. Weinberg. 1977. Urban residential mobility: A review and synthesis. *International Regional Science Review* 2(Fall):41–66.

Rex, J., and S. Moore. 1967. *Race, Community and Conflict.* London: Oxford University Press.

Riley, M. W. 1987. On the significance of age in sociology. *American Sociological Review* 52(February):1–14.

Roistacher, E., and J. S. Young. 1979. Two earner families in the housing market. *Policy Studies Journal* 8(2):227–240.

Rossi, P. H. 1955. *Why Families Move: A Study of the Social Psychology of Urban Residential Mobility.* New York: Macmillan.

Rudel, T. K. 1987. House price inflation, family growth, and the move from rented to owner occupied housing. *Urban Studies* 24:258–267.

Rudel, T. K., and A. Neaigus. 1984. Inflation, new homeowners, and downgrading in the United States. *Urban Studies* 21:129–138.

Ryder, N. B. 1965. The cohort as a concept in the study of social change. *American Sociological Review* 30:843–861.

Saunders, P. 1984. Beyond housing classes: The sociological significance of private property rights in means of consumption. *International Journal of Urban and Regional Research* 8:202–227.

Seek, N. H. 1983. Adjusting housing consumption: Improve or move. *Urban Studies* 20:455–469.

Stapleton, C. M. 1980. Reformulation of the life-cycle concept: Implications for residential mobility. *Environment and Planning A* 12:1103–1118.

Sternlieb, G., and J. W. Hughes. 1986. Demographics and housing in America. Population Reference Bureau, *Population Bulletin* 41:1–34.

Struyk, R. 1976. *Urban Homeownership: The Economic Determinants*. Lexington, Mass.: D. C. Heath.

Sullivan, O., and M. J. Murphy. 1984. Housing pathways and stratification: Some evidence from a British survey. *Journal of Social Policy* 13:147–165.

Thorns, D. C. 1981. Constraints versus choices in the analysis of housing allocation and residential mobility. In C. Ungerson and V. Karn (eds.), *Housing, A Consumer View*. London: Saxon House.

Uhlenberg, P. 1974. Cohort variations in family life cycle experiences of United States females. *Journal of Marriage and the Family* 36:284–292.

Waring, J. M. 1975. Social replenishment and social change: The problem of the disordered cohort flow. *American Behavioral Scientist* 2:237–255.

Watson, S. 1986. Women and housing or feminist housing analysis. *Housing Studies* 1(1)(January):1–10.

7 *George S. Masnick, John R. Pitkin, and John Brennan*

Cohort Housing Trends in a Local Housing Market: The Case of Southern California

Introduction

Long-term projections of households and the types of housing structures they occupy are used by many public and private organizations and businesses for long-range planning and policy-making. Governmental bodies are interested in whether housing supply will be adequate to meet the demand in the years to come, developers whether projects they undertake will sell out, bankers whether housing demand in a particular area will hold firm during the effective life of the financing, suppliers of building materials whether a new plant or warehouse will be justified in a particular market area, and utility companies whether their capacity to serve their customers will be adequate, to name just a few. Besides the number of occupied housing units, projections often call for characteristics of those units, such as tenure, type of structure, and size. To date, no standard methods of projecting housing have emerged (Myers, 1987). This chapter describes one approach used to address the needs for housing forecasts undertaken at a major electric utility company.

George S. Masnick is President of Benchmark Data Services, P.O. Box 771, Hamilton, Montana 59840.

John R. Pitkin is President of Analysis and Forecasting, Inc., P.O. Box 415, Cambridge, Massachusetts 02238.

John Brennan is Senior Information Systems Analyst at Southern California Edison Company, P.O. Box 800, Rosemead, California 91770.

Southern California Edison requires demographic and housing occupancy estimates and projections for some 35 administrative areas in the SCE service territory, which includes population drawn from 11 southern California counties.[1] Estimates and projections of occupied housing units by tenure and type are required for simulation of residential energy sales, for initiatives in conservation planning, and for targeting, evaluating, and properly weighting survey data of Edison customers. A joint-research undertaking of the staff of Analysis and Forecasting, Inc., and the staff of the Electric Systems Planning Division of the Systems Development Department at SCE produced the required estimates and projections.

Many service providers require population estimates and projections to help guide long-range planning activities, but SCE also needs estimates and projections of households and housing characteristics, because the company's product—electricity—is delivered to households (occupied housing units) and is consumed and conserved differently depending on whether the housing units are single family or multifamily and owner or renter occupied. For example, energy-management programs that attempt to help customers conserve electricity during periods of peak use will approach single-family homeowners differently from apartment renters about installation of high-efficiency air conditioners, insulation, and so on. Although it is important to be able to project population growth per se with accuracy, it is the finer breakdown of the population into households and housing types that motivated the research we summarize here.

The housing study analyzed trends between 1970 and 1980 using United States decennial census data, and developed a projection model for households and housing consumption to be used by SCE in its future planning and marketing activities. This chapter reports on one aspect of the overall study—namely, the issue of "local" variations in housing market dynamics. First we describe the method we used to analyze housing trends between 1970 and 1980 in the SCE service territory. Next we highlight certain similarities and differences in patterns of housing occupancy as they changed over the decade of the 1970s for the United States as a whole compared with that portion of southern California served by Southern California Edison. Finally, we consider some of the variation in patterns and trends in housing within the SCE service territory by comparing three counties that show interesting differences, suggesting certain hypotheses about the nature of housing adjustments that take place over the life course of individuals and households.

1. The SCE service territory includes all or part of the following counties: Fresno, Imperial, Inyo, Kern, Kings, Los Angeles (except Los Angeles City), Mono, Orange, Riverside, San Bernardino, Santa Barbara, Tulare, and Ventura.

The California housing market of the 1970s provides an unusual opportunity to examine life course adjustments of households' occupancy of the housing stock. By all accounts the 1970s was a period of unusual household mobility and housing market activity, with new construction and resales of existing homes reaching record levels toward the end of that decade. Between 1976 and 1979 alone, the equivalent of a third of all California households and two-thirds of all homeowners bought (and sold) homes (Lowry, Hillestad, and Sarma, 1983). The fact that this housing boom was in large part fueled by high inflation and speculation about the prospects of future housing-price escalation should not obscure the fact that substantial housing adjustments took place in a relatively short period of time, adjustments that might have been stretched out over a much longer period under "normal" circumstances. These adjustments include a rapid expansion of the housing stock in both "older" and "newer" communities to accommodate the needs of recent in-migrants as well as the new households being formed by the baby-boom cohorts entering the housing market for the first time. The decade also witnessed the conversion of many rental properties to owner occupancy, and the "thawing" of the frozen occupancy of empty-nest households.[2] Many of these aging, long-term occupants moved out of larger single-family housing into newer, smaller, and easier-to-maintain cluster housing, condominiums, apartments, and mobile homes.

We shall view the 1970s in California as a decade in which time raced forward, accelerating and accentuating the many housing adjustments that more typically take place over the life course at a slower pace. The task at hand was to identify typical housing choices and adjustments that households make when they first form and then change over time, and use this information to develop projections of the levels and types of housing consumption that are likely to take place in the future.

The trend analyses and projection model have at their core the concept of "cohort trajectories." A cohort is a group of people who experience the same event during a specified period of time.[3] In demography, cohorts are most commonly defined by birth or marriage (those born or married during a particular period of history). Cohort membership im-

---

2. "Frozen occupancy" is a term coined by Myers (1978) to describe the common occurence of long-term occupancy in neighborhoods of single-family houses populated by late-middle-aged and elderly residents.

3. Because birth cohorts move across age brackets as time passes, they are sometimes called age cohorts. However, that usage may be confusing. Given that the same people (cohort) will occupy different age groups at different points in time, we must clearly distinguish between age groups (static) and birth cohorts (longitudinal). In this chapter, we use the term "cohort" to emphasize the actual experience of a population as it ages over time.

plies, not only a shared experience around the critical cohort-defining event, but also a lasting effect on attitudes and behavior for years following the event. For birth cohorts, the event is not literally birth, but other events following birth that have a cumulative impact on attitudes and behavior as each member of the cohort ages together through life course milestones.[4] The critical condition for birth cohorts is that all living members are the same age at all points in historical time. Events that occur when members of the cohort are normally making significant life course transitions are of particular interest.

For our purposes in this chapter, a period of rapid inflation in housing costs and values, like that which took place in California in the late 1970s, had a lasting impact on cohorts who were making life course transitions in the housing market. Young cohorts entering the housing market for the first time had their transitions slowed by rapidly escalating housing costs. Middle-aged cohorts, who were at the age at which growing incomes and expanding families would normally find them "trading up" in the housing market, borrowed heavily and accelerated their transitions both to avoid being "closed out" because of the anticipated further run-up in housing prices and to reap the benefits of housing-price inflation by investing in "more house" sooner rather than later. Older cohorts who normally might adjust their housing occupancy to reflect less of a need for extra bedrooms, or who would like less of a burden in terms of taxes, maintenance, or repairs, could cash out some of their equity and move to where housing was significantly less expensive and less costly to keep up.

Operationally, this concept of differential cohort behavior in the housing market can be translated into graphs showing cohort trajectories. These graphs plot the numbers (or proportions) of those in a particular birth cohort who occupy a particular type of housing when they reach a specified age (Pitkin and Masnick, 1980). For analytical purposes, the trajectories of different cohorts are displayed on the same graph so each cohort's relative levels of consumption, and its change over time, can be compared with the others'. As we shall see below, every birth cohort tends to follow a distinctive pattern of housing consumption over its life course as the interplay between historical events and life course transitions get articulated in the housing market. These regularities can be observed in the *broad patterns* of change in housing consumption over the life cycle that tend to be similar across cohorts, as well as in the

4. Cohort-defining events could be as benign as the weaning of most of a generation on Dr. Benjamin Spock's *Baby and Child Care* or as traumatic as the Great Depression or a world war.

distinct differences that emerge between cohorts in the *details* of their housing careers. Cohorts establish either higher or lower trajectories depending on a variety of housing market and other economic and social forces, such as interest rates, housing prices, rents, housing supply, incomes, migration rates, marriage and divorce levels, family composition, or ethnicity, as well as intercohort differences in norms, or tastes, regarding desired or appropriate levels of housing consumption. Regularities in these cohort trajectories provide a powerful tool both for understanding past housing trends and for providing a benchmark for projecting future trends.

Trends of the United States versus Those of the Southern California Edison Service Territory

Period versus Cohort Graphs

Table 7.1 presents headship rates, or the proportions of the population in specific age groups who head households, for both the SCE service territory and the entire United States in 1970 and 1980. We shall use these data to illustrate the period (age group) versus cohort (longitudinal) approach to trend analysis. In comparing SCE with U.S. headship rates, we can see that the age variation among headship is similar in the two areas, but the absolute levels were quite different in 1970 and 1980. Except for the very oldest age group, headship rates in the SCE territory are generally higher than those for the entire United States.[5] We graph

Table 7.1. Proportion of the Population Heading Their Own Households: SCE Service Territory versus the Entire United States, by Age Group

	1970		1980	
	SCE	U.S.	SCE	U.S.
15–24	0.157	0.126	0.165	0.159
25–34	0.517	0.469	0.521	0.508
35–44	0.570	0.508	0.602	0.549
45–54	0.574	0.525	0.611	0.556
55–64	0.622	0.583	0.620	0.583
65–74	0.640	0.624	0.660	0.658
≥ 75	0.611	0.616	0.633	0.719

5. Several factors probably stand out in accounting for the higher propensity to form households in southern California compared with the nation as a whole. As an area of high

these data in two very different ways. First, Figure 7.1 presents these data as "period" graphs connecting the points representing age groups' headship rates attained in 1970 and in 1980. By connecting the headship rates attained by each age group in each of the years, the interpretation generally attached to such a graph is that headship rates change over time as the population ages. That is, we generally *interpret* a period graph by following the curve from left to right as if it represents changing behavior over the life course. According to this interpretation, headship increases rapidly in the young-adult ages, then levels off throughout middle age, then rises slightly in older ages before declining somewhat in the oldest age group.

The same data that were plotted in Figure 7.1 can be replotted, as Figure 7.2 shows, following the cohort convention: a line is drawn joining the levels obtained by the same cohort at the beginning and the end of the decade. That is, for example, in 1970 about 15 percent of the cohort that was ages 15–24 headed independent households; in 1980 when the cohort was 10 years older (ages 25–34), the proportion of household heads rose to about 50 percent. As can be seen in Figure 7.2, all cohorts increased their headship as they aged, and no cohort trend showed signs of leveling off over the middle of the life course, as the period curves suggest.

In examining the details of the cohort trajectories comparing U.S. and SCE service territory headship trends, the youngest cohort in the SCE territory (leftmost line segment in the corresponding graph of Figure 7.2) did not speed up its rate of household formation between 1970 and 1980, whereas in the United States as a whole the youngest cohort surpassed the headship levels of the preceding cohorts by ages 25–34. In spite of the slower increase in the transition to household headship

---

in-migration, the SCE service territory population contains a high proportion of residents who do not have adult relatives living close by. Because unmarried adults who are accommodated in existing households are most likely to double up with relatives, geographic separation from kin is likely to translate into greater independence in living arrangements among young adults. Secondly, a higher fraction of California's population is unmarried because of longer delay before first marriage and higher divorce rates than the rest of the country. Thirdly, the housing stock is newer than the rest of the nation's, and therefore more likely to match the needs of smaller household sizes than housing built during historical periods when household sizes were much larger. Clearly, a projection model attempting to incorporate trends in all these factors affecting household formation and housing consumption at the local geographic level would be futile. Lack of benchmark data alone precludes such a model, not to mention the problem of accurately projecting many of these variables into the future. A cohort model captures the effects of many of these variables without directly measuring them.

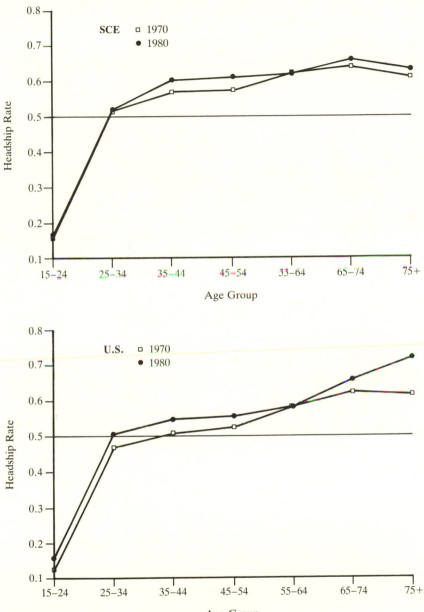

Figure 7.1 Period (Age Group) Representation of the Proportion Heading Households in the Southern California Edison Service Territory and the Entire United States

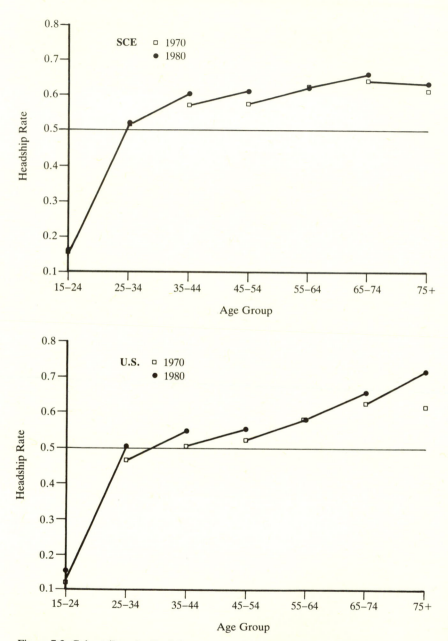

Figure 7.2. Cohort (Longitudinal) Representation of the Proportion Heading Households in the Southern California Edison Service Territory and the Entire United States

among the young SCE cohort, its rate still remains above the U.S. average in 1980. The middle-age cohorts (ages 35–44 to 45–54) in both graphs of Figure 7.2 are on slightly higher cohort trajectories than those that passed immediately before them (their trajectories fan upward). Among older cohorts it can be seen how the transition to headship accelerated in the United States, probably as a consequence of mortality leaving more and more of the elderly population as widows who live alone. Southern California's elderly population is on average younger and contains a higher proportion of married couples because of its higher proportion of elderly who are migrants from outside the state. Elderly in-migrants tend to be couples who are relatively healthy at the time of migration and survive longer jointly.

Cohort Housing Consumption Trajectories

Let us now shift our focus to the types of housing in which households live. We shall distinguish between owner and renter households and between four structure types within each of the tenures. Figures 7.3a–3d and 7.4a–d plot the 1970–80 cohort trajectories of the proportion of households residing in each of eight housing types (two tenure × four structure types) for the United States as a whole and for the SCE service territory. Notice that the vertical scales are set differently for each set of housing trajectories in order to maximize the resolution of the graphs. Also, we use 5-year birth cohorts instead of 10-year groups for the same reason. In this case the cohort trajectory connects, say, the group that was 25–29 in 1970 to the same group in 1980, when it was 10 years older (ages 35–39).

The cohort ownership trajectories during the 1970s showed rapid movement into single-family homeownership during the young-adult years, with fully 65 percent of SCE households falling into this category by ages 45–49 (Figure 7.3a). After age 50, however, cohorts began to reduce their occupancy of single-family owned units, and cohorts in the SCE territory dramatically increased their occupancy of owned mobile homes and apartments as well as showed significant movement into rental apartments and mobile homes.

Although such "trading down" is thought to be an appropriate response for widows and couples in the empty-nest stage of the family cycle, the strong readjustment of housing among the elderly in southern California in the 1970s stands out in strong contrast to the more gradual adjustments shown by the older cohorts in the U.S. trajectories. We shall discuss the latter pattern of "frozen occupancy" in greater detail

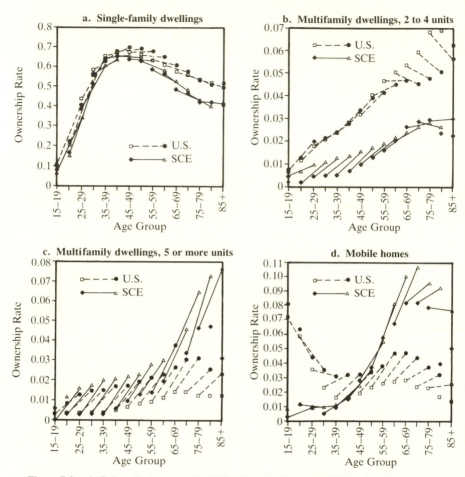

Figure 7.3a–d. Cohort Trajectories for 1970–80 for the Southern California Edison Service Territory and the United States: Proportions Owning Homes, by Age of Household Head and Type of Housing

below when we examine housing trends in several counties within the SCE service territory.

In addition to the gross patterns of housing consumption over the life cycle that we just described, several more subtle trends are revealed in the cohort trajectories in Figure 7.3. First, Figure 7.3a suggests that young adults in southern California, although certainly moving rapidly into single-family homeownership, appear to have slowed down this transition relative to the pace set by the cohorts that immediately precede them in the age structure. In addition, middle-aged cohorts in the United States as well as the SCE territory have clearly achieved record levels of single-family homeownership relative to the cohorts that came before them. In Figure 7.3a the slight fanning up of the cohort trajectories among those over 50 indicates that those who were in the middle-age cohorts in 1980 are on paths that will lead to higher levels of single-family ownership as they move into old age in the years to come than would be inferred from the period curves alone.

The sharp downward trend among the elderly in U.S. cohort trajectories of owner households living in multifamily structures of two to four units is also noteworthy. First, this pattern is opposite what would be inferred (incorrectly) from either set of period curves, where ownership within multifamily dwellings of two to four units continues to rise in the older ages. One hypothesis to explain this trend is that elderly cohorts living in two-to-four-family units in the United States tend to be living in rundown urban neighborhoods in the older cities of this country. During the 1970s, many of these duplex, triplex, and fourplex houses in blighted central-city neighborhoods were either torn down or boarded up, or the elderly (mostly white) residents moved out of these neighborhoods and were replaced by younger nonwhite ethnics.

Shifting attention to the renter trajectories in Figure 7.4a–d, we must question the basis for the persistent decline in single-family rentership (Figure 7.4a) across all cohorts. Although we might expect younger cohorts to make the transition from renter to owner, the sharp downward slopes for the elderly, especially in the SCE territory plots, appear a bit unusual. Relatively few elderly renters are expected to become owners at the late stage in their life cycles. Some of the shift out of single-family rentership is due to the impact of the addition of new multifamily and manufactured housing, which might have captured a higher share of elderly who change residences, especially the new migrants into southern California. We also suspect that some of the decline in single-family rentership in southern California is the result of middle-aged and elderly households having been forced either to buy the unit in which they were living or to be displaced, because the rapid run-up in real estate values in the 1970s prompted landlords to put the units on the market. Those who chose not to buy probably moved to rental apartments and perhaps mobile homes, as is suggested by the rising cohort trajectories in Figures 7.4c and d.

From our discussion thus far of cohort housing-consumption trajectories we can begin to appreciate the interrelatedness of such factors as life

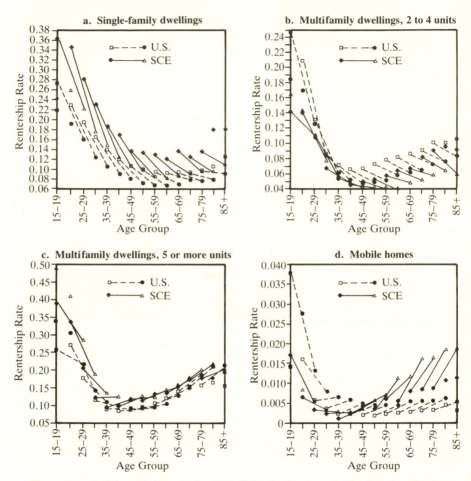

Figure 7.4a–d. Cohort Trajectories for 1970–80 for the Southern California Edison Service Territory and the United States: Proportions Renting Homes, by Age of Household Head and Type of Housing

cycle housing adjustments, competition among different cohorts for access to the available housing stock, the types of new housing being constructed, and the presence of alternative housing that is vacant for occupancy. How this match up between people and housing changes over time will be better understood once we examine cohort trajectories for a few more "local" housing markets in southern California.

Examples of Three Different Housing Markets

The level of "trading down" among the older cohorts depends in part on what housing alternatives are available for empty-nest and elderly house-holds to occupy. We have chosen to present cohort trajectories for three counties that illustrate differences in trends in homeownership. In San Bernardino County (Figures 7.5a–d) the decline in the proportion of single-family homeowners after age 55 is paralleled by an increase in

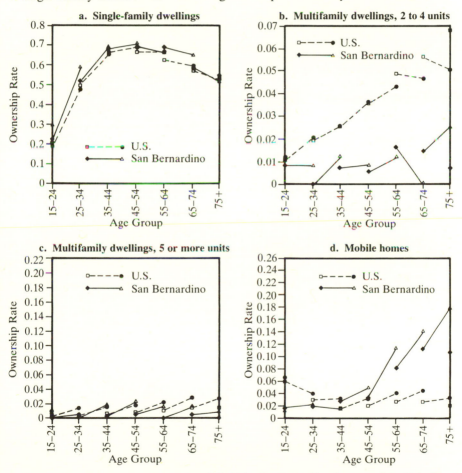

Figure 7.5a–d. Cohort Trajectories for 1970–80 for San Bernardino County and the United States: Proportions Owning Homes, by Age of Household Head and Type of Housing

ownership of mobile homes and very little change in owner occupancy in multifamily structures of two-to-four family units or five-or-more units. In Riverside County (Figure 7.6a–d) there is a slightly more pronounced decline in the proportion of older cohorts in single-family ownership, and once again it is the sharp increase in mobile home occupancy that preserves overall homeownership rates at near 80 percent. Finally, in Orange County (Figures 7.7a–d), the pattern of "trading down" from

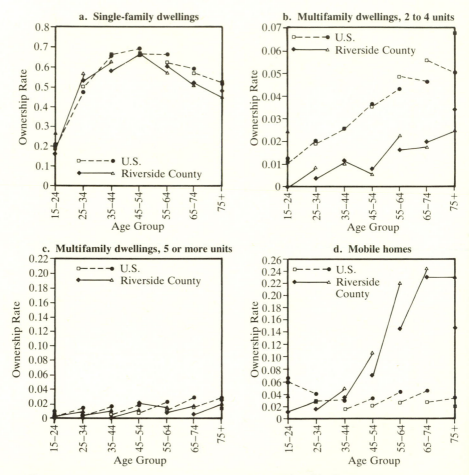

Figure 7.6a–d. Cohort Trajectories for 1970–80 for Riverside County and the United States: Proportions Owning Homes, by Age of Household Head and Type of Housing

single-family occupancy was very pronounced during the 1970–80 decade. Here it can be seen that a shift to condominium ownership (structures of five-or-more units) as well as a strong market for two-to-four family units allowed older cohorts to keep their grip on homeownership while "turning over" the occupancy of the single-family housing stock to cohorts under the age of 50.

We have qualified the words "trading down" and "turning over" with

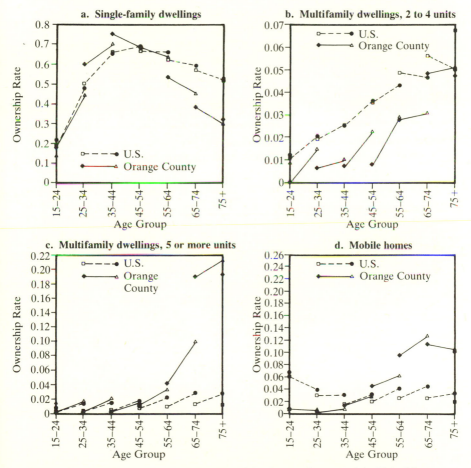

Figure 7.7a–d. Cohort Trajectories for 1970–80 for Orange County and the United States: Proportions Owning Homes, by Age of Household Head and Type of Housing

quotation marks, because declines in proportions of single-family home-owners among particular cohorts do not necessarily mean that individuals have changed their type of housing in all cases. In areas of high in-migration, the new residents could occupy housing entirely different from that of their native counterparts in the same age cohort, thus driving the "average" cohort consumption in new directions. For example, elderly out-migrants from Orange County could vacate single-family housing and move to a different county and into single-family housing once again. Elderly in-migrants could move from rented apartments into mobile homes. Hypothetically, the net result for elderly cohorts in that geographic area is a shift out of single-family houses, but no one, in fact, "traded down." In general, such extreme differences in the housing consumption of in-migrants, out-migrants, and stayers *within the same age groups* do not occur.

Figures 7.5, 7.6, and 7.7 illustrate the importance of localized housing market factors in conditioning the response that cohorts make to housing adjustments over the life cycle. In Orange County, the acceptance of housing alternatives to the traditional single-family structure, namely condominiums, townhouses, and mobile homes, appears to have generated a strong response during the 1970s in housing adjustments among elderly heads of households. In other areas, such as San Bernardino County, the single-family structure reigned supreme, with only manufactured housing serving to lure some elderly out of their stick-built homes. The 1970s experience appears to demonstrate that the elderly will cash out their equity in their homes *if* attractive alternative housing (perhaps offering easier maintenance, greater security, amenities, and maybe even lower cost) can be found nearby. At least this is what the cohort trajectories suggest. Verification of this hypothesis would need to measure motives, housing characteristics, and housing mobility more directly.

Conclusions

The housing projection model developed for Southern California Edison generates rates of household headship and housing consumption for future years that can be applied to projections of population, by age, to arrive at projections of the number of occupied housing units of different structure and tenure characteristics. Limitation of space prevents us from elaborating upon the details of the projection model at this time, but the essence of the model can be stated succinctly. Each individual historical cohort trajectory is extrapolated forward into the future by using information about "typical" adjustments made by older cohorts based on their life course housing adjustments in the past. Although no method of forecasting future patterns of housing consumption is fool-proof, the cohort method is generally superior to most others. Because the cohort method recognizes both the importance of cohort inertia from year to year and the salience of observed historical life course adjustments in housing occupancy in a particular time and place, projections are on track more often than not.

This practical application of the cohort method was what originally motivated the data analysis of actual housing adjustments made over a 10-year span of the life course of southern California residents. However, as is evident in our discussion throughout this chapter, both the analytical and public policy insights generated by the cohort approach should not be overlooked. The fact that different cohorts follow different housing-consumption trajectories over the life course should not be surprising, given the differences between generations in family structure, income and wealth, and life style. But how much are these housing differences a matter of choice and how much a matter of constraint? Also, as new housing is added to the existing stock, it should not be surprising that it differs from the existing stock in location, structure type, size, and perhaps even tenure. How selective is new housing of certain demographic groups, and what impact, if any, does new housing have on cohort housing-consumption trajectories? How important are the differences between recent migrants and natives in their housing-consumption trajectories? Although we have not attempted to answer questions such as these, we have succeeded in demonstrating the existence of cohort differentials in housing trends that make these questions worth asking.

References

Lowry, I. A., C. E. Hillestad, and S. Sarma. 1983. *California's Housing: Adequacy, Availability and Affordability.* Report R-3066-CSA. Santa Monica: Rand Corporation.

Myers, D. 1978. Aging of population and housing: A new perspective on planning for more balanced metropolitan growth. *Growth and Change* 9:8–13.

Myers, D. 1987. Extended forecasts of housing demand in metropolitan areas: The coming downturn. *Appraisal Journal* 55:266–278.

Pitkin, J. R., and G. Masnick. 1980. *Projections of Housing Consumption in the U.S., 1980 to 2000, by a Cohort Method.* Annual Housing Survey Studies, No. 9. Washington, D.C.: U.S. Department of Housing and Urban Development, Office of Policy Development and Research.

8 *John R. Pitkin*

Housing Consumption of the Elderly: A Cohort Economic Model

Introduction

This chapter analyzes two aspects of the housing consumption patterns of the elderly: the choice of whether to head a household and the choice of housing tenure.

For the foreseeable future the growth in the population of elderly is projected to be greater than in any other age group in the United States, raising many policy and planning issues. How the elderly live— whether independently in their own households and, if so, whether they own or rent—will have significant impacts on needs for their housing, on the design of systems for delivering services such as health care, and on aggregate housing demand. In order to plan for these future needs we require projections of the housing patterns of the elderly.

Because the household headship and tenure choices are interdependent in that only heads of households directly select a tenure of occupancy, they are modeled as a simultaneous three-way selection among mutually exclusive consumption alternatives, namely: (1) to live as a nonhead in a household headed by someone else, possibly though not necessarily a relative; (2) to head a household and own one's house

John R. Pitkin is President of Analysis and Forecasting, Inc., P.O. Box 415, Cambridge, Massachusetts 02238.

or apartment; and (3) to head a household and rent one's house or apartment.[1]

These choices are measured by comparing groups of elderly families and individuals in 57 metropolitan areas in the mid-1970s. To allow for systematic differences in life-cycle situations, separate relationships are estimated for three groups: married couples, widows, and never-married and divorced individuals.

We expect these choices to be affected by housing prices and incomes. We also expect them to be heavily influenced by the family or individual's past housing. Housing is consumed in inflexible housing "units," which include houses, apartments, mobile homes, and so on. Households can change their consumption by moving, but most do so only infrequently and live in the same housing unit for several years because of the difficulty and expense of moving as well as idiosyncratic attachments to a particular housing unit. The influence of past housing consumption on current housing patterns is particularly strong for older households, who move less often than younger ones.[2]

The collective impact of the past individual housing consumption choices for a population group is a *cohort effect*. Because the model presented here is of aggregate housing choice and, it will be seen, is to a large extent driven by cohort effects, it is called a *cohort model*. We ask here what effects prices and income have on current housing consumption of the elderly and how they compare with those of past housing choices. This chapter tests the importance of lagged cohort housing choices relative to economic factors in determining housing consumption.

The estimation results show that the lagged cohort effects have coefficients in the expected range of 0.5–1.0 and contribute far more than the price and income terms to the overall explanatory power of the model. This points to the conclusion that the historical experience of elderly cohorts powerfully influences their current and future housing choices, irrespective of their current income and market conditions. The price and income terms have effects which conform well to prior expectations: higher income reduces the number of nonheads of households and increases ownership rates; higher housing prices have the opposite effect; rapid increase in prices encourages retention of homeownership; and high rents for small apartments discourage formation of independent

1. This structuring of alternatives is limited to those available to the population living in households, that is, it excludes the option of living in group quarters such as nursing homes.

2. According to the 1970 U.S. Census, fewer than a quarter of elderly heads of households had moved in the previous five years (U.S. Bureau of the Census, 1973).

households. For an example of a forecasting application of a cohort model, see the chapter by Masnick, Pitkin, and Brennan.

The Need for a Model of Cohort Effects on Housing

There are three clusters of forces that determine the housing consumption of a family or individual at any time: *economic constraints* imposed jointly by the prices or rents the consumer must pay for different housing units and the consumer's financial resources; *life-cycle situations*, determined by age, marital status, and family size, as they alter and shape tastes or needs for particular types of housing units; and *inertia*, which inhibits the prompt adjustment of housing consumption in response to fluctuations in economic constraints or life-cycle changes. Inertia is seen, for example, in the 33 percent of all U.S. householders in 1980 who had lived in the same housing unit since before 1970 (U.S. Bureau of the Census, 1973), and it exists in the costs and difficulty of moving from one housing unit to another. These costs include the often substantial effort needed to find a more suitable housing unit.

Birth cohorts typically experience major life course events, such as family formation, buying a first house, "trading up" to a bigger house, departure of children from the parental home, retirement from the labor force, and widowhood at approximately the same time and under similar economic and housing market conditions. Major national fluctuations that have left their marks on the housing patterns of particular cohorts, or generations, include the Roaring Twenties, the Great Depression, prosperity and low interest rates in the 1950s and early 1960s, and the inflation of the 1970s. Reaganomics promises to shape the housing patterns of today's young families.

The observation of marked variations in housing consumption between different age groups as of a given date led to the development of fixed age-effect models, in which differences between age groups are described by one or more age-specific parameters. For example, Hendershott and Smith (1985) estimated such a model of household headship and Rosen and Rosen (1980) a model of the aggregate ownership rate.

However well such models fit the data, they confound age and cohort effects. We cannot tell to what extent differences in the housing patterns of 70–79-year-olds and 60–69-year-olds in 1980 reflect the effects of age and to what extent they are a passive continuation of differences which had been established earlier in response to fluctuations in the economic and housing-market environment. In this case, members of the earlier cohort raised their families during the depression and World War II, and those of the later cohort were still raising their children during the much more prosperous and affordable 1950s, which allowed them to achieve higher rates of homeownership than the earlier cohort.[3]

Boersch-Supan and Pollakowski (forthcoming) use individual panel data to estimate the effects of lagged individual housing choice on current choice and confirm that housing choices are intertemporally correlated. They find strong differences between the estimates with and without the effects of lagged consumption and conclude that these effects must be accounted for to estimate structural demand parameters from panel data. Because their empirical approach requires special panel survey data, it is of limited applicability for forecasting purposes.

In this chapter we consider housing market–specific cohort effects on the current housing consumption of elderly families and individuals. By restricting the analysis to the elderly we eliminate the effects of variation in age. By making intermetropolitan comparisons we observe *interarea* variations among cohorts rather than intertemporal ones.

Just as different national cohorts have experienced distinctive economic and housing environments through their life courses, members of the same national birth cohorts have also experienced distinctive housing environments, depending on which region and housing market area they have lived in. Levels of income, cost of living, and prices and availability of housing vary substantially between metropolitan areas at any time. Such variations leave their mark on the housing consumption of the cohorts who experience them as surely as variations over time in national economic conditions shape the housing consumption of each generation. For example, in the 57 sample metropolitan areas (SMSAs) in the 1975, 1976, and 1977 Annual Housing Surveys, the rate of homeownership for elderly married couples varied from a low of 61.0 percent in Miami, Florida, to a high of 91.5 percent in the Salt Lake City, Utah, SMSA; and the fraction of never-married and divorced elderly who did not head a household ranged from 16.0 percent in the Spokane, Washington, SMSA to 35.1 percent in the Philadelphia, Pennsylvania–New Jersey, SMSA. Interarea variability among cohorts allows us to measure the force of inertia by comparing the housing consumption of particular cohorts in a later year and measuring the degree to which preexisting differences in housing patterns have been maintained.

---

3. In 1960, when the earlier cohort was age 50–59 years, 34.5 percent of its members were homeowners. In 1970, when the later cohort was that age, 38.6 percent were homeowners (percentages tabulated from 1960 and 1970 U.S. Census 1-in-100 Public Use Sample data files).

An Aggregated Cohort Model

The aggregated model of cohort housing consumption is based on an underlying model of the housing choices of individual families and people. In the model of individual housing choice, each couple or person simultaneously chooses from among a number of discrete housing alternatives.[4] In this case there are three. The choices of the individual couple or person are probabilistic in that the odds that a given alternative will be chosen depend on the characteristics and income of the couple or person and the prices of the various alternatives, as well as the couple's or person's prior housing consumption:

$$h_{ijk} = f_j(a_i, y_i, \bar{\mathbf{P}}_k, \mathbf{H}_i^{-1})$$

where h_{ijk} is the probability that couple or person i in housing market k will choose the jth housing option; a and y are, respectively, the life-cycle situation and income of the couple or person; $\bar{\mathbf{P}}_k$ is the vector of housing prices and costs that confront all households in housing market k; and $\mathbf{H}_i^{-1}$ is a vector of dummy variables, one for each housing alternative, which take the value 1 if the couple or person chose the specified alternative at a particular time in the past, and otherwise take the value 0. The randomness of the choices made by individuals can be attributed to variations in preferences. There is a different equation for each possible choice concerning type of housing and headship, j.

Because of observed sharp variations among the housing choices of population in different life-cycle situations, a, a unique relationship is assumed to exist for the population in each:

$$h_{ijk} = f_j(y_i, \bar{\mathbf{P}}_k, \mathbf{H}_i^{-1} \mid a_i)$$
$$h_{ijk} = f_{ja}(y_i, \bar{\mathbf{P}}_k, \mathbf{H}_i^{-1})$$

These individual choices can be aggregated across all the couples or people in any particular metropolitan area, k:

$$\sum_{i=1}^{N_{ak}} h_{ijk} = \sum_{i=1}^{N_{ak}} f_{ja}(\bar{y}_i, \bar{\mathbf{P}}_k, \mathbf{H}_k^{-1})$$

where N_{ak} is the population in life-cycle situation a in housing market k. Dividing by the population we obtain a relationship between the share

---

4. Models which describe housing choices as sequential (for example, first headship and then whether to own or rent) run the risk of missing interactions among the choices. An increase in headship rate may impact the ownership rate for a group of households, because marginal households are likely to have a lower ownership rate than already established ones.

of the stratum which selects a particular housing alternative and the average income of the stratum, the structure of housing prices in the area, and the lagged housing consumption of the stratum:

$$h_{a \cdot jk} = g_a(\bar{Y}_{ak}, \bar{\mathbf{P}}_k, \bar{\mathbf{H}}_{a \cdot k}^{-1})$$

where $h_{a \cdot jk}$ is the current *housing choice share,* and $\bar{\mathbf{H}}_{a \cdot k}^{-1}$ is the cohort-lagged distribution of aggregate housing choice shares.

Historical data on the housing consumption patterns of U.S. cohorts approaching the 60–79-year age range show persistent marked differences among marital status groups. For example, in 1980 among the cohort of married couples aged 55–59, over 99 percent headed households and 87 percent were owner-occupiers, whereas among the never-married and divorced, 75 percent headed households and 38 percent were owner-occupiers; widows and widowers had intermediate rates of both headship and ownership. Similar differences among marital groups were seen in earlier censuses (Table 8.1), indicating that there are consistent divergences in either the preferences or cohort histories. The model therefore distinguishes three marital-status strata among the elderly: married couples, never-married and divorced individuals, and widows and widowers. Each couple or unmarried person is considered equally as a housing consumer.

Because few of the elderly live with family other than a spouse, variations in family size within marital-status groups are likely to be negligible, and family size is dropped from the model.

The age boundaries of elderly used here are 60–79 years, and for married couples are applied to the wife's age. (An age threshold of 60 years rather than the conventional 65 insures adequate sample sizes. An age ceiling minimizes the possible distortions caused by omitting nursing homes as a residential alternative in the model. Above age 80 the share of the population living in nursing homes is far higher than for that below age 80.)

Income and Prices

Income and prices play an important role in shaping housing consumption. The model therefore includes current money income and selected measures of housing prices.

Current money income indicates the ability of the couple or individual to pay for housing and other goods. For consumers in a similar life-cycle situation, current income should correlate closely to, if not equal, total resources available to pay for current consumption; these resources include income-producing assets, such as savings accounts and stocks,

Table 8.1. Percentage Distribution of Housing Consumption by 55–59-Year-Olds and 60–79-Year-Olds in the United States, by Selected Variables

| | Owner-Occupier Head | | | Renter-Occupier Head | | | |
	Fewer than 5 Rooms	5 or 6 Rooms	7 or More Rooms	Multifamily Structure, 5 or More Units	Other Type of Structure	Nonhead	Total
Ages 55–59							
Married couples							
1960	16.4	41.3	17.6	6.7	16.9	1.1	100.0
1970	16.0	46.6	17.5	6.1	13.1	0.7	100.0
1980	11.0	48.0	28.4	4.3	7.8	0.6	100.0
Never-married and divorced							
1960	8.4	11.5	5.6	15.0	18.5	41.0	100.0
1970	10.7	15.8	5.7	16.7	19.2	31.9	100.0
1980	10.2	20.3	8.0	18.4	17.6	25.5	100.0
Widowed							
1960	13.0	21.3	8.1	11.2	20.1	26.4	100.0
1970	14.0	27.3	8.5	12.6	20.4	17.2	100.0
1980	12.4	32.1	12.8	12.5	15.9	14.2	100.0
Ages 60–79							
Married couples							
1960	17.7	39.9	18.6	6.4	15.0	2.4	100.0
1970	19.7	43.9	14.2	7.8	12.5	1.9	100.0
1980	16.8	48.4	18.6	6.5	8.8	0.9	100.0
Never-married and divorced							
1960	9.8	13.4	7.7	14.1	16.0	39.0	100.0
1970	12.1	15.9	6.4	17.2	17.4	31.0	100.0
1980	13.2	19.9	6.8	19.2	16.2	24.7	100.0
Widowed							
1960	12.8	19.8	8.7	9.0	16.2	33.5	100.0
1970	15.9	24.2	7.3	13.0	17.3	22.4	100.0
1980	15.9	30.0	9.0	15.1	14.8	15.3	100.0

Note: The rows may not add to the exact total of 100.0 because of rounding.

which are reduced by debt repayments and savings. The relationship between current income and total current resources, or *permanent income,* varies over the life cycle. When separate equations for individuals in different life-cycle situations are specified, this source of variation in permanent income is eliminated.

We expect that higher incomes lead to more consumption of the most expensive housing alternative, owner-headship, and less consumption of the least expensive alternative, nonheadship. The effects on the intermediate alternative, renter-headship, will tend to resemble the effects for the *least chosen* of the other two alternatives. Most members of a population stratum with a high average rate of homeownership, such as elderly marrieds and widows, will see rental occupancy as a relatively inferior housing option. Members of a group with approximately equal numbers of owner-heads and nonheads of households, such as elderly never-married and divorced people, will be more evenly split: the owner-heads will view rental occupancy as inferior, and the nonheads will view it as superior relative to their chosen alternative. Income is therefore expected to have little net effect on rental-headship for this latter group and to have a negative effect on rental-headship among couples and widows.

The central price variable is the general level of housing prices in the housing market or SMSA. It determines the cost of all housing alternatives as a class relative to other goods. High housing prices should have the same direction of effect as low income, and low prices the same direction as higher income, namely, to raise owner-headship and lower nonheadship.

The relative prices of different housing alternatives may vary independently of average housing prices. Two relative prices are relevant to the three housing alternatives under consideration: the typical current cash costs of owning relative to renting a housing unit of the same size; and the rent of a typical five-room unit, which is large enough to accommodate a head and a roommate, relative to a typical three-room unit, which is an economical size for a lone householder. The second is the most direct available measure for the price of the alternative of living as a nonhead in a household with others. If large apartments are cheap relative to small ones, it becomes more economical for two individuals to live together rather than head separate households; conversely, when small units are relatively cheap, independent living is favored.

Because owner-occupants in the United States more often than not have realized gains from appreciation in housing prices, it is necessary also to measure this potential benefit of owner-occupancy. Prospective appreciation of house prices has been shown to be a major cause of the rise in homeownership rates during the 1970s (see Hendershott, 1988). This enters the model as a negative price, because it offsets the cash costs of ownership, but is not simply subtracted from cash housing costs, because the gains are only potential until they are realized through sale or refinancing. The expected rate of appreciation on a typical house is assumed to be equal to the recent past rate and is divided by the typical current cash costs of ownership to give the anticipated *rate of return over cost* from owner-occupancy.

The Data

Where the sample size is large enough, aggregated choice measures permit efficient estimation of probabilistic models of individual choice among multiple alternatives. Sample data on housing choices and current values of economic variables in the Annual Housing Survey (AHS) SMSA samples of 1975, 1976, and 1977 meet this condition. The particular sample used here comprises 57 SMSAs in the mid-1970s. These SMSAs are listed in Table 8.2.[5] This sample includes a total of 75,334 elderly families and individuals, an average of 1,322 per SMSA and a minimum of 614.

The lagged cohort consumption terms, $\bar{H}_{a \cdot k}^{-1}$, are housing choice shares tabulated from the 1970 U.S. Census 1-in-100 Public Use Sample for county groups in each SMSA. These cohort-lagged shares are for families and individuals in the same birth cohort as in the mid-1970s AHS data, at ages 55–74 in SMSAs in the 1975 AHS, at ages 54–73 in SMSAs in the 1976 AHS, and at ages 53–72 in SMSAs in the 1977 AHS. The lagged choice shares are defined separately for the three marital-status strata, so that the lagged consumption term for married couples refers to the consumption of married couples, and so forth for the other strata.

It must be pointed out that these are not panel data. The U.S. Census and AHS are independent samples of the same population in different years, so the consumption of a birth cohort is linked over time using age as an index. Use of this procedure requires that age be accurately reported and that the two samples be sufficiently large to be representative of the choice shares of the entire cohort in the SMSA. These conditions are apparently met. It can be assumed that age is correctly reported for a high proportion of census and survey respondents. The size of the AHS samples has been discussed. The 1 percent U.S. Census sample appears

---

5. Two SMSAs in the Annual Housing Survey—Colorado Springs, Colorado, and Saginaw, Michigan—are excluded from the analysis because 1970 U.S. Census data on lagged housing consumption are not available for them.

Table 8.2. SMSAs Included in This Study's Sample

	Year
Albany-Schenectady-Troy, New York	1977
Allentown-Bethlehem-Easton, Pennsylvania–New Jersey	1976
Anaheim–Santa Ana–Garden Grove, California	1977
Atlanta, Georgia	1975
Baltimore, Maryland	1976
Birmingham, Alabama	1976
Boston, Massachusetts	1977
Buffalo, New York	1976
Chicago, Illinois	1975
Cincinnati, Ohio-Kentucky-Indiana	1975
Cleveland, Ohio	1976
Columbus, Ohio	1975
Dallas, Texas	1977
Denver, Colorado	1976
Detroit, Michigan	1977
Fort Worth, Texas	1977
Grand Rapids, Michigan	1976
Hartford, Connecticut	1975
Houston, Texas	1976
Indianapolis, Indiana	1976
Kansas City, Missouri–Kansas City	1975
Las Vegas, Nevada	1976
Los Angeles–Long Beach, California	1977
Louisville, Kentucky-Indiana	1976
Madison, Wisconsin	1977
Memphis, Tennessee-Arkansas	1977
Miami, Florida	1975
Milwaukee, Wisconsin	1975
Minneapolis–St. Paul, Minnesota	1977
Newark, New Jersey	1977
New Orleans, Louisiana	1975
Newport News–Hampton, Virginia	1975
New York City, New York	1976
Oklahoma City, Oklahoma	1976
Omaha, Nebraska	1976
Orlando, Florida	1977
Paterson-Clifton-Passaic, New Jersey	1975
Philadelphia, Pennsylvania–New Jersey	1975
Phoenix, Arizona	1977
Pittsburgh, Pennsylvania	1977
Portland, Oregon	1975
Providence-Warwick-Pawtucket, Rhode Island–Massachusetts	1976
Raleigh, North Carolina	1976
Rochester, New York	1975
Sacramento, California	1976
St. Louis, Missouri-Illinois	1976

(continued on following page)

Table 8.2   *(continued)*

	Year
Salt Lake City, Utah	1977
San Antonio, Texas	1975
San Bernardino–Riverside–Ontario, California	1975
San Diego, California	1975
San Francisco–Oakland, California	1975
Seattle-Everett, Washington	1976
Spokane, Washington	1977
Springfield-Chicopee-Holyoke, Massachusetts	1975
Tacoma, Washington	1977
Washington, D.C.–Maryland–Virginia	1977
Wichita, Kansas	1977

Table 8.3   Descriptive Statistics of the AHS Housing Choice Shares: Tenure and Headship Distributions, by Marital Status, Mid-1970s

	Number of SMSAs	Mean	Standard Deviation	Minimum	Maximum
Married couples					
Owner-head	57	0.803	0.071	0.610	0.915
Renter-head	57	0.184	0.065	0.084	0.403
Nonhead	57	0.013	0.010	0.001	0.059
Never-married and divorced					
Owner-head	55	0.334	0.069	0.187	0.517
Renter-head	55	0.400	0.067	0.270	0.549
Nonhead	55	0.265	0.052	0.160	0.351
Widows and widowers					
Owner-head	56	0.506	0.084	0.282	0.651
Renter-head	56	0.318	0.061	0.206	0.472
Nonhead	56	0.176	0.044	0.091	0.299

to be large enough for our purposes. The smallest sample proportion for each stratum choice is shown in Table 8.3.

There is also leakage into and out of each cohort group through migration, death, and marriage. This will not distort the analysis as long as the arrivers and leavers have the same distribution of housing choices as the stayers. In the absence of direct information on this issue, the small size of most of the flows should prevent serious disturbances from this source. The one exception is the transition from married couple to widow or widower: the frequent retention of housing units occupied when spouses were still alive possibly alters the choice shares of the cohort of elderly widows and widowers. This effect is explicitly recognized in the model by inclusion of a *link-lagged* cohort choice share for married couples in the choice equations for widows and widowers. The coefficient of this term will indicate the strength of the effect of changing population composition.

Summary descriptive statistics of the AHS housing choice shares are given in Table 8.3, and those of the 1970 U.S. Census choice shares are given in the top panel of Table 8.4. Figure 8.1 graphs the housing choice profiles for all three strata of elderly in three SMSAs with very different consumption patterns. We see not only that the overall choice shares vary sharply between areas but also that the intermarital differences vary between areas. For example, there is a much larger share of renter-heads

Table 8.4. Descriptive Statistics: Independent Variables

	Mean	Standard Deviation
Cohort-Lagged Independent Variables		
LOWNM	1.417	0.439
LOWNS	−0.220	0.344
LOWNW	0.394	0.388
LNONHEDM	−3.216	0.696
LNONHEDS	−0.301	0.325
LNONHEDW	−0.493	0.277
Independent Variables		
RENT5E	198.473	27.959
RCOST5E	0.698	0.111
RRENT53E	1.295	0.111
RETURN5E	0.548	0.144
INCOMEM	11.624	1.127
INCOMES	5.688	0.769
INCOMEW	5.053	0.474
YEAR76	0.333	0.471
YEAR77	0.333	0.471
Excluded Variables		
RENT3B	111.746	17.327
RENT5B	142.727	20.153
VALUE5B	1.748e+004	3,764.072
VALUE7B	2.477e+004	4,783.905
CNSTCOST	1.534	0.083
DVAL6070	0.767	0.524
DREN6070	0.746	0.508
DELTAPOP	0.327	0.201

Note: Variables are defined in Table 8.5.

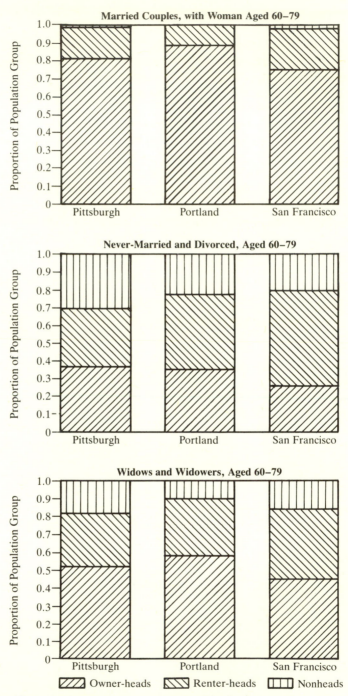

Figure 8.1 Tenure and Headship Status Distributions, by Marital Status, in Pittsburgh, Portland, and San Francisco in the Mid-1970s

among marrieds in Pittsburgh than in Portland, yet renter-heads are more prevalent among never-married and divorced individuals in Portland.

Figure 8.2 plots the relationship between the 1970 and mid-1970s choice shares for three particular choices in the 57 sample SMSAs. Each graph includes a ray from the origin with a slope of 1 to indicate the locus of equality between the two observations for each group. The points are tightly clustered around the line in the graph for married-couple owner-heads. There is more dispersion in the plots for widowed renter-heads and for never-married and divorced nonheads, indicating greater behavioral or sampling variations in the last two cases than in the first.

The income used in the model is the mean money income in the cohort–marital group in the previous year, tabulated from the AHS and deflated to 1975 dollars using the U.S. Consumer Price Index. Inter-SMSA variations in price levels are eliminated by deflating all incomes and housing prices to the national average price level using total nonhousing components in the Bureau of Labor Statistics Urban Family Budget (middle standard) as a cross-geographic price index.

Mean gross monthly rent of an apartment or house with five rooms, as tabulated from the AHS, is used to indicate the general level of housing prices in each SMSA. This benchmark, in fact, correlates quite well with prices for other types of housing units, 0.610 with mean values of five-room owner-occupied single-family houses in the SMSA, 0.730 with the mean values of seven-room houses, and 0.830 with mean gross monthly rents of three-room housing units.[6]

The first relative housing price is the ratio of current owner-to-renter cash costs. Periodic cash costs of ownership are based on the mean value of five-room owner-occupied single-family houses in the AHS. These are calculated as the sum of mortgage interest and amortization, real estate taxes, and utility and maintenance costs. Mortgage payments are calculated assuming a fixed-rate 25-year mortgage for 85 percent of the mean value at the prevailing effective interest rate reported for the SMSA by the Federal Home Loan Bank Board. Property tax rates are imputed from the 1977 and 1972 Census of Governments, and utility costs from the AHS.[7] The denominator of the ratio is the mean gross monthly rent of a five-room housing unit.

The second relative price is the ratio of the mean gross monthly rents of three- and five-room housing units.

6. Reported correlations are for the 57 Annual Housing Survey SMSA samples in the mid-1970s.

7. All ownership expenses could be directly tabulated from the AHS. This measure is not used because we needed to be able to construct consistent cost measures for non-AHS years, especially 1970. (Note that 1970 housing price variables are used as instruments in the model. See below.)

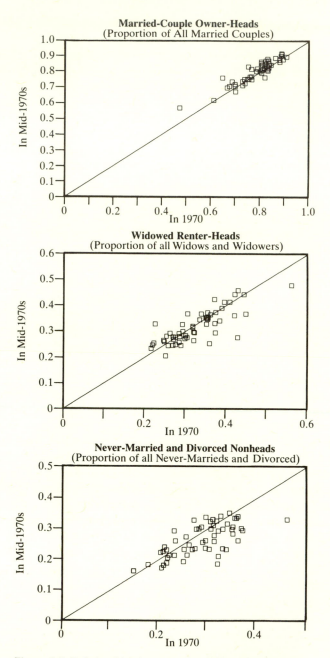

Figure 8.2 Relationships between the 1970 and Mid-1970s Housing Choice Shares, by Marital and Headship Status, for the 57 Sample SMSAs

The final price variable is the rate of return over cost on an average five-room house as of the mid-1970s. Returns are measured on the mean value of five-room houses in the SMSA and assume appreciation to be equal to the average annual increase in mean prices of houses of that size between the 1970 U.S. Census and the AHS. Costs are the annualized current cash costs of ownership, described above. The ratio of the two gives the expected rate of return over cost from owning a typical five-room house in an SMSA.

Econometric Estimation

For purposes of estimation the demand relationships defined above are transformed by taking the log of the ratios of the choice shares as the dependent variables, with renter-head as the reference, or "numeraire," alternative. This gives two equations for each stratum, one which determines the ratio of number of owners to number of renters and a second which determines the ratio of number of nonheads to number of renters. Because the three shares in each stratum include all possible choices, they must sum to one. The two estimating equations can therefore be solved to give the shares of the population choosing each of the three housing alternatives.

With this transformation the equations are estimated by least squares regression. In models such as this one where the dependent variable is a multiway discrete choice, this estimator is efficient as long as the number of cases in each choice category is large. Above we found that this condition is met by the selected SMSAs and population strata.

Because the lagged consumption shares have exactly the same form as the current shares, the lagged cohort housing variables are transformed in the same way to give lagged 1970 log-choice ratios. This facilitates direct measurement of the effects of lagged cohort consumption from the estimating equations.

The equation for each choice excludes the lagged cohort choice ratio for the other choice, owner in the nonhead equation and nonhead in the owner equation, thereby constraining the coefficient to zero.

For couples and the never-married and divorced, this gives:

$$\log \left(\frac{h_{a \cdot jk}}{h_{a \cdot 2k}} \right) = a_{j1} \bar{Y}_{ak} + a_{j2} \bar{p}_{1k} + a_{j3} \bar{p}_{2k} + a_{j4} \bar{p}_{3k}$$

$$+ a_{j5} \bar{p}_{4k} + a_{j6} \log \left(\frac{h_{a \cdot jk}^{-1}}{h_{a \cdot 2k}^{-1}} \right) + \mu_{ak}$$

For widows, this gives:

$$\log \left(\frac{h_{a \cdot jk}}{h_{a \cdot 2k}} \right) = a_{j1} \bar{Y}_{ak} + a_{j2} \bar{p}_{1k} + a_{j3} \bar{p}_{2k} + a_{j4} \bar{p}_{3k} + a_{j5} \bar{p}_{4k}$$

$$+ a_{j6} \log \left(\frac{h_{a \cdot jk}^{-1}}{h_{a \cdot 2k}^{-1}} \right) + a_{j7} \log \left(\frac{h_{b \cdot jk}^{-1}}{h_{b \cdot 2k}^{-1}} \right) + \mu_{ak}$$

for $j = 1$, owner-head, and $j = 3$, nonhead, where $h_{a \cdot jk}$ is the current share of couples or people in life-cycle situation a selecting housing alternative j in SMSA k; $h_{a \cdot 2k}$ is the share of renter-heads; $h_{a \cdot jk}^{-1}$ and $h_{a \cdot 2k}^{-1}$ are the corresponding cohort-lagged shares who selected alternative j and renter-head status, respectively; and $h_{b \cdot jk}^{-1}$ and $h_{b \cdot 2k}^{-1}$ are the lagged share of married couples in the cohort who selected alternative j and rental-headship, respectively; and μ_{ak} is the residual, error, term. Henceforth, I will refer to the variables by the following mnemonic names, which are defined fully in Table 8.5: OWN and NONHED, the dependent variables; LOWN and LNONHED, the cohort-lagged housing-consumption terms; INCOME; and RENT5E, RCOST5E, RRENT5E, and RETURN5E, the current price variables.

The specified choice-share equations are demand relationships, in that they predict the proportion and, by extension, the number of owned and rental housing units occupied by the three strata of elderly. Even the number of nonheads can be thought of as a demand for nonhead accommodations in households. Each demand is expressed as a function of prices and incomes.

Because the price variables must also affect the number of housing units and nonhead accommodations that are *supplied* in an SMSA, the coefficients estimated by single-equation methods may be biased toward understating the effect of prices and rents on housing choices. The bias arises from a correlation between errors in the estimating equation and the price terms. It can be controlled for by the method of a two-stage least squares estimation, in which the affected right-hand variables are first regressed on predictors that are uncorrelated with the dependent variables. In the final, or second-stage, estimating equations, the same right-hand variables are replaced by their predicted values from the first-stage equations. The predicted values are uncorrelated with the dependent variables, and the resulting estimates should be unbiased.

Accordingly, the method of two-stage least squares is used. The first-stage regressors, or instrumental variables, which are excluded from the choice share equations are: the mean gross monthly rents of three- and five-room housing units in 1970; the mean values of five- and seven-

Table 8.5. Definition of Variables Used in the Choice Share Equations

Dependent Variables	
$OWNi_k$	Logarithm of ratio of number of owner-occupiers to number of renters among marital stratum i at ages 60–79, mid-1970s, in SMSA[a]
$NONHEDi_k$	Logarithm of ratio of number of nonheads in households to number of renters among marital stratum i at ages 60–79, mid-1970s[a]

Cohort-Lagged Independent Variables	
$LOWNi_k$	Logarithm of ratio of number of owner-occupiers to number of renters among marital stratum i at ages 55–74, 1970[a]
$LNONHEDi_k$	Logarithm of ratio of number of nonheads in households to number of renters among marital stratum i at ages 55–74, 1970[a]

Independent Variables	
$RENT5E_k$	Mean gross monthly rent of five-room housing unit, mid-1970s
$RCOST5E_k$	Ratio of $RENT5E_k$ to mean monthly out-of-pocket costs of purchasing five-room single-family house, mid-1970s
$RRENT53E_k$	Ratio of $RENT5E_k$ to mean gross monthly rent of three-room housing unit, mid-1970s
$RETURN5E_k$	Ratio of anticipated (= recent) mean appreciation in value to mean periodic out-of-pocket costs of purchasing five-room single-family house, mid-1970s
$INCOMEi_k$	Mean annual money income of marital stratum i at ages 60–79, mid-1970s[a]
$YEAR76_k$ $YEAR77_k$	Dummy variables = 1 if observation is 1976 or 1977, = 0 otherwise

Excluded Variables	
$RENT3B_k$	Mean gross monthly rent of three-room housing unit, 1970
$RENT5B_k$	Mean gross monthly rent of five-room housing unit, 1970
$VALUE5B_k$	Mean value of five-room single-family owner-occupied house, 1970
$VALUE7B_k$	Mean value of seven-room single-family owner-occupied house, 1970
$CNSTCOST_k$	Inter-SMSA index of residential construction costs
$DVAL6070_k$	Proportional increase in median value of five-room owner-occupied houses between 1960 and 1970
$DREN6070_k$	Proportional increase in median rent of three-room renter-occupied housing units between 1960 and 1970
$DELTAPOP_k$	Proportional increase between 1970 and mid-1970s in population aged 18–24

[a]When i = M, stratum is married couples. When i = S, stratum is never-married and divorced people. When i = W, stratum is widows and widowers.

room houses in 1970; the residential construction cost index; the average annual rate of increase in median value of five-room houses between 1960 and 1970; the average annual rate of increase in median rents of three-room housing units between 1960 and 1970; and the rate of increase in population of young adults in the early 1970s.

The differences in year of observation and, by extension, in the amount of time elapsed between the 1970 U.S. Census cohort-lagged choices and the AHS may affect the observed choice shares. To account for these effects, two dummy variables are included, one taking the value 1 if the SMSA is the 1976 AHS and 0 if not, and the other equal to 1 if the SMSA is in the 1977 AHS and 0 if not.

Estimation Results

The results of estimation are shown in Table 8.6.[8] With the exception of the nonhead equation for married couples, the corrected R^2s range from .461 to .682.

The cohort-lagged consumption terms have coefficients between 0.497 and 0.965. The estimated effect is greatest in the owner equation for marrieds and weakest in the owner equation for widows. Their contribution to the explanatory power of the model is indicated by the fact that they have the highest t-statistic of all variables in every equation but one.

The two link-lagged cohort consumption shares for married couples in 1970, which are in the equations for widows, have the expected positive sign and value relative to the own lag terms. In the nonhead equation the coefficient is significant.

Although the income and price variables perform well in the model, *it is the lagged cohort consumption terms that give the model almost all of its explanatory power.* When the price and income terms are omitted from the model, the resulting increase in standard errors is negligible. On the other hand, when the lagged cohort consumption shares are omitted, there is a sharp loss of explanatory power: the standard errors in the ownership equations more than double, and those in the nonheadship equation rise by between a quarter and a half over the full model's.

Most of the price and income terms have the expected signs. Income has the expected sign in all equations, positive in the owner equations

8. Examination of preliminary estimates revealed that two SMSAs in the never-married and divorced equations and one in the widows equation were extreme outliers. These observations, for Madison, Wisconsin, Miami, Florida, and San Bernardino–Riverside–Ontario, California, respectively, are excluded from the estimations presented here. Small sample size and large sampling error may explain the apparent deviance of Madison and San Bernardino. Miami's deviance may result from its traditional large influx of elderly migrants.

Table 8.6.   Estimation Results (method of estimation: two-stage least squares)

Independent Variable	Estimated Coefficient	Standard Error	t-Statistic
Dependent Variable: OWNM			
Intercept	0.605	0.740	0.818
LOWNM	0.965	0.112	8.642
LNONHEDM	−4.060e-002	6.198e-002	−0.655
RENT5E	−3.8413-003	2.011e-003	−1.910
RCOST5E	0.351	0.556	0.630
RRENT53E	−0.918	0.770	−1.193
RETURN5E	1.371	0.597	2.295
INCOMEM	3.070e-002	3.545e-002	0.866
YEAR76	5.080e-002	0.103	0.491
YEAR77	2.984e-002	0.107	0.278

N	57		
R^2	.733		
Corrected R^2	.682		
Sum of squared residuals	2.811		
Standard error of regression	0.245		
Mean of dependent variable	1.529		

Dependent Variable: OWNS			
Intercept	0.631	0.794	0.795
LOWNS	0.727	0.129	5.631
LNONHEDS	−3.030e-002	0.123	−0.247
RENT5E	−4.6193-003	2.957e-003	−2.246
RCOST5E	1.913	0.684	2.798
RRENT53E	−1.801	0.883	−2.040
RETURN5E	1.559	0.672	2.320
INCOMES	4.958e-002	5.477e-002	0.905
YEAR76	0.133	0.103	1.293
YEAR77	0.179	9.974e-002	1.791

N	55		
R^2	.562		
Corrected R^2	.475		
Sum of squared residuals	2.868		
Standard error of regression	0.252		
Mean of dependent variable	−0.187		

Dependent Variable: OWNW			
Intercept	6.635e-002	0.686	9.669e-002
LOWNW	0.497	0.230	2.163
LOWNM	0.152	0.215	0.706
LNONHEDW	9.881e-002	0.192	0.516
LNONHEDM	4.102e-002	5.260e-002	0.780

continued on following page

Table 8.6.   *(continued)*

Dependent Variable: OWNW			
RENT5E	−5.834e-003	2.537e-003	−2.229
RCOST5E	0.829	0.650	1.275
RRENT53E	−0.913	0.744	−1.227
RETURN5E	1.294	0.628	2.060
INCOMEW	0.226	0.121	1.873
YEAR76	0.114	9.036e-002	1.264
YEAR77	0.124	9.813e-002	1.265
N	56		
R²	.670		
Corrected R²	.588		
Sum of squared residuals	2.280		
Standard error of regression	0.228		
Mean of dependent variable	0.469		

Dependent Variable: NONHEDM			
Intercept	1.381	1.903	0.726
LOWNM	−4.390e-002	0.287	−0.153
LNONHEDM	0.629	0.159	3.944
RENT5E	9.706e-003	5.175e-003	1.876
RCOST5E	−0.824	1.431	−0.576
RRENT53E	−0.515	1.980	−0.260
RRETURN5E	−0.173	1.537	−0.112
INCOMEM	−0.226	9.112e-002	−2.482
YEAR76	−0.228	0.266	−0.858
YEAR77	−0.469	0.277	−1.695
N	57		
R²	.461		
Corrected R²	.358		
Sum of squared residuals	18.613		
Standard error of regression	0.629		
Mean of dependent variable	−2.950		

Dependent Variable: NONHEDS			
Intercept	1.165	0.672	1.734
LOWNS	7.897e-002	0.109	0.723
LNONHEDS	0.608	0.104	5.857
RENT5E	−1.030e-003	1.741e-003	−0.592
RCOST5E	0.980	0.579	1.693
RRENT53E	−1.481	0.747	−1.983
RETURN5E	0.867	0.569	1.524

continued on following page

Table 8.6. *(continued)*

Dependent Variable: NONHEDS			
INCOMES	−8.319e-002	4.635e-002	−1.795
YEAR76	9.476e-002	8.687e-002	1.091
YEAR77	8.418e-002	8.441e-002	0.997

N	55		
R^2	.596		
Corrected R^2	.515		
Sum of squared residuals	2.054		
Standard error of regression	0.214		
Mean of dependent variable	−0.417		

Dependent Variable: NONHEDW			
Intercept	0.417	0.490	0.851
LOWNW	9.756e-003	0.164	5.943e-002
LOWNM	−0.211	0.154	−1.376
LNONHEDW	0.727	0.137	5.322
LNONHEDM	8.237e-002	3.754e-002	2.194
RENT5E	−3.233e-003	1.811e-003	−1.785
RCOST5E	1.057	0.464	2.278
RRENT53E	−1.034	0.531	−1.947
RETURN5E	0.731	0.448	1.631
INCOMEW	0.129	8.601e-002	1.502
YEAR76	0.107	6.449e-002	1.664
YEAR77	0.114	7.003e-002	1.632

N	56		
R^2	.741		
Corrected R^2	.677		
Sum of squared residuals	1.161		
Standard error of regression	0.162		
Mean of dependent variable	−0.605		

and negative in the nonhead. It is significant only in the equation for married nonheads.

The measure of the level of housing prices, RENT5E, has the expected sign in four of the six equations, the exception being the nonhead equations for the never-married and divorced and for widows. In the three owner equations the coefficients are negative, of similar magnitude, and significant.

The anticipated rate of return over cost of owning, RETURN5E, has significant coefficients of the expected sign in the three owner equations. These coefficients range from 1.29 in the widows equation to 1.56 for the never-married and divorced. We have no prior expectations about the sign of this variable in the three nonhead equations.

The relative cash cost of renting versus owning, RCOST5E, has the

Table 8.7. Estimated Elasticities of Tenure and Headship Choices, by Marital Status, in Three Selected SMSAs

	Share Renter-Head			Share Owner-Head			Share Nonhead		
	Pittsburgh	Portland	San Francisco	Pittsburgh	Portland	San Francisco	Pittsburgh	Portland	San Francisco
Married Couples, with Woman Aged 60–79									
RENT5E	0.574	0.517	0.604	−0.136	−0.090	−0.252	2.369	2.051	2.766
RCOST5E	−0.167	−0.206	−0.159	0.039	0.036	0.066	−0.652	−0.774	−0.688
RRENT53E	0.985	1.040	0.888	−0.193	−0.163	−0.291	0.324	0.365	0.227
RETURN5E	−0.674	−0.548	−0.518	0.138	0.088	0.179	−0.776	−0.628	−0.605
INCOMEM	−0.239	−0.284	−0.252	0.074	0.058	0.148	−2.544	−2.806	−3.202
Never-Married and Divorced, Aged 60–79									
RENT5E	0.343	0.294	0.293	−0.511	−0.437	−0.736	0.153	0.131	0.063
RCOST5E	−0.553	−0.611	−0.422	0.573	0.707	0.806	0.024	0.064	0.207
RRENT53E	1.357	1.249	0.942	−0.955	−1.110	−1.370	−0.544	−0.691	−0.959
RETURN5E	−0.466	−0.342	−0.280	0.458	0.381	0.513	0.047	0.060	0.161
INCOMES	0.048	0.001	0.033	0.305	0.264	0.346	−0.383	−0.441	−0.491
Widows and Widowers, Aged 60–79									
RENT5E	0.663	0.559	0.668	−0.416	−0.364	−0.632	0.065	0.047	−0.052
RCOST5E	−0.360	−0.396	−0.343	0.128	0.175	0.188	0.263	0.333	0.335
RRENT53E	0.835	0.808	0.726	−0.337	−0.388	−0.446	−0.492	−0.547	−0.601
RRETURN5E	−0.472	−0.364	−0.339	0.294	0.236	0.318	−0.039	−0.025	0.032
INCOMEW	−0.651	−0.627	−0.637	0.403	0.405	0.595	−0.047	−0.037	0.068

anticipated positive sign in the three owner equations and is significant in one. The proxy indicator of the relative cost of living as a nonhead, RRENT53E, has the expected negative sign in the three nonhead equations and is significant in two.

The two equations for each marital stratum are part of a three-equation system which determines the three choice shares, so the combined net effect of the price and income variables on the choice shares can be seen only by solving for the partial derivatives or elasticities. Because the system is highly nonlinear, they both vary according to the choice shares and values of the right-hand variables. Table 8.7 shows elasticities calculated for the price and income variables in three SMSAs with very different housing patterns: Pittsburgh, Portland, and San Francisco (see Figure 8.1, above).

The elasticities confirm the results on the effect of income and relative prices that were seen directly from the estimating equations. In addition they show some surprisingly strong and plausible cross-alternative price effects, including that of owner returns over costs on share of nonheads for marrieds (negative) and that of the relative rent of five- and three-room units on share of owners for the never-married and divorced and for widows (negative). Couples are not as affected by the rents of small apartments and houses. This result indicates that individual elderly homeowners who contemplate selling their houses and moving to rental units are at least as responsive to the rent levels of small, three-room units as they are to those of typical five-room units.

Overall the estimation results on prices and income suggest that elderly never-married and divorced people are more responsive than other strata to relative housing prices and returns on different housing alternatives. Of the price terms, relative rent of five- and three-room units has the largest absolute elasticity in six of the nine combinations of marital status and housing alternatives.

Conclusions and Implications for Projections

In this chapter we have examined the effects of cohort inertia, or past housing consumption, and economic constraints, or incomes and prices, on the housing consumption of the elderly. Although the force of economic constraint is found to have many of the anticipated effects on the current housing choices of the elderly, the force of inertia exerts a far stronger and dominant influence on these choices. Whether an elderly couple or person owned a home, rented, or lived with relatives half a decade ago has a much more decisive impact on whether they do so today than do their income, mortgage interest rates, and housing prices combined.

The empirical estimates show: that higher current income and lower current housing prices alike lead to more homeownership and formation of more households; that higher current ownership expenses and mortgage interest rates and lower expectations of price gains discourage homeownership; and that the current availability of small, inexpensive apartments facilitates the formation of independent households; but the force of inertia inhibits adjustments of housing choices in response to variations in housing prices and incomes. People tend to stay put because finding a suitable new housing unit or housemate and moving are both difficult, and because they may be satisfied with their present housing situations. Also when people are forced to move because of a change in circumstances, their preferences are often unchanged and lead them to find a new housing arrangement similar to the one they left.

Whatever the source of the inertia, its strength compels recognition of its central role in determining the housing patterns of broad population groups. Those who seek to understand, model, or project actual housing choices ignore the effects of cohort inertia at their peril.

The model treats three broad marital-status groups separately, allowing for differences in the preferences and behavior of consumers in different life course situations. The effects of both cohort inertia and economic constraint are found to vary among married couples, widows, and the never-married and divorced.

The same basic cohort model can be extended to encompass choices of size of housing unit and type of structure in addition to the choices of household headship and tenure, which we examined here. It can also be used to describe the housing choices of younger age groups. Although we expect that cohort effects are stronger for the elderly than for younger age groups, the impacts found here are so powerful that even much weaker ones can be expected to play an important role in shaping housing consumption earlier in the life course. Estimation of these effects should be a topic for further research.

The model as estimated can be applied directly to the task of projecting housing consumption for the elderly in any given SMSA. Though we can not foresee future incomes and prices with certainty, we often have accurate information about present housing-consumption patterns and the cohort-lagged housing-consumption terms which affect housing five years in the future. Any information we have about future trends or levels of income, housing prices, and mortgage rates can be used to improve the projections. Longer-term projections can be made by using the 5-year projections to generate the cohort-lagged consumption terms for 10-year projections, the 10-year projections as inputs for 15-year projections, and so forth.

Although the model has been estimated on a cross-section of SMSAs, it can also be used to make national projections. The observed inter-SMSA variation in housing-choice patterns spans the range of observed past and plausible future distributions of housing choices among the elderly population in the United States, and therefore provides a sound statistical basis for projections of national housing consumption of this population group. For example, the homeownership rate for elderly married couples was 76.2 percent in 1960, it rose to 77.8 percent in 1970 and 83.8 percent in 1980[9], as compared with the range of 61.0–91.5 percent in the 57 SMSAs in 1975, 1976, and 1977.

Similarly marked differences have been observed in the housing consumption patterns of cohorts at ages 55–59 years. This implies that the effect of cohort-lagged housing consumption on the elderly has not been and in all likelihood will not in the future be constant. The cohort dimension of the model permits realistic projection of the future consequences of the established housing patterns of different cohorts. Where these patterns are distinctive, models that ignore the effects of cohort inertia promise to yield seriously misleading results.

Long-term projections of national housing consumption, almost uniformly, have assumed fixed age effects and thereby ignored cohort inertia (see, for example, Sternlieb and Hughes, 1986). Pitkin and Masnick (1986), who made national projections with a cohort model, are an exception.

References

Boersch-Supan, A., and H. O. Pollakowski. Forthcoming. Estimating housing consumption adjustments from panel data. *Journal of Urban Economics*.

Hendershott, P. H. 1988. Home ownership and real house prices: Sources of change. *Housing Finance Review* 7:1–18.

Hendershott, P. H., and M. Smith. 1985. Household formations. Pp. 183–203, chapter 7, in P. H. Hendershott (ed.), *The Level and Composition of Household Saving*. Cambridge, Mass.: Ballinger.

Pitkin, J. R., and G. S. Masnick. 1986. *Households and Housing Consumption in the United States, 1985 to 2000: Projections by a Cohort Method*. Research Report RJ86-1. Cambridge, Mass.: MIT and Harvard University, Joint Center for Housing Studies.

Rosen, H. S., and K. T. Rosen. 1980. Federal taxes and home ownership: Evidence from time series. *Journal of Political Economy* 88:59–75.

Sternlieb, G., and J. W. Hughes. 1986. Demographics and housing in America. Population Reference Bureau, *Population Bulletin* 41(1).

U.S. Bureau of the Census. 1973. *Mover Households*. Census of Housing 1970, Final Report HC(7)-5. Washington, D.C.: U.S. Government Printing Office.

9. U.S. Census 1-in-100 Public Use Samples, 1960, 1970, and 1980.

PART 3
PERSPECTIVES ON SPACE, TIME, AND HOUSING STOCK

9 *Eric G. Moore and William A. V. Clark*

Housing and Households in American Cities: Structure and Change in Population Mobility, 1974–1982

Introduction

Residential mobility has been viewed as the mechanism by which households adjust their housing according to changing needs and resources (Rossi, 1955; Clark, 1982). As households grow or shrink, as incomes rise or fall, adjustments are made in the size, quality, and location of their residences. Such a voluntary, or choice, approach to mobility emphasizes the role of rational selection among alternatives. This behavioral perspective downplays the importance of demographic changes and their impact—particularly when associated with changes in local housing and labor markets—on the changing distribution of urban populations. Yet mobility behavior is known to be influenced by age, by changes in household composition, by housing formation and dissolution, and by changes in household relations with work places and with entry to and exit from the labor force (Speare, Goldstein, and Frey, 1975; Stapleton, 1980).

The detailed social-behavioral analysis of these demographic forces within a traditional choice framework is not always feasible, but an understanding of changing patterns of associations between these socio-

Eric G. Moore is Professor of Geography, Queen's University, Kingston, Ontario, Canada K7L 3N6.

William A. V. Clark is Professor of Geography, University of California at Los Angeles, Los Angeles, California 90024.

demographic phenomena and mobility is a necessary basis for assessing the forces of redistribution in the housing stock, at least in the short run. Preceding chapters by Sweet, Kendig, and Pitkin can be made more concrete by applying their respective lessons regarding family life-cycle stages, life course analysis, and cohort histories in the analysis of annual mobility behavior.

Concern for the impacts of demographic events raises the more general issue of the relevance of choice versus constraint in movement decisions. The occurrence of divorce or separation and new household formation often generates moves whose structure has little relation to models of choice among considered alternatives. A similar argument can also be made for moves instigated by serious problems of affordability and by job relocation as well as by direct acts of eviction or displacement. These problems are often associated with households with particular demographic attributes. It is in this context that we need to develop a better understanding of how demographic states and events contribute to mobility and change within our cities.

An additional dimension is imposed by the nature of the local market conditions in which movement behavior occurs. Movement reflects both the sets of events which stimulate desires to move and the distribution of opportunities which allow desires to be translated into action. Stimulating events include changes in household composition, employment, income, and specific housing conditions. The likelihood of such changes occurring is, in aggregate, a function of variables such as age, household size, income, tenure, and duration of residence. The supply of opportunities is influenced by many factors including rates of new construction, growth levels of housing stock and jobs within the local area, availability of financing, and the presence of actions such as rent control in local submarkets. Although the processes which stimulate potential demand for changes in residence are likely to possess strong commonalities across cities, those which control supply are dependent only in part on factors operating at the national level. Most influences on supply have strongly localized components reflecting the differential volatility of local economies and the singular characteristics of local political decisions.

Time as well as space introduces variation into mobility behavior. Significant changes have taken place in the structure of the U.S. population over the last 20 years. Not only has the population aged, primarily as a function of dramatic declines in fertility, but also major shifts have occurred in the composition of households (Hughes, 1980). Average size has fallen and the proportion of single-person and single-parent households has grown. Increases in female labor-force participation have increased financial resources in families with two wage-earners and have altered the distribution of housing preferences as the links to work for two-adult families have grown more important (Waite, 1981). In addition to these societal changes, upswings and downswings in both national and local economies have affected investment, finance charges, and the demand for expansion in local housing opportunities as external migration waxes and wanes.

Analyzing mobility behavior across cities also creates problems for empirical analysis. Differences arise in both the level of mobility and the structure of flows (within cities) from two sources: one is the differences in sociodemographic composition between cities and the other is the differences in local contexts, reflecting variation in local economic growth, housing market conditions, and public policies (Moore and Clark, 1986). However, because the characterization of context results in only one set of values for each city at a given time, the estimation of the relative importance of the different sources of variation requires a relatively large sample of cities to obtain reliable coefficients for the contextual variables. At the same time, the detailed specification of intracity flows necessitates access to microlevel data containing origins and destinations for individual households. In combination, these considerations generate a demand for large samples whose responses are comparable across cities. Only two sources satisfy this demand: the Public Use Sample tapes associated with the U.S. decennial censuses and the source used in this chapter, the Annual Housing Survey SMSA samples.

A General Framework

In this chapter we present a view of mobility which emphasizes the explicit links between housing submarkets and household flows within individual cities. It is a framework which includes both stocks and flows and which permits analyses of the relationships between levels of mobility and structural differentials in mobility across cities and over time. The framework is designed to take specific advantage of the rich data source provided by the Annual Housing Survey.

The primary focus is on the way in which mobility influences the redistribution of households within the housing stock of a metropolitan area rather than on the behavioral mechanisms by which choices are made between housing alternatives (see, for example, Fischer and Aufhauser, 1988). Following our previous work (Moore and Clark, 1986), the basic unit of observation is the dwelling unit. Mobility is conceptualized both as a series of transfers between dwelling units of different types by households with different attributes and as changes in occupancy of dwelling units over time. The advantages of this perspective are: it focuses on issues of turnover and redistribution of population within the housing stock, which tends to be a more immediate concern of public policy and programs than the decision-making processes of individuals; and it yields a basis for dealing with change, because the locational fixity of dwelling units is a more attractive analytic unit than the much more amorphous concept of household, which can change in quite dramatic ways over even short periods of time.

An initial step in linking housing and households is to characterize the sectors of the housing market between which flows occur. Because housing and financial policies and programs differentiate between owner-occupied and rental units, between public and private sectors, and between city and suburban jurisdictions, an appropriate starting point is to construct sectors based on the following: *location*—city versus suburbs; and *tenure*—owning versus renting, with rental properties further divided into public- versus private-sector units.

This dimensional structure generates six sectors. Movers into these sectors can be identified and their origins classified on the same basis. We can identify two additional origins, "in-migrants" and "others," the latter classification comprising those who transferred from origins which do not fall within the established categories—primarily institutions. Finally, there is the set of "stayers," those who have not moved in the prior 12 months. These relations are set out in Figure 9.1. Each of the observed flows to a given destination (f_{ij}, m_j, s_j) can then be associated with a vector of sociodemographic attributes characterizing the household composition, racial make-up, and incomes of the movers. Note that we cannot identify out-migrants from the city, nor can we tell unambiguously whether the transferring households existed as separate households at their previous locations. It is therefore not possible to calculate true transition proportions from each of the origin categories (Rees, 1986).

The purposes of the ensuing analysis are to examine how the parameters of the table format in Figure 9.1 vary over time in selected U.S. cities and to assess the degree to which the composition of given flows is dependent both on the sectoral framework of local housing markets and on sociodemographic differentials within these urban populations.

The Annual Housing Survey

The Annual Housing Survey was initiated in 1974 with the objectives of providing data to "administer existing programs effectively, to evaluate possible new programs, and to monitor and evaluate the availability of adequate housing at affordable prices, particularly for low income house-

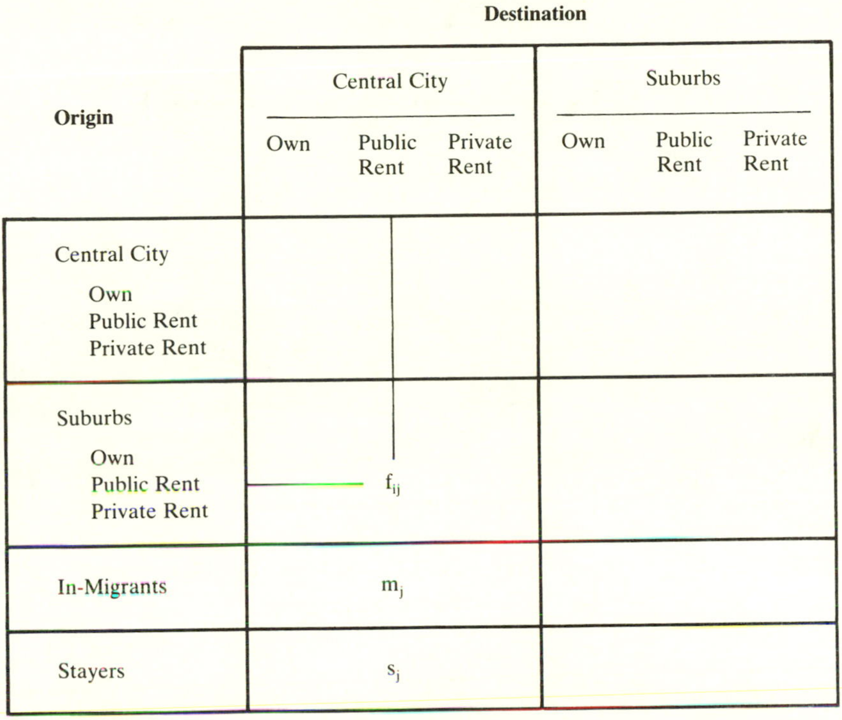

Destination

Origin	Central City			Suburbs		
	Own	Public Rent	Private Rent	Own	Public Rent	Private Rent
Central City Own Public Rent Private Rent						
Suburbs Own Public Rent Private Rent		f_{ij}				
In-Migrants	m_j					
Stayers	s_j					

f_{ij} = moves from origin i to destination j
m_j = in-migrants to destination j
s_j = stayers in destination j

Figure 9.1 A Framework for Analyzing Last-Move Data

holds" (Dahmann, 1986). The survey consists of two separate samples: a national sample collected each year from 1974 to 1981 and every other year since; and a series of metropolitan samples undertaken on a rotational basis, such that approximately 15–20 cities have been sampled each year within a three-to-four-year cycle (see Moore, 1987, for details). A critical aspect of both samples is that the same dwellings are surveyed in each sample period with appropriate additions to reflect local stock modifications.

Figure 9.2 provides an overview of the observable relationships obtained from the Annual Housing Survey, in which a given dwelling unit is surveyed at regular intervals and, at each interview point, information is obtained on the mobility experience of the occupants over the prior 12 months. The potential for the analysis of local dynamics is immense and

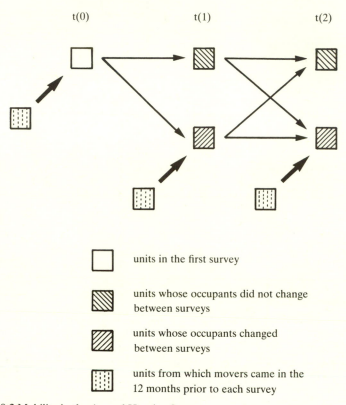

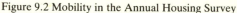

Figure 9.2 Mobility in the Annual Housing Survey

can be pursued along two major strategic lines. One strategy is to compare the structure of local mobility over time by analyzing movement behavior over the previous 12 months across cities and for successive survey periods. This permits the assessment of variation in movement response under varying national and local economic and policy conditions and the identification of the relative importance of shifts in the composition of population and housing to overall mobility.

The second strategy is to make more direct use of the longitudinal property of dwelling-unit linkage. By comparing the occupancy of the same units over time, we can assess the net redistributive effects arising from the flows of population through dwelling units. These effects are measured in terms of changes in the distribution of economic, social, and demographic characteristcs in different housing sectors, controlling for changes within the stock itself. In particular, it is then possible to identify the relative roles played by aging in place (changes that occur to those

Table 9.1. The Six Cities Used in This Study
and Their Sample Sizes

	Years Surveyed	Sample Size
Atlanta	1975, 1978, 1982	3,825
Detroit	1974, 1977, 1981	3,923
Kansas City	1975, 1978, 1982	4,126
Philadelphia	1975, 1978, 1982	5,258
Phoenix	1974, 1977, 1981	5,121
San Diego	1975, 1978, 1982	4,490

households who do not move between survey periods), internal mobility, and in-migration in effecting redistribution in different segments of the stock. For example, as mobility declines in the owner-occupied sector, we might observe that the average age of that population increases rapidly with a higher incidence of "empty-nesters" (Miron, 1988) than in periods of higher mobility.

A longer-term goal would then be to integrate the two different strategies, because changes in period-specific mobility produce redistributional shifts over more extended periods. In this study, which is part of a larger research effort, we focus on the first strategy of comparing successive sets of movers and stayers rather than on changing occupancy of the dwelling unit. The responses associated with movement experience over the prior 12 months provide the most direct link between demographic events and movement response.

In this study we used a recently constructed linked file for six cities from the SMSA samples (Table 9.1). These cities were carefully chosen to provide a broad regional coverage of cities with highly varied industrial mixes and differentiated growth experience over the last decade and a half. Each city was surveyed three times between 1974 and 1982, and the file linked dwelling units that were present in each survey period, thus removing the direct effects of new construction.

Questions relating to mobility are retrospective and refer to the characteristics of the last move if it occurred within the prior 12 months. Therefore, they cannot be used to compute annual flow rates, because multiple moves in a 12-month period were not recorded.[1] Analyses are therefore confined to measurement of the likelihood of "at least one move" in the last 12 months and to the structure of transfers of last moves.

1. In 1982, a question was asked about the number of moves by an individual in the last 12 months, but more detailed information refers only to the most recent move.

Analysis

To demonstrate the real links between demographic events and mobility, we have organized the analysis to explain the underpinnings of overall mobility, the nature of flows measured as last-move transitions, and the composition of these transitions.

Overall Levels of Mobility

Much of the previous research on intercity comparison of mobility rates focuses on total rates, undifferentiated by dwelling or household characteristics (Goodman, 1982; Long and Boertlein, 1978). The central argument follows earlier systemic ideas of White (1970), who suggested that the internal dynamism of an organism is a function of its rate of growth, which itself is a function of levels of in-migration. Growth creates new opportunities that initiate chains of adjustment, which have a multiplier effect on the number of internal moves.

Although there is much to be gained by such aggregate comparisons, a breakdown of sector-specific turnover rates by city and year reveals additional important findings about mobility (Table 9.2). Each of these rates is adjusted for new construction, such that the measure relates to movement into the existing stock. The mobility of individual cities exhibits both a substantial variation and a marked consistency in the rank ordering over time. Those cities with rapid growth rates and high levels of in-migration have consistently higher levels of mobility than those with slower growth rates and lower levels of in-migration (Figure 9.3), a finding consistent with both Goodman (1982) and Long and Boertlein (1978). The expanding cities of the Southwest—San Diego and Phoenix—lie at one end of the spectrum, with the large metropolises of the Northeast and Midwest— Philadelphia and Detroit—lying at the other. Kansas City and Atlanta occupy the middle ground, with the higher growth rate of Atlanta being associated with a mobility rate closer to that of San Diego and Phoenix.

Over time, little difference is observed between the first and second survey periods, but there is a significant drop in mobility in the third period, particularly in the suburban owned sector. Although much has been written recently about the decline in mobility at the national level (Rogerson, 1987), it is difficult to tell whether the declines observed in our samples reflect the same demographic forces of population-aging and larger young cohorts competing for limited opportunities. Short-term downswings in national and regional economies, if associated with a general increase in unemployment, will also produce a decline in new construction and in the multiplier effect of new opportunities within a given area.

Table 9.2. Percentage Distribution of Households Who Have Moved in the Last 12 Months, by City, Year, and Sector

		Central City			Suburbs		
	Total	Own	Public Rental	Private Rental	Own	Public Rental	Private Rental
Atlanta							
1975	21.7	4.7	23.7	34.6	8.0	15.4	50.4
1978	23.0	6.9	18.2	35.5	9.4	31.4	48.7
1982	18.4	3.4	13.2	32.1	3.5	26.1	44.1
Philadelphia							
1975	10.6	3.3	9.3	21.7	4.1	23.6	32.5
1978	12.8	4.5	15.5	28.2	5.4	20.5	32.8
1982	10.0	3.1	7.1	24.9	3.9	21.3	25.2
Kansas City							
1975	19.1	4.9	45.7	42.0	6.4	38.3	49.1
1978	20.5	10.5	39.6	39.0	9.1	49.3	42.8
1982	15.6	4.2	33.2	36.8	3.7	38.7	43.8
San Diego							
1975	26.3	7.8	43.0	45.8	9.2	53.4	46.1
1978	25.3	7.7	20.6	44.3	10.9	22.0	47.7
1982	21.3	4.0	27.5	37.7	4.3	28.9	41.9
Detroit							
1974	12.4	5.2	23.2	29.9	6.6	19.0	32.2
1977	15.2	7.0	20.1	33.0	7.6	25.9	34.6
1981	12.2	3.7	25.0	27.0	4.5	26.5	34.9
Phoenix							
1974	21.4	8.2	36.1	52.6	6.7	44.5	58.9
1977	25.7	11.0	38.2	52.5	11.1	51.2	54.6
1981	21.3	6.6	35.9	49.9	7.2	29.5	45.7

The structure of the propensity to move within given sectors of a city shows much higher levels of consistency across cities than the overall rates of mobility. The findings of another of our studies more limited than this one (Moore and Clark, 1986) are confirmed in the present study. The consistently high ratio of moves for rented as opposed to owned units is present for all cities and years. Also, private-rental units have higher mobility rates than public rentals, and the suburbs generally exhibit higher rates than the central city, even after the adjustment for new construction, which is highly suburban oriented.

A more rigorous analysis of these relationships, including race, can be undertaken by fitting a linear logit model (Feinberg, 1980) to the 6 × 3 × 2 × 3 × 2 × 2 table formed from the following variables: *city* (six categories: Atlanta, Detroit, Kansas City, Philadelphia, Phoenix, San Diego); *year* (year 1, year 2, year 3); *location* (central city, suburbs);

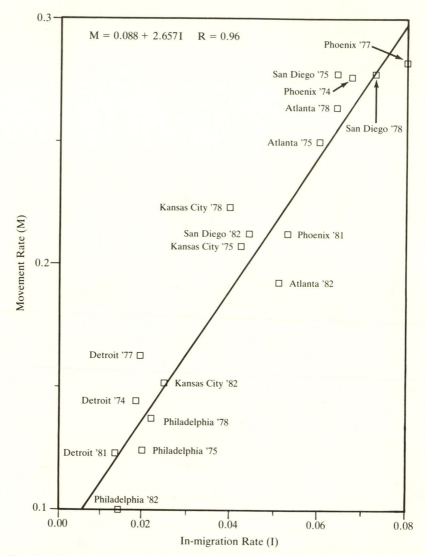

Figure 9.3 Relation between In-migration and Mobility

tenure (own, private rental, public rental); *race* (nonwhite, white); and *move* (move, no move), with *move* as the dependent variable.

In this model, *move* is considered to be the response variable, and it is the log odds of "move versus no move" (or the logit of the probability of moving) which is the dependent variable. The remaining variables are regarded as explanatory variables, whose distribution is taken as fixed by design. The modeling produces a parsimonious representation of the responses with respect to the explanatory variables in terms of a sufficient set of parameters associated with main effects and interactions between the explanatory variables. The CATMOD procedure (SAS Institute, 1985) was used to fit the models and generate parameter estimates. CATMOD uses a chi-square statistic to estimate goodness of fit between observed and predicted responses for cells in the multiway table defined by the explanatory variables.

If all observations are included in one model, the analysis tends to be swamped by the own-rent contrasts (see also Table 9.2), so the modeling was done separately for owner-occupied and rental sectors. We present the salient results in Table 9.3 in terms of the relative odds of having moved for selected variables, controlling for the influence of other variables. In the owner model, the city effects are strong but do not change their relative magnitude over time (the city-year interaction is not significant). The strength of the effects are presented in terms of the relative odds of having experienced a move in each city compared with Atlanta. Thus the relative effect of being in Phoenix as opposed to Atlanta increases the likelihood of having moved by 54.6 percent, whereas location in Philadelphia reduces the odds by 23.7 percent. In the same panel we show the specific effects associated with year, location, and race for all the cities combined. (For each variable, the first element listed serves as a reference point, with a value of 1.000, for the other elements in that variable.) The increase in mobility in 1977–78 and the even more dramatic decline in 1981–82 are marked; also, central cities have consistently lower mobility and nonwhites higher mobility over the entire set of cities.

The situation for renters is somewhat more complex, in part because of the additional dichotomy between public and private units. Tenure is highly significant, with public rentals having substantially lower movement rates than private rentals. However, the interaction terms are difficult to interpret, largely because of small numbers of public rentals in most cells, so we have not included odds ratios for the public-rental sector in Table 9.3.

If we focus attention on the numerically dominant private-rental sector, we find considerable consistency. This is demonstrated by the set of odds ratios in the bottom panel of Table 9.3. Again, we calculate the relative likelihood of being a recent mover across cities and over time, using Atlanta as the reference city, but this time the city-year effect must be included. Yet the pattern is still very stable. The statistical significance of the city-year effect is almost entirely due to the low value for Detroit in 1974 (even so, the only result is a switch in the order of

Table 9.3. Relative Odds of a Move in the Last 12 Months, by Sector and Other
           Selected Variables

Owner-Occupied Sector			
City		Year	
Atlanta	1.000	1974–75	1.000
Detroit	0.903	1977–78	1.343
Kansas City	0.988	1981–82	0.704
Philadelphia	0.763	Race	
Phoenix	1.546	Nonwhite	1.000
San Diego	1.066	White	0.768
Location			
Central city	1.000		
Suburbs	1.436		

Private-Rental Sector			
	1974–75	*1977–78*	*1981–82*
City-Year			
Atlanta	1.000	1.000	1.000
Detroit	0.356	0.708	0.722
Kansas City	1.152	0.913	0.991
Philadelphia	0.500	0.582	0.547
Phoenix	1.645	1.597	1.554
San Diego	1.354	1.206	1.317
Race-Year			
Nonwhite	1.000	1.000	1.000
White	1.012	1.002	0.648
Location-Year			
Central city	1.000	1.000	1.000
Suburbs	1.296	1.296	1.296

Note: Odds are computed from the parameters of the models fitted to the Annual
Housing Survey data. For each variable, the first category is the reference category, for
which the value is 1.000; the other values are defined relative to the reference category.

Philadelphia and Detroit at the low end of the mobility spectrum). Although the city-year interaction is significant for renters, the direct year
effect is much weaker for renters than for owners, suggesting that, although the indirect effects of growth, new construction, and changes in
local mortgage financing may be the strongest influences on local-
movement intensity, their impact is primarily within the owner-occupied
sector. As in the owner case, central cities have lower mobility than
suburbs, but the higher mobility for nonwhites becomes evident only in
the last survey period (1981–82).

The Structure of Flows

The "flows" in this section are last-move transitions, which provide an indicator of the intensity of the relations between the various sectors of the housing market within a metropolitan area. Although the redistributive outcome between two points in time is not readily estimable, one indicator of the redistributive potential of mobility is the relative magnitude of the interchange, or degree of openness, between city and suburb. The larger the intersector changes relative to the intrasector changes, the greater is this potential. If we consider the 2 × 2 subtable formed by aggregating flows over tenure categories, we obtain:

	Central City	Suburbs
central city	m_{11}	m_{12}
suburbs	m_{21}	m_{22}

Then the cross product ratio $\beta = (m_{11}m_{22})/(m_{21}m_{12})$ is a size-independent measure of association (Feinberg, 1980). Because of the diagonally dominant nature of mobility, we chose to measure the variable $\Omega = 1/\beta$ (Ω is the degree of openness of the system of flows) such that, as Ω approaches zero, the matrix is composed entirely of intrasector moves. For all 18 observations, the values of Ω are small (<0.2), as might be expected; nevertheless, there is a clear relationship ($r = 0.76$; see Figure 9.4) between the overall mobility rate and its degree of openness. This finding is consistent both with the general conclusion of Emmi (1986), that declining mobility rates for the city as a whole are associated with increasing isolation and fragmentation of metropolitan systems, and with the more specific comments of Berry and Elster (1983) regarding the growing isolation of the central city in older industrialized areas of the Northeast.

Frey (1985) provides some clues to the underpinnings of these changes, particularly in regard to the declining propensities of households to move back to the central city in the late 1970s as compared with the late 1960s. Although standard explanations tend to be couched in terms of a preference for suburban lifestyles together with a continued dispersion of employment, an important factor is the increasing heterogeneity of suburbs, which means a greater ability to satisfy changing needs through *intrasector,* as opposed to *intersector,* moves. In all the cities except Kansas City, a significant increase occurred in the rented-

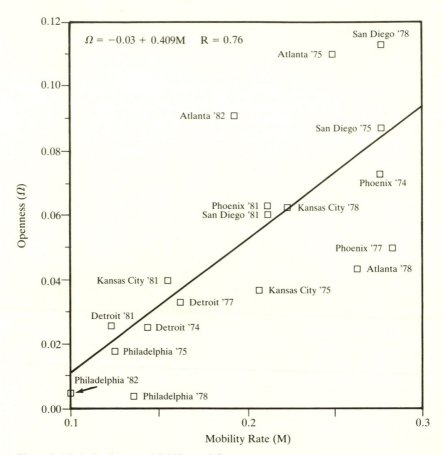

Figure 9.4 Relation between Mobility and Openness

owned ratio of suburban units over the study period; at the same time the range of family types became more diverse in the suburbs, with declines in the proportion of households containing two adults and children under 18, and the proportion of nonwhites increased. These changes suggest that the "central city–suburb" dichotomy also has limitations for analysis, because the increasing heterogeneity encourages analyses based on moves between individual jurisdictions within the suburbs; this is certainly not a new idea, having been central to Tiebout's notions (Tiebout, 1956) of choice between bundles of public services, but it cannot be pursued using the Annual Housing Survey data, which provides only a central city–suburb dichotomy.

We can extend the analysis of openness by including tenure in the characterization of origin and destination states. We constructed a 2 × 2 table of central city–suburb interactions for each tenure combination associated with household transfers (own-own, rent-rent, own-rent, and rent-own) and calculated the corresponding values of Ω in each case. The relationship between the aggregate measure and the measures of openness for each tenure category can be estimated. In each case the relation is linear, with the constant term not significantly different from zero; this implies that, when the slope of the fitted regression line is higher, the degree of openness for a given level of mobility is also higher. In Table 9.4, these regression coefficients indicate that the degree of openness is consistently smaller for transfers within the same tenure category (own-own and rent-rent) and consistently greater for transfers between tenure categories (own-rent and rent-own). This suggests that the role played by transfers between tenure categories is different from that of transfers within the same category in relation to the reasons for moving. This issue will be examined in greater detail later in the chapter.

In addition to a decline in mobility and in the openness of metropolitan systems, there has also been a noticeable decrease in the role of ownership as a movement destination. This change is generated from two different directions: first, there has been an overall decline in access to homeownership, and second, there has been an increase in transfers from owned to rented units associated with the growing number of divorced, separated, and widowed individuals. Table 9.5 shows the dramatic increase in the likelihood of a mover becoming a renter after having been an owner and the decreasing likelihood of a renter becom-

Table 9.4. Regression/Correlation Coefficients for the Relation between Housing Sector and Overall Openness of Central City–Suburb Interactions

	Relation with Ω_T	
	β	r
Tenure transfer		
Own-own	0.74	0.52
Rent-rent	0.92	0.87
Own-rent	1.44	0.69
Rent-own	1.55	0.67
Race		
White	1.26	0.81
Nonwhite	0.87	0.53

Table 9.5.   Changing Structure of Own-Rent and Rent-Own Transfers

	Own-Rent		Rent-Own	
	Central City	Suburbs	Central City	Suburbs
Atlanta	1.29	2.42	0.32	0.48
Detroit	1.38	3.19	0.31	0.59
Kansas City	0.95	1.90	0.83	1.02
Philadelphia	1.64	1.15	0.82	1.37
Phoenix	2.04	2.63	0.64	0.52
San Diego	1.98	1.88	0.77	0.35

Note: The values are the relative likelihood of making the given transfer from the tenure and location of origin in 1981–82 as opposed to 1974–75 (which has a value of 1.00).

ing an owner. This is a pervasive trend and holds both in central cities and suburbs, irrespective of the rate of growth of individual cities. It is reflective of much more general demographic changes on the one hand and shifts in economic conditions, particularly those relating to housing finance, on the other.

The Composition of Flows

Traditional analyses of mobility since the seminal work of Rossi (1955) have focused on the movements of integral households and have paid little, if any, attention to the demographic forces of household formation or break-up as contributors to mobility. However, the flows of migrants are not undifferentiated. Increasingly we find that movers are a combination of single persons, single-parent families, and integral households. The dissolution and recombination of families are also important demographic forces that generate mobility in their own right. A recognition that flows are composed of different actors and their households is the stimulus for this attempt to disentangle the composition of flows.

A problem in analyzing the mobility behavior of newly formed households (either through union or dissolution) is the availability of suitable data; even with the richness of the Annual Housing Survey, it is not possible to introduce a great deal of precision. Two methods are feasible. The first identifies whether the respondent, or reference person (formerly designated the head of the household), was present in the household at the previous survey or whether the reference person for that household has changed (i.e., Has the structure of the household changed in a significant way?). The second method makes use of the reasons given for mov-

Table 9.6. Upper- and Lower-Bound Estimates of the Percentage of Movers Who Formed New Households

	Method				Method	
	1	2			1	2
Atlanta				San Diego		
1975	27.0	16.1		1975	35.0	17.2
1978	31.5	22.9		1978	30.9	15.1
1982	29.8	17.8		1982	27.3	17.4
Philadelphia				Kansas City		
1975	38.9	28.6		1975	26.3	19.7
1978	38.7	22.1		1978	32.0	25.8
1982	38.7	25.4		1982	29.0	23.8
Detroit				Phoenix		
1974	32.7	21.7		1974	32.8	14.7
1977	35.9	23.1		1977	30.6	15.4
1981	37.6	23.1		1981	30.4	15.8

Method 1: Percentage of households in which reference person or respondent changed.
Method 2: Percentage of households who said that they moved for reasons of family formation or break-up.

ing and identifies those households who gave household formation or break-up as a reason for the move (Table 9.6). Because respondents give only one reason, they might not point to the change in structure as the primary reason (some may say it involved preferences for housing or location with respect to work or schools). As a consequence the values from the second method constitute a lower bound. On the other hand, the first method tends to give an overestimate, because changes in the notion of who was head, as well as temporary absences from the household, do not contribute to significant changes in household composition. Even when viewed with the upper and lower bounds, there is no question that the contribution of household-composition changes to mobility is substantial. The fact that these changes are relatively more important in low-mobility cities (Detroit and Philadelphia) than in high-mobility cities (Phoenix and San Diego) suggests that the impacts of lower mobility are primarily felt in the areas of voluntary behavior.

The importance of household formation and break-up also reflects to some degree the changing character of households themselves. The declining importance of the traditional family with two adults and children of school or preschool age experienced during the decade of the 1970s has been well documented (Hughes, 1980). These findings are reiterated in our sample (Table 9.7). Across the cities, the average decline in the proportion of households comprising two adults and children is about 5

Table 9.7.   Percentage Distribution of Household Types, by
General Population and Mover Profiles, and Odds
Ratios of Their Changing Structure

	FT1	FT2	FT3	FT4
Atlanta				
1975				
Population	18.0	33.0	6.0	43.0
Movers	24.3	32.5	9.2	34.0
Odds ratio	1.35	0.98	1.53	0.79
1982				
Population	23.4	36.7	7.1	32.8
Movers	30.4	34.1	10.4	25.2
Odds ratio	1.30	0.93	1.46	0.77
Kansas City				
1975				
Population	21.7	34.5	5.4	38.4
Movers	27.2	29.0	10.6	33.2
Odds ratio	1.25	0.84	1.96	0.86
1982				
Population	24.1	36.9	5.7	33.3
Movers	33.3	29.6	11.4	25.8
Odds ratio	1.38	0.80	2.00	0.77
Philadelphia				
1975				
Population	18.6	35.8	5.0	40.6
Movers	24.4	30.4	13.4	31.9
Odds ratio	1.31	0.85	2.68	0.79
1982				
Population	21.3	38.7	6.2	33.8
Movers	27.8	28.1	14.0	30.0
Odds ratio	1.31	0.73	2.26	0.89
San Diego				
1975				
Population	24.8	38.4	5.9	30.8
Movers	26.7	38.0	7.3	28.1
Odds ratio	1.08	0.99	1.24	0.91
1982				
Population	24.3	41.1	6.1	28.5
Movers	25.2	36.5	10.9	27.4
Odds ratio	1.04	0.89	1.79	0.96
Detroit				
1977				
Population	20.5	35.2	6.6	37.7
Movers	27.5	30.4	10.5	31.6
Odds ratio	1.34	0.86	1.59	0.84
1981				
Population	22.6	36.3	6.7	34.4
Movers	33.7	26.9	10.3	29.1
Odds ratio	1.49	0.74	1.54	0.84

(continued on following page)

Table 9.7. *(continued)*

	FT1	FT2	FT3	FT4
Phoenix				
1977				
Population	20.8	38.4	5.4	35.4
Movers	23.0	33.8	9.2	31.6
Odds ratio	1.11	0.88	1.70	0.89
1981				
Population	21.9	40.1	5.1	32.9
Movers	25.5	33.8	9.2	31.6
Odds ratio	1.16	0.84	1.80	0.96

FT1 = single-person households.
FT2 = 2 or more adults with no children.
FT3 = single-parent families.
FT4 = 2 or more adults with children.

percent over the study period, with the other three categories all experiencing gains. The shift in the mover profiles is similar, although traditional families are somewhat less likely to be movers than other household types. The most noticeable increase is in the likelihood of movers being single-parent families or single persons, a phenomenon which is also a function of the higher likelihood of members of these two groups being renters than owners. The fact that overall mobility declines in the face of forces which should generate increases in movement intensity indicates the strength of other factors, most notably the shifts in national and local economic conditions.

The profiles of reasons for moves taking place provide further insight into the composition of flows and their demographic context. The original responses were detailed and required aggregation for analysis. Corresponding to previous work in this area (e.g., Clark and Onaka, 1983), reasons were grouped into six major categories: *work*—including relocations relating to entry to and exit from the labor force; *family*—moves relating to household formation and break-up; *housing*—moves relating to adjustments of housing consumption to meet changing needs or preferences; *cost*—moves relating to affordability; *displacement*—moves relating to eviction, acquisition for conversion, and disasters; and *other*—moves for miscellaneous reasons and those for which no reason is given.

The total profiles for each city (Table 9.8) show strong commonalities. The traditional emphasis on housing adjustment is shown to account for fewer than 40 percent of moves in all cities. The main differences are between the low-mobility cities of Detroit and Philadelphia and the rest.

In the low-mobility cities, family-related moves are relatively more important and work-related moves are significantly less. However, much stronger differences are observed between household types and between sector destinations (see Tables 9.8 and 9.9). Families with two adults and children are much more likely to move for traditional housing reasons, whereas single persons and single-parent families are more likely to move for family-related reasons. As might be expected, single-parent families, in general, are more likely to have to move for reasons of affordability or displacement, and they are also much less likely to move for work-related reasons than the other household types. Single persons would probably have benefited from being differentiated by age, because younger individuals would dominate the work component and older individuals the family component.

With respect to the analysis by sector, the strongest differentials are between owner-occupied and rented units. The responses for renters illustrate just how limited the traditional housing adjustment model is for this group, because most cities indicate that fewer than 30 percent of renters move for housing-related reasons. Renters are much more likely to cite changes in household composition, affordability, or displacement as reasons for moving, whereas owners consistently cite housing reasons for 50–65 percent of all moves.

A more rigorous assessment of the effects of housing-sector and socio-demographic variables is provided for each city in our study by fitting multiple-response logit models to a $2 \times 2 \times 4 \times 3 \times 2 \times 2 \times 4$ table made up of the following variables: *current tenure* (own, rent); *previous tenure* (own, rent); *household type* (single person; single parent; 2 or more adults with no children; 2 or more adults with children); *year* (year 1, year 2, year 3); *current location* (central city, suburbs); *previous location* (central city, suburbs). The coding schemes prevent the household type from being defined for Detroit and Phoenix in 1974, so the full model was fitted to the other four cities. In each case, the year was not a significant factor, indicating that the reason profile remained stable. Current location was significant only in San Diego, where central-city residents are much more likely to have relocated for work-related reasons than suburban residents, a contrast which was not found elsewhere. The remaining variables (current tenure, previous tenure, household type, and previous location) were all highly significant, and a main-effects model was sufficient to describe the data (Feinberg, 1980).

Table 9.10 presents the important results of this analysis. Using a multiple-response model (SAS Institute, 1985), we consider four possible outcomes: moved for family-related reasons, moved for work-related

Table 9.8. Percentage Distribution of Reasons for Moving, by City, Year, and Household Type

| | Reason for Move | | | | | | Percentage of Population |
	Work	Family	Housing	Cost	Displacement	Other	
Atlanta							
1975							
FT1	25.2	25.7	23.4	2.7	8.5	14.6	24.3
FT2	21.4	18.9	38.0	1.2	4.7	15.9	32.5
FT3	26.1	15.9	30.4	2.6	9.5	15.6	9.2
FT4	26.2	3.7	46.2	3.0	7.3	13.5	34.0
1982							
FT1	25.5	20.1	22.8	0.6	9.2	21.8	30.4
FT2	28.5	14.5	31.9	2.0	5.5	17.5	34.1
FT3	0.0	33.5	36.8	4.9	10.0	14.7	10.4
FT4	28.5	12.9	36.2	3.2	9.2	15.7	25.2
Kansas City							
1975							
FT1	21.2	23.2	22.5	8.0	8.2	16.9	27.2
FT2	24.2	24.3	32.8	4.9	3.8	10.0	29.0
FT3	4.6	34.9	38.3	9.0	8.9	4.4	10.6
FT4	22.6	8.0	48.9	4.9	6.6	9.1	33.2
1982							
FT1	22.0	29.1	25.2	3.4	3.9	16.4	33.3
FT2	15.4	23.5	32.1	8.3	5.9	15.2	29.6
FT3	13.1	25.8	31.7	1.6	11.5	16.3	11.4
FT4	24.8	16.6	41.1	3.7	7.1	6.6	25.8
Philadelphia							
1975							
FT1	12.6	32.2	14.2	7.1	5.0	28.8	24.4
FT2	22.2	34.5	23.7	4.2	3.6	12.7	30.4
FT3	2.1	46.9	35.2	2.0	5.4	8.4	13.4
FT4	25.3	14.7	45.5	3.0	1.6	9.9	31.9
1982							
FT1	14.0	24.2	30.4	1.1	8.2	23.5	27.8
FT2	17.9	34.3	27.1	0.0	2.2	18.5	28.1
FT3	2.2	33.6	32.8	6.4	10.5	14.5	14.0
FT4	19.9	11.7	49.4	3.8	6.6	8.6	30.0
San Diego							
1975							
FT1	15.6	31.1	23.8	4.9	10.4	14.2	26.7
FT2	21.3	12.5	34.8	2.9	7.1	21.4	38.0
FT3	16.1	24.5	19.8	9.8	13.7	16.1	7.3
FT4	24.5	7.0	40.8	2.9	8.8	16.1	28.1
1982							
FT1	23.8	23.8	20.0	3.5	6.7	22.2	25.2
FT2	25.4	14.0	31.4	4.2	8.3	15.8	36.5
FT3	11.6	36.7	30.2	10.0	3.8	7.7	10.9
FT4	23.5	6.9	40.7	9.3	4.7	14.9	27.4

(continued on following page)

Table 9.8.   *(continued)*

	Reason for Move						Percentage of Population
	Work	Family	Housing	Cost	Displacement	Other	
Detroit							
1977							
FT1	9.4	32.6	25.2	3.1	5.4	24.2	27.5
FT2	17.1	24.3	38.4	1.8	3.1	15.3	30.4
FT3	4.7	23.7	40.5	10.4	3.0	17.7	10.5
FT4	13.5	13.6	48.4	5.0	3.3	15.2	31.6
1981							
FT1	14.5	28.1	27.2	4.1	5.8	20.3	33.7
FT2	12.1	28.0	34.0	1.0	3.8	21.1	26.9
FT3	4.3	25.8	46.0	1.2	4.8	17.9	10.3
FT4	9.0	11.6	54.7	2.4	2.5	19.9	29.1
Phoenix							
1977							
FT1	22.3	24.7	22.1	1.6	11.4	17.9	23.0
FT2	26.1	12.1	31.1	2.1	5.9	22.7	35.5
FT3	17.2	20.8	28.4	8.7	13.3	11.5	7.5
FT4	20.2	6.1	44.8	4.7	4.9	19.2	34.0
1981							
FT1	23.6	17.3	27.5	2.4	3.5	25.8	25.5
FT2	24.8	14.7	33.4	3.4	4.4	19.3	33.8
FT3	14.6	29.2	34.3	2.8	8.3	10.8	9.2
FT4	21.1	11.6	34.4	4.9	5.3	22.8	31.6

FT1 = single-person households.
FT2 = 2 or more adults with no children.
FT3 = single-parent families.
FT4 = 2 or more adults with children.

reasons, moved because of displacement, and moved for housing-related reasons. Housing-related reasons constitute the reference category, and the relative odds of the other three responses are modeled. The model parameters then permit calculation of the odds ratios of having moved for a specific nonhousing reason as compared with a housing reason for given combinations of independent variables.

We can use Atlanta to illustrate the results set out in Table 9.10. We see that current renters there are 2.89 times as likely as owner-occupiers to cite family reasons for moving relative to housing reasons. Previous location is even more discriminating, with previous renters being 6.00 times as likely as previous owners to cite family reasons. What emerges from this analysis is a remarkable degree of stability in the structure of responses. We have noted that the year does not interact in a significant

Table 9.9. Percentage Distribution of Reasons for Moving, by City, Year, and Sector Destination–Tenure

	Reason for Move						Percentage of Population
	Work	Family	Housing	Cost	Displacement	Other	
Atlanta							
1975							
C-own	12.7	12.4	37.3	6.1	6.6	24.9	1.5
C-rent	15.8	18.5	29.4	7.1	4.0	25.3	14.3
S-own	23.8	5.9	58.2	0.0	1.0	11.2	19.3
S-rent	25.6	18.8	30.5	1.1	9.6	14.4	65.0
1982							
C-own	4.6	7.7	64.5	0.0	0.0	23.3	2.2
C-rent	15.2	16.9	24.6	5.8	10.3	27.2	23.1
S-own	21.6	12.4	57.0	0.0	2.1	6.9	8.0
S-rent	27.9	19.2	26.7	1.3	8.3	16.5	66.7
Philadelphia							
1975							
C-own	3.9	36.1	48.0	0.0	0.0	12.0	6.3
C-rent	11.6	29.2	25.7	7.6	4.5	21.5	23.7
S-own	23.7	10.7	51.6	3.5	0.0	10.5	19.4
S-rent	15.8	33.5	24.2	4.7	6.7	15.1	50.6
1982							
C-own	9.3	48.1	38.1	0.0	0.0	4.5	7.1
C-rent	11.4	23.5	34.4	1.0	8.7	21.0	34.0
S-own	15.9	25.6	51.2	0.0	0.0	7.3	17.8
S-rent	19.1	22.6	27.6	4.2	8.3	18.2	41.1
Kansas City							
1975							
C-own	12.0	14.7	64.4	0.0	0.0	8.9	5.9
C-rent	22.4	20.6	26.9	9.2	9.2	11.7	36.4
S-own	21.9	9.7	55.2	2.5	4.8	6.0	14.6
S-rent	21.2	23.7	30.7	5.7	6.5	12.0	43.1
1982							
C-own	12.8	9.6	61.2	6.7	6.5	3.2	5.7
C-rent	17.6	26.2	26.6	4.6	5.5	19.5	35.9
S-own	18.9	15.6	55.2	1.7	6.9	1.7	11.2
S-rent	21.5	26.2	27.4	4.9	6.3	13.3	47.2
San Diego							
1975							
C-own	14.9	14.4	62.4	0.0	2.1	6.3	9.3
C-rent	19.5	20.0	28.4	4.7	9.7	17.7	61.2
S-own	15.7	5.2	60.7	1.3	1.3	15.8	7.4
S-rent	21.8	15.5	27.2	5.0	10.1	20.5	22.1
1982							
C-own	22.0	6.0	55.0	0.0	0.0	17.1	5.0
C-rent	26.3	16.6	27.8	6.6	5.7	17.0	58.7
S-own	6.5	12.4	57.8	2.2	3.7	17.5	4.6
S-rent	17.9	21.6	30.3	6.7	9.4	14.1	31.7

(continued on following page)

Table 9.9.   *(continued)*

| | Reason for Move | | | | | Percentage of Population |
	Work	Family	Housing	Cost	Displacement	Other	
Detroit							
1974							
C-own	4.8	25.4	57.0	3.1	0.0	9.6	9.0
C-rent	8.7	18.8	31.3	8.7	5.3	19.8	31.5
S-own	18.1	11.2	48.7	1.7	0.9	9.5	27.8
S-rent	17.3	32.6	24.5	6.2	8.1	11.3	31.8
1981							
C-own	2.4	16.7	38.2	9.9	0.0	32.9	5.8
C-rent	10.2	24.1	40.9	4.2	6.9	13.6	25.5
S-own	3.6	21.1	56.8	0.0	0.0	18.6	19.4
S-rent	15.4	24.0	31.6	1.7	5.1	22.2	49.4
Phoenix							
1974							
C-own	15.7	11.3	48.1	4.1	1.1	19.7	15.3
C-rent	21.4	18.3	27.8	2.8	13.2	16.5	44.0
S-own	17.0	1.6	58.2	3.2	1.7	18.5	9.5
S-rent	33.5	15.3	28.7	3.1	6.3	13.1	31.2
1981							
C-own	17.0	3.8	56.8	1.3	0.0	21.1	9.8
C-rent	22.0	17.5	30.0	2.5	6.5	21.5	46.2
S-own	22.0	12.8	43.5	4.2	3.1	14.4	11.3
S-rent	25.5	18.0	25.2	5.7	4.2	21.5	32.7

C-own = central-city owner-occupied units.
C-rent = central-city rented units.
S-own = suburban owner-occupied units.
S-rent = suburban rented units.

way with any of the other variables. For the odds ratios presented in Table 9.10, there is a high level of consistency across the cities for any particular reason comparison for any given contrast among the independent variables. Thus, the range of values for "family versus housing" reasons for the rent versus own contrast in current tenure is from 1.89 to 2.89; for a "work versus housing" reason the range is from 1.40 to 2.43; and for "displacement versus housing," from 1.42 to 2.43. Other profiles show even more consistency. Further, we can readily identify the aberrant cases. San Diego has a particularly high incidence of "family versus housing" reasons among the family-type contrasts (values of 3.75 and 3.52 for single persons and single parents versus families with children, respectively). Thus, single persons and single parents are almost four

Table 9.10. Relative Odds of Having Moved for Selected Reasons
Relative to Housing Reasons, by Selected Variables, 1974–82

	Reason for Move		
	Family vs. Housing	Work vs. Housing	Displacement vs. Housing
Current tenure			
(Rent vs. own)			
Atlanta	2.89	2.43	2.43
Kansas City	2.89	1.40	1.42
Philadelphia	1.95	1.71	2.10
San Diego	1.89	2.19	2.43
Previous tenure			
(Rent vs. own)			
Atlanta	6.00	2.03	0.81
Kansas City	5.67	1.68	1.12
Philadelphia	5.19	1.67	0.83
San Diego	4.09	1.40	0.76
Family type			
(Single person vs.			
2 or more adults			
with children)			
Atlanta	2.01	1.32	1.22
Kansas City	2.35	1.41	1.59
Philadelphia	2.18	2.10	2.44
San Diego	3.75	1.47	1.14
(Single parent vs.			
2 or more adults			
with children)			
Atlanta	2.09	0.64	1.49
Kansas City	1.76	0.80	1.43
Philadelphia	1.82	0.91	2.32
San Diego	3.52	0.73	1.95
Current location			
(City vs. suburbs)			
Atlanta	1.05	1.19	1.67
Kansas City	1.19	1.49	1.25
Philadelphia	1.16	1.21	1.24
San Diego	1.10	2.69	1.41
Previous location			
(City vs. suburbs)			
Atlanta	2.01	0.66	1.40
Kansas City	1.49	1.21	1.21
Philadelphia	1.90	1.49	1.31
San Diego	1.71	0.84	0.84

Note: Values give the relative odds of having moved for the stated reason
versus a housing reason for each of the contrasts shown on the left-hand side
of the table. Computations are based on the fitted logistic model for each
city.

times as likely as two-adult families with children to cite family reasons for moving rather than housing reasons. This suggests that the particular character of San Diego, with both a high population turnover and a large immigrant population, generates a distinctive local-housing demography compared with the other cities.

The second intercity contrast of interest in Table 9.10 involves the pattern of responses for "work versus housing" reasons by previous location. In both Atlanta and San Diego, respondents who had previously lived in the city were relatively less likely to cite work reasons than housing reasons, whereas the converse was true in Kansas City and Philadelphia. This suggests that the internal redistribution of jobs in the latter two cities may be a more significant influence on relocation than in the former. This would also lead to the expectation that, if Detroit and Phoenix, for example, had been included in the model, we would have found a value greater than 1.0 for Detroit and less than 1.0 for Phoenix.

Finally, the odds of a displacement versus a housing-related move, as might be expected, are greatest for single-parent and single-person households and for renters. This is most strongly observed in Philadelphia, although high values are also observed in Atlanta and San Diego, which may reflect conditions of booming property markets, condominium conversions, and escalating rents.

What emerges clearly from this analysis is that, as changes continue to take place in the composition of households in the larger society, these changes will be reflected in the dynamics of local housing markets. In particular, our analysis points to the critical role of the rental as opposed to the owner-occupied sector in accommodating these shifts in demographically driven mobility behavior. If access to ownership continues to be reduced (Morrow-Jones, 1986) then pressure will build at an ever increasing rate within the rental sectors, much of it attributable to moves which do not fall within the traditional notions of voluntaristic behavior.

Conclusion

In this chapter we have compared selected aspects of mobility in six different cities at three different times between 1974 and 1982 using the SMSA samples from the Annual Housing Survey. This is the first time that such a study has been undertaken, and it serves as a useful comparison to previous work, which has depended either on national surveys (e.g., Butler et al., 1969) or on detailed studies of individual cities or regions (e.g., Speare, Goldstein, and Frey, 1975). The results can also be compared with those of Frey (1985), which focus on demographically based comparisons over intercensal periods but do not consider the role of tenure.

One set of results relates to systemwide properties of mobility for a metropolitan area. The very strong association between levels of in-migration and internal mobility (Figure 9.3) provide corroboration for earlier work by both Goodman (1982) and Long and Boertlein (1978). This relationship was extended to show that a second strong association existed between overall mobility and the level of interchange between central city and suburbs; however, low-mobility cities (notably Detroit and Philadelphia) were far less open than those with high mobility (particularly Phoenix and San Diego).

The general structural relations between housing sectors, household types, and mobility tended to be quite stable across the six cities and over time. High relative mobility tended to pervade all sectors of the local market and not be sector specific (e.g., if mobility is high for Phoenix relative to Philadelphia, it is also high for city owners in Phoenix relative to city owners in Philadelphia). Some differences were detected along racial lines, with nonwhites having consistently higher mobility than whites, although the overall racial effect was not as strong as city, tenure, or year effects. Temporal variation was significantly greater for owners than for renters, with mobility increasing from 1974–75 to 1977–78 and then declining even more dramatically to 1981–82. Although separate evidence is needed, this is strongly suggestive of a greater sensitivity of the owner-occupied sector to national economic shifts, an inference which is supported by the subsequent finding that demographically induced mobility is much more strongly concentrated in the rental sector of the market.

Over time, a number of changes occur which affect the overall structure of mobility. As several writers have observed (e.g., Hughes, 1980; Stapleton, 1980; Morrison, 1986), there has been a shift away from the traditional family with two adults and children toward other household types, particularly single-person and single-parent households, each of which is more likely to be a renter, to live in the central city, and to be a mover. Additionally, access to homeownership has become more difficult, increasing the relative significance of moves within the rental sector of the market. The joint effect of these two changes is further influenced by the increasing numbers of rental units being constructed in suburban jurisdictions, which permits a higher proportion of moves to rental units to be satisfied within the same locational sector of the local market.

There is little doubt that demographic events and processes are intertwined with mobility levels and patterns. The study reported here establishes that the mobility process in North American cities in the late twentieth century is increasingly divided between a housing-adjustment process (primarily for owners) which is largely voluntaristic and a more constrained and less voluntaristic process for renters in general and disadvantaged subgroups in particular. The evolution of these two processes and their redistributive consequences are an essential focus of continuing research.

References

Berry, B. J. L., and S. Elster. 1983. What Lies Ahead for Urban America. Paper presented at The Metropolis: A Conference in Honour of Hans Blumenfeld. University of Toronto.

Butler, E. W., F. S. Chapin, Jr., G. C. Hemmens, E. J. Kaiser, M. A. Stegman, and S. F. Weiss. 1969. *Mobility Behavior and Residential Choice.* National Cooperative Highway Research Program, Report No. 81. Washington, D.C.: Highway Research Board.

Clark, W. A. V. 1982. Recent research on migration and mobility: A review and interpretation. *Progress in Planning* 18:1–56.

Clark, W. A. V., and J. Onaka. 1983. Life cycle and housing adjustment as explanations of residential mobility. *Urban Studies* 20:47–57.

Dahmann, D. C. 1986. Decisions on the redesigned American Housing Survey national sample and 44 metropolitan area samples. Population Division, U.S. Bureau of the Census, Washington, D.C. (mimeo).

Emmi, P. C. 1986. On the stability of housing sector interaction: Evidence from 42 metropolitan areas. *Journal of Regional Science* 26:745–760.

Feinberg, S. 1980. *The Analysis of Cross-Classified Categorical Data* (2d ed.). Cambridge, Mass.: MIT Press.

Fischer, M. M., and E. A. Aufhauser. 1988. Housing choice in a regulated market: A nested multinomial logit analysis. *Geographical Analysis* 20:47–69.

Frey, W. 1985. Mover destination selectivity and the changing suburbanization of metropolitan whites and blacks. *Demography* 22:223–244.

Goering, J. M. 1979. *Housing in America: The Characteristics and Uses of the Annual Housing Survey.* Annual Housing Survey No. 6. Washington, D.C.: U.S. Department of Housing and Urban Development.

Goodman, J. 1982. Linking local mobility rates to migration rates: Repeat movers and place effects. Pp. 209–223 in W. A. V. Clark (ed.), *Modelling Housing Market Search.* London: Croom-Helm.

Hughes, J. W. 1980. Demographic and economic change: Implications for residential mobility. Pp. 59–78 in W. A. V. Clark and E. G. Moore (eds.), *Residential Mobility and Public Policy,* Vol. 19. Urban Affairs Annual Reviews. Beverly Hills: Sage.

Long, L. H., and C. G. Boertlein. 1978. Urban Residential Mobility in Comparative Perspective. Paper presented at the International Sociological Association Meetings, Uppsala, Sweden.

Miron, J. R. 1988. *Housing in Postwar Canada: Demographic Change, House-hold Formation, and Housing Demand.* Montreal: McGill-Queen's University Press.

Moore, E. G. 1987. *The Analysis of Residential Mobility Using the American Housing Survey.* Mimeo. Department of Geography, Queen's University, Kingston, Ontario.

Moore, E. G., and W. A. V. Clark. 1986. Stable structure and local variation: A comparison of household flows in four metropolitan areas. *Urban Studies* 23:185–196.

Morrison, P. A. 1986. *Changing Family Structure: Who Cares for America's Dependents.* Rand Note N-2518-NICHD. Santa Monica: Rand Corporation.

Morrow-Jones, H. A. 1986. *A Multistate Analysis of the Transition from Renting to Owning a Home in the United States.* Working Paper WP-86-10. Boulder: University of Colorado, Population Program, Institute of Behavioral Science.

Rees, P. H. 1986. Choices in the construction of regional population projections. Pp. 126–159 in R. Woods and P. Rees (eds.), *Population Structures and Models.* London: Allen and Unwin.

Rogerson, P. 1987. Changes in U.S. national mobility levels. *The Professional Geographer* 39:344–350.

Rossi, P. H. 1955. *Why Families Move.* Glencoe, Ill.: Free Press.

SAS Institute. 1985. *Statistical Analysis System.* Cary, N.C.: SAS Institute.

Speare, A., S. Goldstein, and W. Frey. 1975. *Residential Mobility, Migration and Metropolitan Change.* Cambridge, Mass.: Ballinger.

Stapleton, C. 1980. Reformulation of the family life cycle concept. *Environment and Planning A* 12:1103–1118.

Tiebout, C. M. 1956. A pure theory of local expenditure. *Journal of Political Economy* 64:416–424.

Waite, L. 1981. U.S. women at work. Population Reference Bureau, *Population Bulletin* 36(2).

White, H. C. 1970. *Chains of Opportunity: System Models of Mobility in Organizations.* Cambridge: Harvard University Press.

10 *Patricia Gober*

The Urban Demographic Landscape:
A Geographic Perspective

Introduction

One of the most significant demographic changes of the past several decades is the transformation of American households. This transformation involves a decline in average household size and a shift away from households consisting of married couples with children to less traditional types of families and nonfamilies (Kobrin, 1973, 1976a, 1976b; Norton and Glick, 1979; Sweet, 1984). The largest and most rapidly growing segment of the latter category is persons living alone.

The increasing complexity of households has important territorial ramifications, particularly at the intraurban scale. The nature of households affects the demand for housing with particular space, location, tenure, and price attributes. Changes in household size and composition are also important in the residential mobility process, because local moves traditionally have been seen as the mechanism for matching households' space and locational needs with available housing.

The purpose of this chapter is to examine the territorial properties of household size, composition, and change. The first section reviews theories of intraurban residential location in light of their relevance to household patterns and changes therein. The goal of the second section is to

Patricia Gober is Professor and Chair of the Department of Geography, Arizona State University, Tempe, Arizona 85287–0104.

match these theories to empirical patterns in Phoenix and other U.S. cities. The third section proposes alternative life courses for different types of neighborhoods.

Residential Location

Three models of residential location inform the intraurban distribution of households: the neoclassical trade-off model, the ecological model, and the life-cycle model. These models take a "demand side" approach to residential location, stressing the way households choose housing and locations, as opposed to a more "supply side" perspective, emphasizing the way choices are constrained by financial and governmental institutions, real estate agents, and landlords.

The Neoclassical Trade-Off Model

The trade-off model of residential location posits a relationship between the consumption of housing space and travel, or commuting, costs (Alonso, 1960, 1964; Muth, 1961, 1965, 1969; Wingo, 1961; Mills, 1972; Ramanos, 1976). Assuming employment opportunities are at the city center, locational choice is a trade-off between commuting costs and housing, or space, costs. Households that relocate outward substitute increased commuting costs for lower space costs.

One of the major criticisms of the neoclassical model concerns whether the space–commuting cost trade-off is the overriding consideration in residential location (Bassett and Short, 1980). More behavioral approaches have shown that households bring other factors like dwelling attributes, quality of the physical environment, and the social status of the neighborhood into their decision-making framework (Short, 1978).

The relative weightings of space costs, commuting costs, and other factors also vary with household type and life course trajectory. Not all households are, as the neoclassical economists have assumed, nuclear families with one working spouse. Stapleton (1980) outlined the way alternative living arrangements might operate in a trade-off framework. The dual-career family, for example, considers two sets of commuting distances, proximity to childcare-givers, and the relative importance of each spouse's income in locational decisions. For female single parents entering the work force for the first time, a new set of commuting costs is factored into the locational decision, and housing preferences are subject to severe income constraints.

The Ecological Approach

The ecological approach to residential location applies the concepts of ecology to urban areas. Originating with the Chicago school of sociologists, urban ecologists argued that competition for residential space resulted in the process of invasion and succession, whereby new immigrants to the city occupied older housing near the city center and pushed earlier groups outward. Each succeeding wave of immigration and the expansion of the central business district produced a chain reaction with each preceding group moving toward the edge of the city (Burgess, 1925).

Empirical work in this tradition took the form of social area analysis using areal data to examine patterns of residential differentiation (Shevky and Williams, 1949). Of the three dimensions of residential structure (family, social, and ethnic status), family status best incorporated variation in household types. At one end of the family-status dimension were areas with many families, high fertility, low rates of female labor-force participation, and many single-family dwellings. At the other end were those with few families, few children, many working females, and many multiple-family structures. When mapped, the family-status factor corresponded to Burgess's concentric zones, with family households decentralized on the periphery of the city and nonfamilies concentrated near the city center.

As household structure has increased in complexity, the family-status dimension has become an increasingly narrow and fuzzy dimension of residential location. Narrowness results from the relative rarity of the stereotypical nuclear family. The male breadwinner, his nonworking spouse, and their children constitute fewer than 15 percent of all households (U.S. Bureau of the Census, 1982, 1985). Further, they are found in conjunction with a wide variety of other living arrangments. In a study of "family types" in Cleveland, Guest (1972) found low intercorrelations among the different types of families in his study, indicating that most neighborhoods contained a relatively wide range of family types. To differentiate areas, therefore, according to how closely they conform to the norm of married couples with children captures only a narrow slice of all households and ignores the multidimensionality of contemporary household structure.

Fuzziness of the family-status dimension stems from its growing interaction with social status. In 1983 the median household income for married-couple households was $27,286, and $36,110 when the wife was employed outside the home. For female heads of other families, this figure was only $11,789, giving rise to the "feminization of poverty"

(U.S. Bureau of the Census, 1984). The significant gap in income between married couples and single parents means that household structure correlates with socioeconomic status and should, as a result, assume some of the spatial properties of that dimension as well.

The Life-Cycle Approach

The life cycle of the family is a third theme around which to organize notions of residential location and mobility. As they age, people pass through a life cycle from marriage to childbearing, child-launching, and widowhood (Sabagh, van Arsdol, and Butler, 1969). Local-level changes in residence are thought to arise as families adjust their housing in response to changing space needs related to progression through the life cycle (Rossi, 1955; Speare, Goldstein, and Frey, 1975; Carliner, 1975).

In terms of housing, the expected life-cycle progression is from a rented room or apartment for newly formed households through a sequence of larger apartments into owner-occupied housing. The largest units are occupied by persons between the ages of 45 and 55, when real income reaches its peak and space requirements are high. Later, when space needs and income decline, the shrinking household moves into a smaller house or returns to the rental sector (Bourne, 1981). As shown in the chapter by Sweet, this idealized life-cycle progression is not followed universally but is more a central tendency. Kendig's life course chapter suggests also how complex and diverse is the true behavior.

This ideal progression also has a spatial imprint. The central city is usually thought of as the staging area for newly formed households. When children arrive, families move to new suburbs, and subsequently into older suburbs or exurbs as the family matures. Empty-nesters and the widowed retire back to the city, perhaps in rental accommodations (Bourne, 1981).

Just as people progress through a life cycle, so also are neighborhoods thought to undergo life cycles (but see the cautions in the Myers chapter on filtering). Hoover and Vernon (1959) describe the evolution of neighborhoods from single-family residences inhabited by young families with children, to a transition stage when apartments and other multiple-family structures are constructed, to downgrading when single-family quarters are subdivided to accommodate an increasingly poor and minority population, to a thinning-out stage in which density falls because household size declines. Bourne's (1981) model has the neighborhood moving from "suburbanization" (consisting of young families with small children), to infilling with multiple-family rental units (creating a greater mix of household types), to downgrading (with older families and fewer children), to a thinning-out phase (in which nonfamilies represent the dominant household type), and finally to renewal (the return of young families with children) or rehabilitation (involving few children).

One of the major problems of the life-cycle concept is that an increasing segment of our population passes through living arrangements not covered by the life-cycle model. Using data from the Income Survey Development Program (ISDP), Koo (1985) found that over 11 percent of households are single-headed families, 2.2 percent are multifamilies, and 2.8 percent are cohabiting persons of the same or opposite sex. Added to these are a sizable portion of the 24.4 percent of persons living alone who are divorced or have never married, a subset of the 22.3 percent who are childless couples with no intention of bearing children, and those nuclear families containing adult children and/or other adults. Although the exact size of the non-life-cycle group is not known, it obviously represents a significant and growing segment of households nationwide.

In addition, people enter and leave household situations with much greater frequency than the life-cycle model suggests. Using ISDP data, Koo (1985) investigated the instability of households types and found that approximately 19 percent of all households experienced some change in composition during a 13-month period beginning in 1979. Rates of instability vary from a low of 6.2 percent for divorced females living alone to a high of 84.8 percent for households with two or more unrelated persons. Surprisingly, even supposedly stable groups like married couples with minor children and those with both minor and adult children exhibited relatively high rates of instability; 16 percent in the case of the former, and 34 percent for the latter.

Coming at the same problem from a different angle, Richards, White, and Tsui (1987) computed household survival times—the length of time spent in particular household arrangements. Median survival times are 6.94 years for nuclear families, 4.76 for persons living alone, 4.16 for couples without children, 3.9 for single parents, 3.16 for other families, and 1.78 for unrelated persons living together. These are altogether consistent with Koo's instability rates and demonstrate that households are dynamic units with a high propensity for change from one year to the next.

Equally problematic is that, even when people do progress through a traditional life cycle with respect to their living arrangements and changes therein, their housing tenure, residential location, and mobility behavior do not always conform to what the model predicts. Doling (1976), McLeod and Ellis (1982), and Kendig (1984) demonstrate that income and social status are at least as important as the life-cycle stage in explaining housing tenure. High-income households become homeowners much sooner in the life cycle than their low-income counterparts.

Empirical attempts to relate mobility rates to life-cycle conditions and transitions point to further weaknesses in the model. Chevan (1971), for example, found that mobility was more responsive to overcrowding than undercrowding. Households expanding in size are more likely to move in response to life-cycle forces than ones that are contracting. Underlying this resistance to smaller accommodations is the law of cumulative inertia—that mobility declines as length of residence increases (Myers, McGinnis, and Masnick, 1967; Clark and Huff, 1977; Huff and Clark, 1978). At later stages of the life cycle when households are shrinking, life-cycle forces are offset by cumulative inertia, and households remain in place rather than move to smaller accommodations.

Coupe and Morgan (1981) investigated relationships between family life cycle, housing needs, and residential mobility among owner occupants in Northampton, England. They found that demographic change did not necessarily predispose households to move to acquire more space. Three-quarters of households with additional members and growing children moved in response to home complaints (need for more space), but 55 percent of contracting or stable households also moved for the same reason.

Extrapolating this process onto areas, Myers (1978) found a strong correlation between housing age and population age, attributing this to the immobility of households in owner-occupied housing. Immobility gives rise to a process that Myers calls "frozen occupancy," and has created an extreme shortage of single-family homes for young families in the San Francisco Bay Area.

Moore (1972) explored the effects of mobility on areal population change. He identified four types of neighborhoods: (1) High mobility and rapid change in population characteristics occur in areas affected by ghetto encroachment. (2) Areas with high mobility yet stable population characteristics contain inflexible housing like small apartments, requiring high levels of mobility to maintain a population of, for example, young singles or childless marrieds. (3) Low mobility and rapid change in population characteristics occur in middle-aged, single-family neighborhoods where older children leave parents to age in place. (4) Low mobility and stable population characteristics occur in closely knit, ethnic neighborhoods.

Although the life-cycle and other theories of residential location offer a context within which to view the distribution of different types of households, they are flawed by their overreliance on the nuclear family as the dominant household form. The next section looks at empirical patterns of household size and change in Phoenix and other U.S. cities, with an eye toward reformulation or increased specification of these theories.

Empirical Patterns and Processes

Household Size and Composition

Inherent in all three models of residential location—the neoclassical, ecological, and life cycle—is that household size should increase with distance from the city center. Families with children, in the neoclassical model, place greater emphasis on space in the space–commuting cost trade-off. Social area analysis has consistently shown that large households tend to be found in recently constructed single-family housing on the periphery, and the life cycle of neighborhoods begins with a suburbanization phase characterized by an influx of families with children to new, single-family housing.

Empirical evidence has tended to support this expectation. In 1970 household size in the Phoenix metropolitan area declined in a regular fashion with distance from the city center (Gober, 1980). White (1982) examined the role of intraurban mobility in altering household sizes between central cities and suburbs for the intervals 1965–70, 1970–75, and 1975–79, and found that families who migrated from central cities to suburban rings were larger in mean size than families that composed the counterstream. White concluded that central-city decline and suburban growth are accentuated by these opposing-stream differentials.

More recent research on Phoenix, however, indicates that patterns in household size and change are increasing in complexity. The largest declines in average household size between 1970 and 1980 occurred in Phoenix's suburbs (Table 10.1). While Phoenix experienced a decline of only 0.35 persons per dwelling unit, decreases in suburbs were 0.47 in

Table 10.1. Change in Household Size in Phoenix-Area Communities from 1970 to 1980

	Total	Glendale	Mesa	Phoenix	Scottsdale	Tempe
Household size						
1970	3.14	3.40	3.27	3.09	3.35	3.33
1980	2.73	2.92	2.80	2.74	2.55	2.73
Change from						
1970 to 1980	−0.41	−0.48	−0.47	−0.35	−0.80	−0.60
% change	−13.1	−14.1	−14.4	−11.3	−23.9	−18.0

Source: U.S. Bureau of the Census, 1972, 1983.

Mesa, 0.48 in Glendale, 0.60 in Tempe, and 0.80 in Scottsdale. The effect was to equalize household size across the metroplitan area and to push two suburbs, Scottsdale and Tempe, below household size in the central city (Gober, 1987).

A more comprehensive view of household size is achieved by disaggregating the growth in households into six categories: (1) married couples with children, (2) childless couples, (3) female single parents, (4) other families—a residual category containing families not included in categories 1, 2, and 3, (5) persons living alone, and (6) unrelated persons living together (Table 10.2). Families accounted for 62.5 percent of the metropolitan area's growth in households but varied from 74.6 percent and 70.0 in family-oriented suburbs like Glendale and Mesa to only about 50 percent in Scottsdale and Tempe. In Scottsdale, in spite of an overall growth in population in excess of 30 percent and a gain in households of 70 percent, married couples with children declined by a third. This decline led Scottsdale High School to close in 1984.

Tempe experienced a shift toward unrelated adults of the same and opposite sex living together. Over a fifth of Tempe's increase in households resulted from a gain in cohabiting adults. This gain was related to the growth of Arizona State University from 26,000 in 1970 to 39,000 in 1980.

Table 10.2. Percentage Distribution of Increases in Households, by Household Type and Community within the Phoenix Area, 1970–80

	Total	Glendale	Mesa	Phoenix	Scottsdale	Tempe
Increase in number of households	242,126	22,468	34,965	98,698	14,167	19,720
Families	62.5	74.6	70.0	55.1	49.1	51.1
Child[a]	16.2	33.4	27.5	12.6	−9.3	12.5
Couple[b]	32.3	28.3	31.9	24.5	42.1	24.5
Single[c]	6.4	6.9	5.3	8.2	6.4	6.5
Other[d]	7.6	6.0	5.3	9.8	9.9	7.6
Nonfamilies	37.4	25.5	30.1	45.0	51.0	48.8
Alone[e]	26.9	19.4	22.0	31.0	39.3	26.7
Unrelated[f]	10.5	6.1	8.1	14.0	11.7	22.1

Source: U.S. Bureau of the Census, 1972, 1983.
[a]Married couples with children under 18 years.
[b]Married couples without children under 18 years.
[c]Female single parents with children under 18 years.
[d]Families that do not belong to above categories.
[e]Persons living alone.
[f]Unrelated persons living together.

The dramatic decline in average household size in Tempe and Scottsdale reflects the growing demographic specialization of suburbs. In 1970 all Phoenix's suburbs were skewed toward large households and married couples with children. Over the decade, they developed more strongly specialized characters: Scottsdale's toward childless marrieds and singles, consistent with its role as a cultural and entertainment center; and Tempe's toward cohabitation and a university town. At the same time, suburban Mesa and Glendale continued to house married couples with children and to emphasize schools, parks, libraries, and other family-centered activities.

Relatively small household-size declines in Phoenix stemmed, in large part, from the city's role as the home of the metropolitan area's minority populations. Among minorities, households shifted toward single parents and other families without married couples in contrast to white Anglos, who shifted toward very small households like persons living alone. In several minority tracts, average household size actually increased, married couples with children increased as a proportion of all households, and persons living alone and childless couples decreased. These demographic trends were diametrically opposed to national and metropolitan-wide shifts in household composition and size and tended to mitigate the central city's overall decline in average household size.

Phoenix trends bode ill for the traditional relationship between household size and distance from the city center. As residences for black and Hispanic populations, central cities will stabilize in household size while nonminority suburbs shift toward nonfamilies and very small households. The differentiation between demographically specialized suburbs may prove to be more significant than the traditional central city–suburb distinction.

When Phoenix's census tracts are disaggregated by age of housing (young, middle-aged, old), type of housing (single-family and multiple-family), and ethnicity of resident population (minority and white Anglo), the decline in household size with older housing is restricted to areas dominated by single-family housing (Figure 10.1) (see Gober, 1986, for a more detailed discussion of how and why tracts were disaggregated by these three variables). For that subset of neighborhoods that maintains its single-family character, the life-cycle model continues to provide a useful explanation of population change. The newest housing contains the largest households, and household size declines with age of housing as the household structures shift toward childless couples, persons living alone, and smaller households in general.

The relationship between age of housing and household size breaks down, however, in multiple-family housing. There is no longer a decline

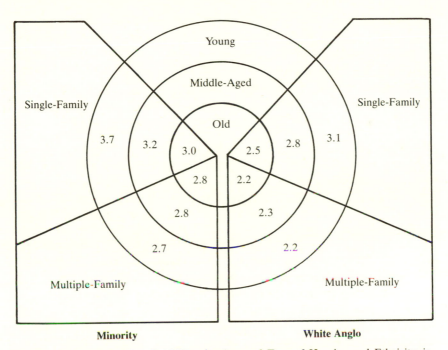

Figure 10.1 Average Household Size, by Age and Type of Housing and Ethnicity, in Phoenix, 1980

in average household size from young to old housing. The thinning out of households is disproportionately concentrated in newly constructed suburban apartments and condominiums. Between 1970 and 1980 average household size declined from 3.0 to 2.2 in peripheral tracts dominated by newly constructed apartment districts.

The evolution and growth of these districts arose from both demographic and economic forces. Household formation among babyboomers was intense during the 1970s, stimulating apartment construction at the periphery. Rapid in-migration of young and old households from outside the metropolitan areas further increased the number of small households and placed additional stress on the local housing market. These demographic events occurred at the same time as the decentralization of urban offices, industries, and retail activity, subventing the 1950s notion of the suburban bedroom community devoid of employment. Suburbs gained parity with the central city as employment centers—a process called urbanization of suburbs. Nearby jobs further enhanced the desirability of suburban apartment complexes.

One interesting wrinkle is that some of the metropolitan area's small-

est households are now coincident with the largest. The greatest dispar-
ity in size between single- and multiple-family neighborhood dwellings
occurs in recently constructed housing where very small households
dominate apartment complexes in contrast with relatively large households in nearby single-family housing.

Aging in Place

If one accepts Koo's (1985) estimate that 19 percent of all households are
unstable over a 13-month period, it is reasonable to conclude that the
magnitude of demographic change in the city occurs much more quickly
than we have traditionally believed. The notion of "aging in place" gives
the false impression of a slow and gradual process in contrast with rapid
population change resulting from mobility. In fact, the 19 percent of
households that are reconfigured in shortly over a year is comparable in
volume to the 18 percent that change residences annually. Household
restructuring is a highly dynamic process and probably as important as
residential mobility in changing areas' population characteristics.

In addition to masking the speed of change, the aging in place notion
leads us to expect only certain types of population change. We are led to
anticipate life-cycle changes like nest-emptying and widowhood but to
ignore the myriad other household changes such as those occurring with
marriage or remarriage when one spouse moves into the other's quarters, when a cohabiting couple marries but does not change residence,
when adult children move back to the parental home, and when divorce
breaks up the nuclear family but leaves one spouse, often the custodial
parent, in the original home. Focus on life-cycle changes and its
ancilliary concept, aging in place, results in an underestimation of the
magnitude, frequency, and areal impacts of *in situ* changes in household
structure.

Population Change and Residential Mobility

Recognizing that areal population change can result from restructuring
in place as well as from residential mobility, I operationalized Moore's
(1972) four-celled model and specifically related the extent of household
restructuring that occurred in metropolitan Phoenix between 1970 and
1980 with levels of population turnover in census tracts (Figure 10.2).
The model included four types of demographic experience—low household change and low turnover, low household change and high turnover,
high household change and low turnover, and high household change
and high turnover. Low turnover coupled with small shifts in household

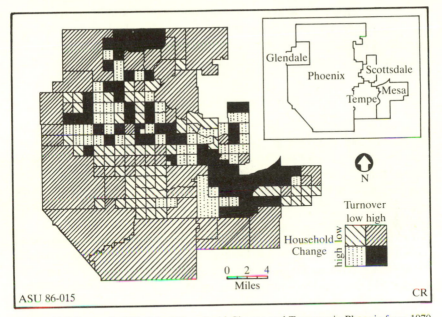

Figure 10.2 Four-celled Model of Household Change and Turnover in Phoenix from 1970 to 1980

composition was concentrated in old, single-family neighborhoods. Low turnover but high compositional change occurred in middle-aged, single-family neighborhoods where child-oriented households were converted to empty nesters. High turnover but low household change occurred in older multiple-family areas. Moore uses the term "high through-put" for the combination of high mobility with small change in population characteristics, because high turnover is required just to maintain a population structure of young singles and newly married couples. The fourth category of high turnover and high household change occurred in middle-aged and young neighborhoods dominated by multiple-family housing. These neighborhoods bore the brunt of household restructuring in Phoenix, and shifted from a diverse mixture of relatively large households in 1970 to highly specialized structures dominated by persons living alone in 1980. Mobility here served to replace households with dissimilar ones.

That high levels of household change occurred in conjunction with both high and low rates of population turnover indicated that mobility was sometimes but not always associated with household change. Results suggest that the view of mobility as a necessary corollary of household change is far too simplistic to capture the diversity of demographic change in Phoenix. High rates of turnover for census tracts do not necessarily imply high rates of household restructuring. Under certain circumstances, residential mobility was the dominant vehicle for household change, whereas under different conditions, it was the mechanism for maintaining a constant household structure (Gober, 1986).

Neighborhood Life Courses

Traditional theories of how neighborhoods change and the role played by mobility in that change are based on a very narrow view of how people progress through a life cycle and how that process is played out in urban space. We need to consider how the neighborhood life-cycle model can be amended to incorporate more appropriately the diversity of contemporary households and their progression through a multiplicity of different life courses.

One major flaw is that the life-cycle model conceives of a newly built-up area as dominated by single-family units; the area is gradually infused with multiple-family dwellings as it ages. It is more often the case, at least in Phoenix, for predominantly single-family neighborhoods to maintain that orientation and for new multiple-family housing to be constructed at the periphery. In 1970, 90 percent of all housing units in 78 of 189 census tracts were single-family dwellings. Almost a third of these 78 tracts maintained that percentage in 1980; three-quarters of the tracts had more than 70 percent single-family dwellings. At the other end of the spectrum were tracts dominated by recently constructed multiple-family housing in both 1970 and 1980. They are now, and probably will remain as, districts dominated by large apartment complexes.

The emergence of these large apartment districts and the relative stability of many single-family neighborhoods demonstrate the need to disaggregate by housing type when considering the demographic life courses of neighborhoods.

The Single-Family Neighborhood

The law of cumulative inertia will probably hold in single-family neighborhoods irrespective of their household compositions. The "holding power" of single-family housing enables it to accommodate a wide range of living arrangements and changes therein. This fact, in conjunction with high rates of homeownership, encourages *in situ* changes in composition and low mobility. Just as married couples have remained in place when children left home, so also will the increased number of single parents remain when their children leave home. The myriad other household changes outside the life-cycle framework should also result in at least one member of the original household remaining in place in the reconfigured household unit.

Population and housing will continue to age in tandem, although single-family neighborhoods will contain a greater mix of household types. Groups heretofore outside the home-buying market have flocked to single-family neighborhoods, inexorably changing their composition. Single-family neighborhoods can expect to see more individuals entering and leaving nuclear families, setting up residences with married or unmarried partners, and moving in with roommates, parents, and siblings.

The Multiple-Family Neighborhood

In contrast with the immobility but frequent *in situ* population restructuring in single-family areas, multiple-family areas should experience higher mobility but less household change with age. These expectations stem from the inflexibility of apartments to accommodate increases, decreases, and changes in household structure and tenure status. Although one might expect the age of population in older apartments to be older than that in more recently constructed apartments, the household structure should vary little with housing age and should maintain its strong orientation toward childless couples and nonfamilies. That household size did not decline as age of housing increased in Phoenix is consistent with this expectation.

Summary and Conclusions

Residential-location and neighborhood-change theories need to incorporate the way contemporary households are sorted out in urban space. In an era when half of all marriages end in divorce, two-thirds of married women are employed outside the home, childlessness is on the rise, and unmarried couples of the same and opposite sex maintain households, our locational models cannot assume that households are nuclear families that progress through a normal life cycle with this progression being played out in the life cycle of neighborhoods.

Because household structure is more complicated and household change more frequent, progression through the life course now entails persons entering and leaving families, sometimes through very unusual routes, and other persons never marrying and/or bearing children. We also need to understand more clearly the way household characteristics and transitions affect residential location and geographic mobility on much finer scales than the one involving movement between central cities and suburban rings. On the neighborhood scale, we need to understand how the connections between households and housing are played out in different residential contexts. The proposed model of expected changes in single- and multiple-family areas is a first step toward these ends.

References

Alonso, W. 1960. A theory of the urban land market. *Papers and Proceedings of the Regional Science Association* 6:149–157.

Alonso, W. 1964. *Location and Land Use: Toward a General Theory of Land Rent.* Cambridge, Mass.: Harvard University Press.

Bassett, K., and J. R. Short. 1980. *Housing and Residential Structure: Alternative Approaches.* Boston: Routledge & Kegan Paul.

Bourne, L. S. 1981. *The Geography of Housing.* New York: Wiley.

Burgess, E. W. 1925. The growth of the city. Pp. 47–62 in R. E. Park, E. W. Burgess, and R. D. McKenzie (eds.), *The City.* Chicago: University of Chicago Press.

Carliner, G. 1975. Determinants of household headship. *Journal of Marriage and the Family* 37:23–38.

Chevan, A. 1971. Family growth, household density and moving. *Demography* 9:45–58.

Clark, W. A. V., and J. O. Huff. 1977. Some empirical tests of duration-of-stay effects in intra-urban migration. *Environment and Planning A* 9:1357–1374.

Coupe, R. T., and B. S. Morgan. 1981. Towards a fuller understanding of residential mobility: A case study of Northampton, England. *Environment and Planning A* 13:201–215.

Doling, J. 1976. The family life cycle and housing choice. *Urban Studies* 13:55–58.

Gober, P. 1980. Shrinking household size and its effect on urban population density patterns: A case study of Phoenix, Arizona. *The Professional Geographer* 32:55–62.

Gober, P. 1986. How and why Phoenix households changed: 1970–1980. *Annals of the Association of American Geographers* 76:536–549.

Gober, P. 1987. Geographic Ramifications of the Changing American Household. Paper presented at the annual meetings of the Association of American Geographers in Portland, Oregon, April.

Guest, A. M. 1972. Patterns of family location. *Demography* 9:159–171.

Hoover, E. M., and R. Vernon. 1959. *Anatomy of a Metropolis.* Cambridge, Mass.: Harvard University Press.

Huff, J. O., and W. A. V. Clark. 1978. Cumulative stress and cumulative inertia: A behavioral model of the decision to move. *Environment and Planning A* 10:1101–1119.

Kendig, H. L. 1984. Housing careers, life cycle and residential mobility: Implications for the housing market. *Urban Studies* 21:271–283.

Kobrin, F. E. 1973. Household headship and its changes in the United States, 1940–1960, 1970. *Journal of the American Statistical Association* 68:793–800.

Kobrin, F. E. 1976a. The fall in household size and the rise of the primary individual in the United States. *Demography* 13:127–138.

Kobrin, F. E. 1976b. The primary individual and the family: Changes in living arrangements in the U.S. since 1940. *Journal of Marriage and the Family* 38:233–239.

Koo, H. P. 1985. Short-term Change in Household and Family Structure. Unpublished paper of the Research Triangle Institute.

McLeod, P. B., and J. R. Ellis. 1982. Housing consumption over the family life cycle: An empirical analysis. *Urban Studies* 19:177–185.

Mills, E. S. 1972. *Studies in the Structure of the Urban Economy.* Baltimore: Johns Hopkins University Press.

Moore, E. G. 1972. *Residential Mobility in the City.* Commission on College Geography Resource Paper No. 13. Washington, D.C.: Association of American Geographers.

Muth, R. 1961. Spatial structure of the housing market. *Papers and Proceedings of the Regional Science Association* 7:207–220.

Muth, R. 1965. The variation of population density and its components in South Chicago. *Papers and Proceedings of the Regional Science Association* 8:173–183.

Muth, R. 1969. *Cities and Housing.* Chicago: University of Chicago Press.

Myers, D. 1978. Aging of population and housing: A new perspective on planning for more balanced metropolitan growth. *Growth and Change* 9:8–13.

Myers, G. C., R. McGinnis, and G. Masnick. 1967. The duration of residence approach to a dynamic stochastic model of internal migration: A test of the axiom of cumulative inertia. *Eugenics Quarterly* 14:121–126.

Norton, A. J., and P. C. Glick. 1979. What's happening to households? *American Demographics* 1:19–22.

Ramanos, M. C. 1976. *Residential Spatial Structure.* Lexington, Mass.: Lexington Books.

Richards, T., M. J. White, and A. O. Tsui. 1987. Changing living arrangements: A hazards model of transitions among household types. *Demography* 24:77–97.

Rossi, P. 1955. *Why Families Move.* Glencoe, Ill.: Free Press.

Sabagh, G. M., M. D. van Arsdol, and E. W. Butler. 1969. Some determinants of intra-metropolitan residential mobility: Conceptual considerations. *Social Forces* 48:88–89.

Shevky, E., and M. Williams. 1949. *The Social Areas of Los Angeles.* Los Angeles: University of California Press.

Short, J. R. 1978. Residential mobility. *Progress in Human Geography* 2:419–447.

Speare, A. S., S. Goldstein, and W. H. Frey. 1975. *Residential Mobility, Migration and Metropolitan Change.* Cambridge, Mass.: Ballinger.

Stapleton, C. M. 1980. Reformulation of the life-cycle concept: Implications for residential mobility. *Environment and Planning A* 12:1103–1118.

Sweet, J. A. 1984. Components of change in the number of households, 1970–1980. *Demography* 21:129–140.

U.S. Bureau of the Census. 1972. *1970 Census of Population and Housing—Phoenix PHC (1)-160.* Washington D.C.: U.S. Government Printing Office.

U.S. Bureau of the Census. 1982. *Trends in Child Care Arrangements of Working Mothers.* Current Population Reports, Ser. P-23, No. 117. Washington, D.C.: U.S. Government Printing Office.

U.S. Bureau of the Census. 1983. *1980 Census of Population and Housing— Phoenix PHC80-2-284.* Washington, D.C.: U.S. Government Printing Office.

U.S. Bureau of the Census. 1984. *Money Income and Poverty Status of Families and Persons in the United States: 1983.* Current Population Reports, Ser. P-60, No. 145. Washington, D.C.: U.S. Government Printing Office.

U.S. Bureau of the Census. 1985. *Household and Family Characteristics: March 1984.* Current Population Reports, Ser. P-20, No. 398. Washington, D.C.: U.S. Government Printing Office.

White, R. B. 1982. Family size composition differentials between central city–suburb and metropolitan-nonmetropolitan migration streams. *Demography* 19:29–51.

Wingo, L. 1961. *Transportation and Urban Land.* Baltimore: Johns Hopkins University Press.

11 *William C. Baer*

Aging of the Housing Stock and Components of Inventory Change

Introduction

In discussing housing demography this chapter focuses on housing units rather than on households. It shows the dynamics at work on the stock over time, concentrating on what happens to housing once built. Traditionally, this kind of discussion has examined housing depreciation or loss rates. Although useful, such discussions concentrate upon central tendencies, upon what happens to the stock in general with little regard to the particulars. Such discussions unwittingly impede thinking about the immense variety of change that actually takes place in the stock and about when these changes tend to occur. These housing-unit particulars will be stressed here, and in many ways serve as counterpoint to the household changes discussed in chapters by Patricia Gober and Hal Kendig.

First we examine past efforts to describe what happens to housing units over time. Shortcomings in these approaches lead us to examine a supplementary view stressing housing "vintages" by tenure and by types of change. Tenure appears to be an important determinant of the propensity of a housing unit to undergo change—a consideration widely acknowledged in the real estate field but rarely examined in the literature.

William C. Baer is Associate Professor in the School of Urban and Regional Planning, University of Southern California, Los Angeles, California 90089.

By contrast, the various types of change (besides demolition) that can happen to the stock have been mentioned in the literature but little discussed (but see Apgar et al., 1985:ch. 4). My data come from the little-used Components of Inventory Change, both the published and unpublished tables and cross-tabulations provided by the U.S. Bureau of the Census (tapes are not available) (U.S. Bureau of the Census, 1983a,b).[1] I conclude by stressing that explicit consideration of the varieties of change and their link with tenure enriches our understanding of how the stock ages and declines in quality, and what actions owners take to stave off (or at least take maximum advantage of) that decline.

Housing Depreciation Curves

Housing's durability as a special attribute is widely remarked upon. Thus, determining housing's longevity is a basic issue for housing demography, yet traditionally it has been explored through economists' and appraisers' depreciation curves. This determination has proved far more intractable than has establishing people's longevity. Maintenance, rehabilitation, and restoration can, theoretically, prolong a unit's life indefinitely. Witness the European castles still used as habitations. But castles and manors of the rich aside, it has proved difficult to establish the general longevity of a more typical unit in the United States.[2]

Estimates for single-family or low-density multifamily units tend to range from 75 to 100 years.[3] For units surviving 100 years, Gleeson

1. There are three distinct but related sources for housing data from the U.S. Census: the decennial Census of Housing; the American (formerly Annual) Housing Survey (AHS), which uses a smaller sample but surveys more frequently and uses the same unit each time; and the Components of Inventory Change (CINCH), which, decennially, uses the AHS sample but adds to it units involved in a conversion or merger and a small supplemental sample of units derived from nonresidential space. None of these sources agrees with the others as to exact counts of housing, and each has strengths and weaknesses, but for the purpose here the CINCH data would seem to be the best. See Apgar et al., 1985:ch. 4, for a discussion of some of these differences.

2. One problem is learning the age of a unit. The age categories in the U.S. Census, for instance (our best source) are not very informative about housing over 50 years old. The oldest units are lumped together as built in 1939 or earlier. Nor are the age estimates precise (see Appendix 1). England, by contrast, apparently has substantially better records for longevity, allowing estimates of the number of units up to 150 years old. For a fascinating account of what can be done with such data, see O'Dell, 1986.

3. Cannaday and Sunderman (1986), for instance, citing three local studies that calculated the typical economic "life" of a single-family unit (87.5 years in St. Louis; 75–88.8 years in Minneapolis; 88 years overall in the United States), themselves concluded that 88 years was a reasonable estimate for Champaign, Illinois. Grether and Mieszkowski (1974), however, had earlier estimated that single-family units in New Haven continued to depreci-

(1985) estimated that their expected life was about another 20 years. Even units that survived to 150 years (about 4 percent of the original stock), he calculated, had an estimated life of another 18 years because, "as less desirable units are eliminated from the stock, those remaining are more likely to be unique and maintained with special care" (p. 655).

Most losses are due to deliberate demolitions following complete depreciation of the unit, hence depreciation affects longevity (Chinloy, 1983:145). Efforts to examine this facet attempt to derive theoretically (Chinloy, 1979; Hulten and Wycoff, 1980) or construct empirically (Smith, 1973; Follain and Malpezzi, 1980; Chinloy, 1983; Cannaday and Sunderman, 1986) depreciation curves—again with mixed results. There is, for instance, debate over the path of the curve.[4] The alternatives most frequently discussed are illustrated in Figure 11.1 (as adapted from Cannaday and Sunderman, 1986). From top to bottom they include: (1) a horizontal line (dubbed the "one hoss shay" after Oliver Wendell Holmes's subject in his poem "The Deacon's Masterpiece") that shows no depreciation until a sudden and complete loss of value (like a light bulb that continues to illuminate like new until suddenly burning out); (2) curves with a concave function, showing limited depreciation initially but accelerating in the later years; (3) reverse "S" curves; (4) a straight-line decline; and (5) curves with a convex function (typical of the accelerated depreciation so beloved by real estate investors for income tax deduction purposes [Hulten and Wycoff, 1980:90–94]).

Regardless of the depreciation path, these efforts must be approached with caution. First, the empirical work typically pertains only to low-density units, and usually single-family detached units at that. There are few estimates for multiunit structures (but see Hulten and Wycoff, 1980), although structures with five or more units contain almost 18

---

ate until they were about 100 years old. Gleeson (1984), in the course of developing a life table for structures of one to three units in Indianapolis, also estimated that the expected life when new was about 100 years. Taking a rather different approach, Smith (1973) estimated that the average life of a housing unit in the United States could be 154 years.

4. Accountants and the IRS, for instance, have used a variety of formulas, including straight-line and accelerated depreciation such as double declining balance or sum-of-the-years digits, although these typically are at odds with economists' theories of depreciation (Hulten and Wycoff, 1980).

Empirical works have explored a diverse variety of curves. Cannaday and Sunderman (1986), for instance, after reviewing past empirical efforts, tested four of the most commonly proposed curves. They concluded that a path that is concave (i.e., with initially a less rapid decline than straight-line) best estimates depreciation, and that a reverse sum-of-the-years digits curve (curve number 3 in Figure 11.1) best represents this depreciation in simplified form (a finding substantially different from, say, that of Follain and Malpezzi (1980).

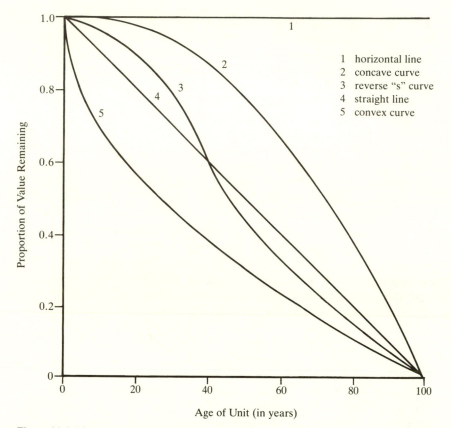

Figure 11.1 Alternative Types of Paths for Depreciation

percent of the nation's housing stock. Second, these estimates usually are unable to separate land from improvements—hence virtually ignore the value of nondepreciating land (but see Smith, 1973, and Cannaday and Sunderland, 1986:270). Third, maintenance and replacement further compound the analyses. It is comparatively easy to replace critical parts of a housing unit (heaters, plumbing, wiring, roofing, foundations), rendering unclear what the "true" age of a unit is even if we know its vintage. Appraisers often use "effective" age, but even this concept is difficult to operationalize (Cannaday and Sunderland, 1986:256, 262).[5]

The seemingly straightforward problem of determining the life of a "typical" housing unit has yet to be resolved, but it would appear that

5. Nevertheless, Chinloy (1983:150) estimated that Canada's total housing stock would decline by an additional 2 percent each year without maintenance expenditures.

just as the "typical"life-span of people is better presented by partitioning the populace into gender and, perhaps, section of the nation in which they live, so also estimates of housing's longevity should be approached in terms of tenure and type of structure, as well as particular housing market (Follain and Malpezzi, 1980). However, even partitioning the stock to derive these curves does not adequately account for the complex reality of some units. Housing units don't necessarily decline in value; they may appreciate, at least initially, as shown by Chinloy (1983). Others both decline and appreciate periodically, dependent upon the level of maintenance or rehabilitation of the unit, or upon externalities in the investment and disinvestment decisions for nearby properties. Still other units may change not only their condition but even their essence. A quantitative depreciation curve cannot capture these qualitative changes, as we will show. Nor can housing policy be appropriately fashioned based solely upon change denoted through simple depreciation curves. A broader perspective is warranted. One such perspective would adopt a longitudinal, life course approach to viewing housing as it ages. Such an approach would borrow conceptualizations and techniques from demography.

A Life Course Approach to Housing Longevity

Although there is perhaps no demographic equivalent to a housing depreciation curve, there are already some nascent applications of demography to the housing stock. A housing mortality table is one example developed by Gleeson (1981, 1984, 1985). He found, for instance, that a Gompertz curve, originally developed in conjunction with actuarial efforts for determining people's longevity, better fits housing than it does people. Although suggesting a number of interesting uses for such tables (e.g., estimates of future housing-stock loss, housing replacement as part of a housing-needs estimate; estimates of loss by vintage), he attempts no explicit explanation of why the losses occur (Gleeson, 1981, 1984). A qualitative approach to supplement his quantitative orientation would be helpful in this regard.

Another basic demographic curve—a morbidity rate—has apparently not yet been explored for housing. Substandard housing units are similar to sick people, for housing can fall into and out of poor health too. Although he didn't couch it this way, Burke (1982), for instance, found that of the nation's 3,610,000 substandard units in 1974 (defined by plumbing facilities that were incomplete or shared with another unit), about a quarter of them had been made standard ("well") by 1980, and another quarter had been removed from the stock. But he also found that at least 465,000 units that were of standard quality in 1974 had dropped to a substandard condition by 1980—a "morbidity rate" of 0.001/year.[6]

Morbidity rates in turn suggest some estimates of the cost to cure the substandard condition. Certainly this is an ongoing concern for housing policy. An early effort was undertaken in San Francisco by Wolfe (1967), who explored a "continuous condition aging model" of housing based on data in the Real Property Survey of 1939 and the use of Markov matrices. It is an interesting approach despite conceptual problems with the evaluative classifications of housing condition used in that survey (Baer, 1976). There are other similarities between people and housing units that a life course approach might explore. They can be only touched upon here. People are captives of unique family compositions through blood and marriage. Whether or not they benefit from this arrangement, individuals as family members are bound together by these biologically and socially created links. These links in turn influence, for better or worse, an individual's life chances (i.e., through social status, economic inheritance, and social contacts [who the family knows]). Similarly, housing units are usually "born" into (or become) a "neighborhood"—a collection of durable housing units (and infrastructure) whose fortunes over time are interlinked by externalities, and which, like a family, may develop social reputations or pedigrees over the years that further influence their fortunes.

The longitudinal emphasis of housing demography also helps illustrate the importance of individuality and the individual trajectories for one's life course. Housing units, like people, gain their special identities and increase their heterogeneity over long periods of time. The era and the location where they were "born" leaves a lasting imprint on their character, as do subsequent events and the ravages of time. Like older people, older housing—older single-family houses in particular—may develop a unique character that is denied to the more homogenized young, or recently built. The importance of such "vintage" analysis is well developed in the chapter on filtering by Myers, but see also the more general review by Baer and Williamson (1988). Clearly housing analysis can learn much from demography's longitudinal emphasis, for the two fields deal with so many common problems. But the very successes this transfer would enjoy in clearly revealing some facets of hous-

---

6. In measuring units with less severe "ailments"—cracks or holes in walls or ceilings—Burke (1982) found that 57 percent (2,285,000) of them with these conditions were "cured" by 1980, but that an even larger number (2,943,000) of "well" units had succumbed to these conditions by the same year—a morbidity rate of 0.009/year. Unfortunately, in neither event did he relate this incidence of ailment to the age of the unit.

ing suggests that it may obscure others. To speak of persons' or a house-holds' "stages" in their life cycles, or their places on the income-earnings curve, for instance, implicitly assumes some regular, inexorable progression along a trajectory of change. Central tendencies are emphasized to the detriment of learning about the dispersion of life course paths and their separate rates of change.

The same problems occur with housing analysis. Mortality rates and depreciation curves also show relatively smooth, nonfluctuating rates of change, and most show an incremental yet inexorable decline. These accounts, too, ignore—indeed obscure—patterns of dispersion in the life course of units. In so theorizing about housing decline, experts are apt to commit two kinds of mistakes: first, to assume incremental and continuous change where lumpiness and discontinuity may prevail (e.g., erroneously assume a city of perfectly "malleable" growth and decline [Vousden, 1980]); and second, when theorizing about neighborhood life cycles, to commit a variant of the ecological fallacy—attributing the characteristics in general to every unit in particular. Doing so robs us of an appreciation for the diversity of aging-derived characteristics which actually exists.

To understand better the wide variation in trajectories that housing units can experience (a variation which might be informative to demography too), I will discuss the multiple changes that can happen to individual housing units, and show how these changes are significant in understanding changes in the overall housing stock.

Measuring the Change in Existing Units

This section provides a qualitative counterpart to the traditional housing depreciation curve. It shows the variety of change that can take place in a unit over time besides mere depreciation, and attempts to broaden the perspective on possible changes over time, noting in particular that some of these changes are not of degree (as in depreciation) but of fundamental essence.

Categories of Change

Monitoring change in the housing stock has fallen largely to the U.S. Bureau of the Census. Its accounting system—the Components of Inventory Change (CINCH)—is built around two basic events: *additions* to and *removals* from the stock. These events are more complex than their terms imply. Besides new construction, additions include a variety of non-new construction sources: moving units onto a site, making two units from one, and so on. Similarly, removals take a variety of forms, and some removals are not necessarily permanent. They are artifacts of the Census Bureau's accounting ledgers, which are based on number of housing units (rather than amount of housing space) and on changes in a unit's location. A permanent removal—that is, a loss of space—occurs only from *demolitions* or *disasters*. More usually a "removal" is merely a reconfiguration or a relocation of existing space: reconfiguration if the space changes use or the number of units changes; relocation if the unit is moved to a different site. Thus, most removals are correlative with non-new construction additions. Despite some seeming artificialities, the CINCH system is a useful accounting device, for it can track the irregular changes that take place in the housing stock.

Figure 11.2 (adapted from CINCH) enumerates these basic changes and organizes them sequentially according to their basic results. In effect, the figure presents a qualitative supplement to quantitative mortality tables or quantitative depreciation curves. Unlike a mortality table it accounts for both temporary and permanent removals. Unlike depreciation curves it shows discontinuous change and abrupt changes in the essence of the units themselves.

The first column in Figure 11.2 lists the basic ways that new space is added to the housing stock. The last column lists the basic ways that space is permanently removed. These categories are obvious and self-explanatory.

The second, third, and fourth columns, however, reflect not-so-obvious accounting changes. The second column accounts for all those units (once built) that experienced no change during the measurement time period. They remained, as the Census expresses it, as "same units." The third and fourth columns reflect change that results in either both gains *and* losses or gains *or* losses of residential units or residential space—but in no event involves either new construction or a permanent removal. The case of moving a house or mobile home is a straightforward example of both an accounting loss and a gain. The unit is removed from one place and added at another. In aggregate there is no net change in units (although there may be genuine gains or losses by geographic location). In the case of *mergers* (combining two or more units into fewer ones) or *conversions* (splitting one unit into two or more), the issue is more complex. In both cases the ledger is debited on the removal side and credited on the additions side.[7]

---

7. The CINCH tables tend to show conversions and mergers as neither removed nor added, but rather as units "changed." It is more accurate, however, to think of them as being removed from one category or size of unit and added to another.

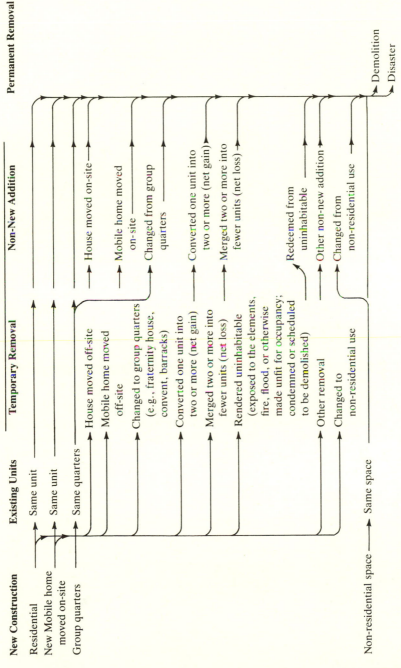

Figure 11.2 Basic Sequence of Components of Inventory Change

257

In still other cases, a "removal" involves a different kind of accounting—placing the unit either in a "suspended animation" category or in a nonresidential-unit category. Although not available at the moment, it subsequently can be redeemed for housing space. For example, units that have become uninhabitable by reason of, say, partial damage by fire, deterioration, or because they are condemned or intended for demolition, are removed from the stock of habitable units in the accounting system, although they are still standing. If some of these units are later salvaged or redeemed to habitable condition, they are then added back as part of "non-new" construction additions.[8] So also can space be reclaimed from "group quarters" (barracks, sorority houses, prisons, a unit where five or more unrelated individuals lived, convents, and other institutional quarters) or from nonresidential use.

In general, built space (both residential and nonresidential) is initially registered on the left of the table and over time tends to move to the right. This "path" is due to owners shifting their space to different housing submarkets over time in an effort to stave off the rate of depreciation by seeking higher yields from their properties. Although we have no concrete evidence, it is likely that some units cycle several times between the categories in the second, third, and fourth columns prior to being permanently removed (the last column).

Components of Inventory Change and Depreciation Curves Combined

Combining CINCH data with a depreciation curve can best be depicted three-dimensionally, for we need to show discontinuous shifts to different submarkets along the depreciation curve. Figure 11.3 illustrates these points with one example, but to simplify the three-dimensional presentation the curve is depicted both in a sectional view (as is traditionally done) and in a "plan" view (looking at the curve from above).

At the top of the figure we see that the path of the overall depreciation curve for this example property may well be made up of a set of shorter curves, reflecting the path of decline as the space is shifted to different submarkets (e.g., different tenure, different-sized units, different uses). In many instances it is probable that the depreciation curve traditionally depicted is really the envelope curve that comprises these

---

8. If instead such units are subsequently demolished rather than being returned to usable condition, they will again be registered as a loss, resulting in double counting (Gleeson, 1981:185).

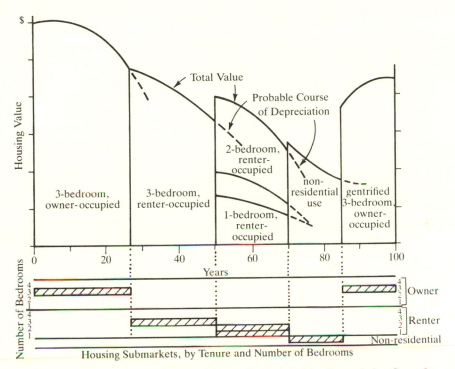

Figure 11.3 Components of Inventory Change Combined with a Depreciation Curve for the Life Course of One Sample Property

individual curves. That is, the owner, at some point in the unit's existence, facing the prospect of a rapidly depreciating asset, seeks to shift it to a different submarket where the rate of depreciation will be less. (The dashed lines represent the probable course of depreciation were the unit to continue in the same submarket). In the lower portion of the figure, we see more clearly the discontinuity from, first, shifting a three-bedroom single-family unit from owner-occupied to renter-occupied; later, subdividing it into a two-bedroom and a one-bedroom unit; still later, shifting it to nonresidential use such as an office (old houses near universities are examples); and finally, with the advent of gentrification, restoring it to its original tenure and use. The *appreciation* shown in this portion of the curve reflects an instance where a unit is one of the first on the block to gentrify, and later enjoys additional positive externalities from surrounding units following suit.

Two major points emerge from this illustration. First, the periodic discontinuity of the depreciation curve is revealed as the unit is shifted to a new submarket (it might even have been moved to a new site). Second, depreciation (and quality in general) is in part contextual—not absolute. Shifting the unit to different submarkets in the pursuit of higher revenues may deter the rate of depreciation. For instance, the distribution in the quality of units offered in a rental market is different from that offered in the owner-occupied market, hence the competition (and amount of return less depreciation) may change as well simply by shifting the tenure. Relocating the unit to a different site or subdividing it is merely a more extreme example of shifting to a different market.

Magnitudes of Change

How much of the stock is affected in the ways just described? Table 11.1 shows the relative magnitude of the basic types of change. These changes are condensed from the detailed listing in Figure 11.2 into five categories: (1) units which remained the same over the period; (2) recycled units (that is, those units not removed from the inventory but nevertheless reconfigured in a basic characteristic such as location or size); (3) units rendered unavailable for occupancy although the space still exists; (4) units permanently removed (the space has been eliminated); and (5) other removals—a residual category.

The top panel of the table shows the disposition of the 1973 housing stock. Here we see that the vast majority (92 percent) of the units remained unchanged. About 2 percent were permanently removed, and another 4 percent changed an aspect of their fundamental characteristics (changed the site on which they were located, changed size through subdivision or merger, and so on), and an additional 2 percent became unavailable for residential use.

The bottom panel of the table shows the relative contribution of different sources of housing to the 1980 stock. (Because it is a bigger base, the percentage changes for the same number of units are smaller). Here new construction dominates the additions (although not for low-income households, which are more likely to look to non-new construction as a source of supply [Baer, 1986]). Seemingly, only a small percentage of the stock is affected by these changes in any one year (recall that the data are for a seven-year period). Perhaps this is why these data have been largely ignored by housing analysts. Yet much of the housing stock is comparatively new (in 1980, about 63 percent of the nation's housing stock was less than 40 years old; 23 percent was less than 15 years). Depreciation curves suggest that the probability of change increases with age. As the average age of the national housing stock (like the

Table 11.1. Disposition of 1973 Housing Stock and Sources of 1980 Housing
Stock

	Number of Units (in thousands)	Percentage of Units
Disposition of the 1973 Stock to 1980		
	1973 Stock	
Total units	*77,245*	*100.0*
Same units	*70,725*	*91.6*
Recycled units	*3,287*	*4.2*
House moved off-site	315	0.4
Mobile home moved off-site	1,708	2.2
Conversion	384	0.5
Merger	880	1.1
Units rendered unavailable	*1,105*	*1.5*
Became uninhabitable	582	0.8
Converted to nonresidential use	523	0.7
Other removals	*320*	*0.4*
(Includes conversions to group quarters)		
Permanent removals	*1,808*	*2.3*
Demolition	1,547	2.0
Disaster (fire, flood, etc.)	261	0.3
Sources of the 1980 Stock since 1973		
	1980 Stock	
Total units	*89,292*	*100.0*
Same units, 1973–80	*70,725*	*79.2*
Recycled units	*4,177*	*4.6*
House moved on-site	602	0.7
Mobile home moved on-site	2,181	2.4
Conversion	925	1.0
Merger	469	0.5
Units reclaimed from unavailable	*712*	*0.8*
Redeemed from uninhabitable	147	0.2
Converted from nonresidential	565	0.6
Units from other sources	*559*	*0.6*
Other non-new additions (includes conversions from group quarters)		
New construction	*13,119*	*14.7*

Sources: U.S. Bureau of the Census, 1983a:tables A-3 and A-5; U.S. Bureau
of the Census, 1983b.

Note: The columns do not add to exactly 100.0 because of rounding.

Table 11.2.   Age Categories (Vintages) of Housing and Number of Units (in thousands), by Tenure

| | Owner-Occupied | | Renter-Occupied | | |
	Number	%	Number	%	Total
Newer units[a]	10,517	65	5,662	35	16,179
Mature units[b]	20,170	72	7,859	28	28,029
Older units[c]	14,289	56	11,242	44	25,531

Source: U.S. Bureau of the Census, 1983a:table A-1.
[a]Built between 1965 and October 1973 (7–15 years old by 1980).
[b]Built between 1940 and 1964 (16–40 years old by 1980).
[c]Built in 1939 or earlier (over 41 years old by 1980).

population) tends to increase, the rates for these changes will increase too.[9]

The Timing of Inventory Change

Using published and unpublished CINCH data we can determine the kinds of removal and their incidence among different vintages by tenure (as we will see tenure is an important determinant of these changes). To simplify the analysis, we aggregate the multiple age-cohort classifications provided by the Census Bureau into three basic categories as shown in Table 11.2. The age divisions are somewhat arbitrary, but, as we will see, the results are so clear-cut that they suggest there would be little difference if somewhat different groupings were chosen. Nevertheless, there is the basic problem of the accuracy in the number of units in each age category (see Appendix 1).

Of note in the table is the comparatively high number of rentals among the older units. In part this may reflect the fact that over 40 years ago there was a higher percentage of units built for renters than today. It also reflects the transition over time in tenure from owner-occupied to renter-occupied. This change in tenure is an important aspect of the depreciation curve.

Detailed results of this analysis are found in Appendix 2. Figure 11.4 summarizes those results in terms of the three basic categories of change

9. The May 11, 1988, *Wall Street Journal* (p. 25) reported that because of the apartment glut in the Southwest (from overconstruction and the depressed economy) lenders and developers razed 10,000 units in Houston in 1987, and expected to demolish another 8,000 in 1988. Most of these required extensive repairs, the expense of which was impossible to recover through increased rents during the glut. One savings and loan reportedly destroyed a 356-unit complex rather than replace a leaking roof.

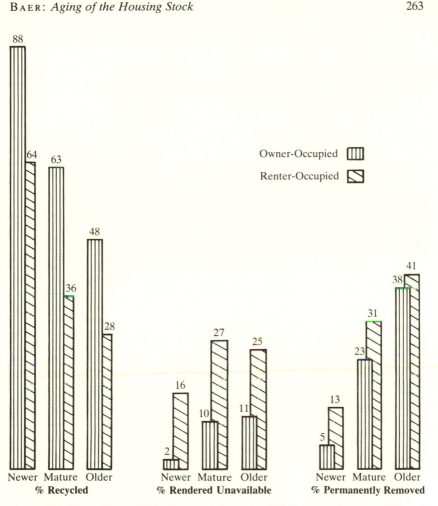

Figure 11.4 Disposition of Units Removed from the 1973 Inventory between 1973 and 1980, by Tenure and Vintage

shown in Table 11.1 ("same units" and "other removals" are not shown). The overall results are clear-cut: Older units tend to be removed permanently (or to be rendered unavailable), and newer units tend to be switched to another category of residential use. Rental units are more apt than owner-occupied units to be permanently removed.

Looking at Figure 11.4 in more detail, we see at the left of the figure, for example, that of the older units (those built in 1939 or earlier) which underwent change between 1973 and 1980, 48 percent of the owner-occupied units were recycled, whereas only 28 percent of the rental units were. In other words, owner-occupied units have a decidedly higher probability than renter-occupied units of being recycled through relocation, conversion, or merger. One reason for this, perhaps, is that owner-occupied units are usually in better repair than rentals, or they are more advantageously located, thereby being more amenable to recycling.

But there is also another reason for the high incidence of recycling among owner-occupied units, based on the physical characteristics of the units produced in different eras, and on what can physically be done with them. Although not shown in Figure 11.4, analysis of the underlying data in Appendix 2 reveals that a major reason for this greater incidence of recycling is the large number of newer owner-occupied mobile homes that are moved to another site. They constitute 58 percent of *all* units moved off-site (mobile homes and houses) for *all* vintages. This high percentage is due in part to the relatively short life of older mobile homes that were constructed some years ago with lower standards than at present, but it is due even more to the greatly increased numbers of mobile homes that were produced from the late 1960s on. Thus, mobile homes lend themselves to being recycled at a more advantageous location by virtue of their inherent ease of being moved.

By contrast, merger and conversion recycling tends to occur more in the rental stock. This type of recycling tends to reconfigure the stock without relocating it—often because this involves multifamily units which are very difficult to move.

The next major group in Figure 11.4 represents housing units rendered unavailable for residential occupancy. In some respects a similar picture to the recycled groups is disclosed. Rental units are more apt to become unavailable for residential use than are owner-occupied units, whether they become unfit for habitation, or because they are switched to nonresidential use. Although rental units constitute only about 35 percent of the total housing stock, they constitute 79 percent of all unavailable units. Of the three different vintages, older units are most apt to fall into this "unavailable" category regardless of tenure, no doubt often because of physical condition or obsolescence. They constitute some 68 percent of all those changed to "unavailable." Within this vintage, rental units are once again the more susceptible to change. Most older "unavailables" (78 percent) came from the rental stock.

The next group in Figure 11.4 is the permanent removals. Here again, an expected pattern emerges. Rental units are more apt to be permanently removed than owner-occupied, and older units are the most likely vintage to be removed for both owner-occupied and rental units. This category represents removals by deliberate demolitions (the traditional "end of the line" of a depreciation curve) as well as removals due to unintended disasters. Given the scant attention in the literature devoted to natural disasters we would expect that delibertate demolitions make up the majority of these permanent removals. Examination of Appendix 2 reveals that demolitions account for 85 percent of all permanent removals and that rental units account for 69 percent of all demolitions. While we would expect the older vintage (especially rentals) to bear a disproportionate incidence of removals—and they do—we might also expect natural disasters to strike this vintage and tenure group disproportionately. They do not. Losses to natural diasters display no clear-cut pattern, either by vintage or tenure. Advanced depreciation does not necessarily invite loss from natural disaster.

Reentry to the Depreciation Curve

We know that recycled units simultaneously constitute both removals and non-new additions. Although empirical analyses have ignored these non-new additions (Gleeson, 1984), these units should have been shown as having been extinguished at some point along the depreciation curve, and the resultant reconfigured space of non-new additions should have been shown as commencing new depreciation curves. (Figure 11.3 dealt with this problem by showing the individual depreciation curves of the subdivided units, and their joint values.) But what of units removed because of their residential unavailability? How is their depreciation shown along the curve? They may be "parked" in a nonresidential use or languishing in a state of "uninhabitability"—perhaps to return to residential use, perhaps not. (Again, Figure 11.3 showed total value, regardless of the fact that the space was no longer used for residential purposes.)

We also want to know the volume of this type of non-new additions. Do newer or mature units have a higher propensity to return to an "available" status than older units? Do owner-occupied units, which in general have a higher propensity to be recycled, in the case of being "unavailable" ultimately contribute larger numbers of non-new additions to the stock than rentals? My previous findings would suggest that they do, that a unit higher on its depreciation curve has a higher probability of re-entry to residential status than one down lower on the depreciation curve. The unpublished CINCH data reveal a surprising result, however. Of the units unavailable for habitation, roughly the same number (by vintage) were returned as were removed during this seven-year period. Older rentals predominated as the state in which the unit returned, particularly units transformed from nonresidential use. Unfortunately, we don't know how many of these had been residential units prior to their nonresidential use, so we don't know what proportion returned to the residential fold to continue their downward decline compared with the proportion "new" to residential use but nevertheless in older (pre-1940) structures.

The Role of Tenure and Vintage

Not surprisingly, I found that the older vintage units were the most susceptible to change. This finding is consistent with other findings: the older the unit, the higher the depreciation rate (Chinloy, 1983; Cannaday and Sunderman, 1986). But I also introduced the matter of tenure, a facet of housing depreciation and mortality rates most others have ignored (but see Follain and Malpezzi, 1980, who found that rental units depreciated faster than owner-occupied ones). The CINCH data are limited to cross-tabulations, so the analysis is limited, but some clear-cut findings emerged. I found that owner-occupied units are less apt to be removed in any fashion (other than being relocated) than are rental units. Even if removed they are more apt to be recycled. This result is consistent with Follain and Malpezzi's (1980:93) finding.

One reason for this higher incidence of change is that rental units tend to be less expensive.[10] We would expect that, as owner-occupied units decline in quality and value, there will be a propensity for their owners first to convert them to rentals and later perhaps to take more drastic action like conversion or merger or change to nonresidential use. These tenure changes come about for a variety of reasons: the owner's desire for an income property; children inheriting their parents' property; or an owner-occupant's inability to sell the property to another owner-occupant because of the lack of adequate financing, which may result in a sale to a speculator who specializes in renting deteriorated units. In many cases the rental category provides flexibility to investors unclear about long-term trends. Decisions to rent the property are temporary and reversible, dependent only upon terms of the lease.

Despite the traditional view about tenure change accompanying neighborhood change over the long term, only slight evidence for this trend to rentals was found in the CINCH data, and it should be viewed with caution. The unpublished CINCH data suggest that, for all vintages, units

10. We cannot measure this directly, but crude indications are: the capitalized value of median rent at, say, 10 percent, resulting in a $29,040 value per rental unit in 1980, compared with the median owner-occupied value of $51,300; and the comparison of 1980 median incomes for renters ($10,500) and for owner-occupants ($19,800), with the assumption that renters and owners devote roughly the same percentage of their incomes to housing costs.

switched from owner-occupied to rental at the annual rate of 0.002, and for the older units at an annual rate of almost 0.003. These are low rates of tenure change, but it must be remembered that during the period of study they occurred in the face of high conversion rates in the opposite direction—from rental units to owner-occupied condominiums.[11]

Depreciation and Structure Type

Earlier we noted that most empirical studies on depreciation either use single-family or low-density multifamily units, or use aggregated data that ignore structure type altogether. Although only summarized here for reasons of space, the CINCH data provide more detail on the qualitative aspects of depreciation. First of all, they reveal that the options open to owners are very much dictated by structure type. Single-family detached units, for instance, are easily moved, easily subdivided, but rarely merged; large multifamily units are rarely moved, but easily subdivided or merged.

Second, owner-occupied single-family detached units are primarily moved (31 percent of all nonpermanent removals) or subdivided (38 percent), and are less typically used for nonresidential use (15 percent). Owner-occupied structures of two to four units are predominantly merged (88 percent of all nonpermanent removals).[12] By contrast, renter-occupied single-family detached units had lower rates of being moved (20 percent) or converted (11 percent) but higher rates of being rendered uninhabitable (30 percent) or of being used nonresidentially (35 percent). Renter-occupied structures of two to four units were also predominantly apt to be merged (66 percent) or rendered uninhabitable (14 percent). Rental structures of five units or more had the highest incidence of being rendered uninhabitable (46 percent) (perhaps because of fire sweeping through a multistory unit), or having the units merged (19 percent), or going to nonresidential use (17 percent).

Conclusions

Three relationships have been established. First, the older the unit, the more apt it is to be removed (not counting mobile homes). This finding is not surprising—it accords with common sense and real estate experi-

---

11. Because many units went in or out of vacancy status without indication of tenure in the unpublished table, the tenure of these vacancies (if it were known) could swamp these results.

12. There were too few owner-occupied units in structures with five or more units to provide an adequate analysis.

ence as well as with the more theoretical depreciation curves and mortality tables. But this "removal" is not necessarily some action signifying the "end of the line" in the way that depreciation suggests. Many removals are merely prelude to some other configuration of the space.

Second, this finding of age-related decline provides background and context to depreciation curves. Figures 11.2 and 11.3, for instance, are not only qualitative counterparts to depreciation curves, they also reflect a behavioral counterpart on the part of owners. They are diagrams of the variety of investor responses to depreciation as well as to acts of nature (fire, flood, earthquake, storm) which accelerate the depreciation process. As units age, they suffer the ravages of nature and/or the effects of a change in occupancy in their unit or their neighborhood. Their owners do not necessarily observe this decline passively by withholding maintenance and lowering their rents or their expectations of future values. Nor do they necessarily actively respond with increased maintenance or by remodeling. Some owners take more drastic action. They may move their units, subdivide them, merge them, or switch them to nonresidential use. Any of these is a radical and discontinuous change, not an incremental response to gradual rates of depreciation.

Third, my findings stress the importance of tenure in predicting the incidence of life course change of a unit. Tenure is an importance facet of housing demography. It applies to both households and housing units. Renter-occupied is more apt to be the tenure at the end of a unit's existence than at the beginning. In many respects this pattern is the obverse of households, who in their earlier years are renters but aspire to owner status for their later ones. Indeed, the reasons for this obverse are found in the differences between the depreciation curve and the household earnings curve. Crudely put, the former starts high and descends, the latter starts low and ascends (until retirement).

To conclude, I note that to date these various changes in the stock have not been accorded much importance in the literature, because, in comparison with the total stock (so much of which is comparatively new), the amount of these changes is small. But the rate of change increases with age. In the future, as the nation's stock ages along with its people (because of reduced demand for new construction), these types of change can be expected to increase. And, just as we have seen increased analyses of the aging population, so also in the future we can expect increased attention to the aging housing stock. Moreover, as the housing stock matures, its aging is increasingly apt to elicit socialized rather than individualized responses, to elicit policy that shifts more of the burden of owning older units from individual owners to the public at large (e.g., through low-interest maintenance and rehabilitation loans and grants)—in just the way our aging population has shifted much of the burden of growing old from themselves (and their families) to the larger society.

Appendix 1
Estimating the Age of the Nation's Housing Stock

Estimating depreciation curves requires estimates of units' ages. These are easier to make locally than by a national survey like the Census of Housing. But local estimates are not readily available. Accordingly, the information is asked of the units' inhabitants—an unreliable source.

Demographers need not rely solely upon people's responses to questions about their ages. Frequently people are not wholly candid about this, and other records are available to demographers. By contrast, there is little reason to lie about a housing unit's age, but it is often a matter of conjecture to the occupant and even the owner (if the two are not the same). Building permits are our only official source, but they do not cover older units well, and their information is not widely circulated in any event. Most people don't take the time to inquire closely about their units' or structures' exact ages.

Accordingly, national estimates of the age of our housing stock are somewhat conjectural. The unpublished Components of Inventory Change data reveal the magnitude of the problem. Depending upon the age of the unit, its tenure, and the number of years in a vintage category, up to a fifth of the respondents may disagree as to the year of construction. Nor is this disagreement confined to bordering categories (i.e., Was the unit built between 1960 and 1964, or between 1965 and 1970?). The most extreme case involves the rental units that were estimated in the 1973 survey to have been constructed between 1965 and March 1970. By the time of the 1980 survey almost 19.7 percent of the respondents had changed the estimates to a different vintage of construction, and almost 5 percent of the respondents had changed the estimate to one of construction in 1939 or earlier! Because the census provides no independent source of age, we have no way of knowing whether the earlier respondents were better vintage estimators than the later ones.

Table 11.A-1 illustrates the problem more generally. Not surprisingly, renter-occupants are less clear about vintage than owners, and moderate-aged units generate more confusion about their age than do very new or very old units. In any event, the table serves as a caveat when examining characteristics of units classified by age in the Census of Housing.

Table 11.A-1.   Percentage Distribution of Respondents' Disagreements on Dates of Units' Construction, by Vintage (with a seven-year interval between surveys)

1973 Classification of Year when Unit Was Built	Respondent	Percentage Assigning a Different Classification in 1980		
		Built Later	Built Earlier	TOTAL
4/1970–12/1973	Owner		1.8	1.8
	Renter		0.5	0.5
1965–3/1970	Owner	1.1	9.9	11.0
	Renter	0.1	19.6	19.7
1960–1964	Owner	2.8	7.8	10.6
	Renter	4.9	8.6	13.5
1950–1959	Owner	3.2	4.3	7.5
	Renter	6.0	7.5	13.5
1940–1949	Owner	5.6	5.7	11.3
	Renter	6.8	11.9	18.7
1939 or earlier	Owner	3.2		3.2
	Renter	3.6		3.6

Source: U.S. Bureau of the Census, 1983b: table U-S-1.

Appendix 2

Table 11.A-2. Number (in thousands of units) and Percentage Distribution of Units Removed from Stock during 1973–80, by Tenure and Method of Removal

| Vintage and Tenure | Total Units | Total Removals | Permanently Removed | | Recycled | | | | Rendered Unavailable | | Other Removals |
			Demolitions	Disasters	Mobile Home Moved Out	House Moved Out	Conversion	Merger	Rendered Un-inhabitable	Converted to Non-residential	
					Owner-Occupied						
Numbers											
1965–10/1973	10,517	1,028	26	23	772	93	16	22	6	12	58
1940–64	20,170	642	98	50	191	45	100	67	19	42	30
1939 or earlier	14,289	809	259	47	65	37	122	160	36	60	23
TOTAL	44,976	2,479	383	120	1,028	175	238	249	61	114	111
Percentages											
1965–10/1973	10,517	100	3	2	75	9	2	2	1	1	5
1940–64	20,170	100	15	8	30	7	16	10	3	7	4
1939 or earlier	14,289	100	32	6	8	5	15	20	4	7	3
					Renter-Occupied						
Numbers											
1965–10/1973	5,662	235	21	9	107	21	2	21	17	22	15
1940–64	7,859	570	167	11	81	31	14	83	54	100	29
1939 or earlier	11,242	1,817	681	78	43	37	83	355	294	170	76
TOTAL	24,763	2,622	869	98	231	89	99	459	365	292	120
Percentages											
1965–10/1973	5,662	100	9	4	45	9	1	9	7	9	6
1940–64	7,859	100	29	2	14	5	2	15	9	18	5
1939 or earlier	11,242	100	38	4	2	2	5	19	16	9	4

Sources: U.S. Bureau of the Census, 1983a:table A-5; U.S. Bureau of the Census, 1983b.

Acknowledgement

This research was supported by a grant from the National Science Foundation (No. 8704256). It was further facilitated by use of unpublished data from the Components of Inventory Change for 1980, supplied by the U.S. Bureau of the Census. The views and opinions expressed are solely the author's, as are any errors.

References

Apgar, W. C., Jr., H. J. Brown, G. Masnik, and J. Pitkin. 1985. *The housing outlook: 1980–1990*. New York: Praeger Publishers.

Baer, W. C. 1976. The evolution of housing indicators and housing standards. *Public Policy* 24:361–393.

Baer, W. C. 1986. The shadow market in housing. *Scientific American* 255(5, November):29–35.

Baer, W. C., and C. B. Williamson. 1988. The filtering of household and housing units. *Journal of Planning Literature* 3(2, Spring):127–152.

Burke, P. 1982. *Changes in Housing Quality 1974–1980*. Processed. Washington, D.C.: Division of Housing and Demographic Analysis, Department of Housing and Urban Development.

Cannaday, R. E., and M. A. Sunderman. 1986. Estimation of depreciation for single-family appraisal. *AREUEA Journal* 14:255–273.

Chinloy, P. 1979. The estimation of net depreciation rates on housing. *Journal of Urban Economics* 6:432–443.

Chinloy, P. 1983. Housing repair and housing stocks. Pp. 139–158 in G. W. Gau and M. A. Goldberg (eds.), *North American Housing Markets into the Twenty-First Century*. Cambridge, Mass.: Ballinger.

Follain, J. R., Jr., and S. Malpezzi. 1980. *Dissecting Housing Value and Rent*. Washington, D.C.: The Urban Institute.

Gleeson, M. E. 1981. Estimating housing mortality. *Journal of the American Planning Association* 47:185–194.

Gleeson, M. E. 1984. Application of a mortality model to subsidized housing. *Environment and Planning A* 16:901–916.

Gleeson, M. E. 1985. Estimating housing mortality from loss records. *Environment and Planning A* 17:647–659.

Grether, D. M., and P. Mieszkowski. 1974. Determinants of real estate values. *Journal of Urban Economics* 1:127–146.

Hulten, C. R., and F. C. Wycoff. 1980. Economic depreciation and the taxation of structures in United States manufacturing industries: An empirical analysis. Pp. 83–119 in D. Usher (ed.), *The Measurement of Capital*. Chicago: University of Chicago Press, National Bureau of Economic Research.

O'Dell, A. 1986. Towards a Model of the Housing Stock and Its Physical Condition. Paper prepared for the International Research Conference on Housing Policy, Gavle, Sweden, June.

Smith, W. F. 1973. Should a house last 300 years? *Socio-economic Planning Science* 7:723–737.

U.S. Bureau of the Census. 1983a. *1980 Census of Housing. Components of Inventory Change* (United States and Regions). August. Washington, D.C.: U.S. Government Printing Office.

U.S. Bureau of the Census. 1983b. *1980 Components of Inventory Change. Detailed Losses from the 1973 Inventory—Unpublished Tabulations.* Processed. Washington, D.C.

Vousden, N. 1980. An open-city model with nonmalleable housing. *Journal of Urban Economics* 7:248–277.

Wolfe, H. B. 1967. Models for condition aging of residential structures. *Journal of the American Institute of Planners* 33:102–196.

Filtering in Time:
Rethinking the Longitudinal Behavior
of Neighborhood Housing Markets

Filtering is a central concept used to describe changes in the housing market and in neighborhoods. The general notion is that of a trickle-down process whereby older houses are handed down from richer to poorer families. However, this process is highly complex, involving multiple behavioral dimensions (often evaluated with regard to different political values), and data are not available for measuring all aspects. This has led to divergent definitions for filtering, as summarized in a recent review by Baer and Williamson (1988).

The scholarly disarray is further emphasized by the anomaly of gentrification, which was recognized in the 1970s. The experience of preceding decades led most observers to view downward filtration as inexorable or normal. With the reversal of this process in some locations during the 1970s, old theories were called into question. Gentrification should not be viewed as an exception to the filtering process; instead, we must construct a revised theory of filtering that can explain the range of events experienced in different decades.

This chapter returns to the basics of filtering in an effort to build a more intellectually robust theory. At root, filtering is a longitudinal process that matches households with different income levels to housing units with different prices and quality levels. Filtering involves *change over time* in this matching, and necessarily includes change in each of the components as well. Many decision-making factors play a role in explaining these changes, including consumer decisions, landlord maintenance and investment decisions, and government policies. Yet I will argue that these decisions are best understood if placed within an explicit temporal context. The chapter draws upon some of the temporal emphases of life course theory as reviewed in the chapter by Hal Kendig. It also bears relation to William Baer's discussion of physical housing changes over time and relates as well to the spatial models of temporal change discussed in the chapter by Patricia Gober.

A theory of filtering must emphasize time, not just because the filtering process is longitudinal, but for more specific reasons as well. First, with regard to the housing stock, the great durability of housing units means that they last for a long period of time. New construction today will live on well into the future, but with passing time important changes occur to dwellings. Moreover, construction at different points in historical time reflects conditions of the respective period: level and type of demand, as well as the contemporary technology and fashion. Thus, each vintage, or cohort, of houses carries forward the imprint of the historical period in which they were constructed. As time passes, the units of certain vintages may become more outdated or obsolescent, with important implications for their subsequent filtering.

Time plays a parallel role with regard to consumer demand. Households serve long time spans in the housing market—perhaps 40–50 years. These housing careers are shorter than the life expectancy of their dwellings, guaranteeing that multiple occupants will pass through the same dwelling. As discussed at several points in this volume, households move through the housing market according to a general life cycle pattern, yet generations of households differ from one another in the size of their respective cohorts and in their other family and economic behavior. Successive generations also face very different market conditions at a given point in their lives, such as when trying to first buy homes. Thus, the household life cycles of different generations may diverge from one another.

This chapter views filtering as the longitudinal joining of supply and demand, with emphasis on the several temporal dimensions of filtering. The interaction between aggregate household life cycles and the aggregate dwelling life cycles gives rise to the filtering observed in each period. But each cohort of households and vintage of houses may follow a life cycle differing from their predecessor's. To assist in describing the interplay of these multiple temporal dimensions, I will adopt the demographer's notion of time, identifying three dimensions: historical time or period, life cycle time or age, and cohort or vintage. This framework can be applied to both houses (or neighborhoods) and the population of consumers, helping to integrate more coherently different aspects of filtering that are raised in the literature. And we can use the temporal framework to reassess key assumptions of classic filtering theory. The ultimate goal is to arrive at a more robust theory of filtering that is less dependent upon past historical circumstance and more reliable for generating insights about the future of filtering and gentrification.

The Filtering Tradition

The early definition by Ratcliff is widely cited: "This process . . . is described most simply as the changing of occupancy as the housing that is occupied by one income group becomes available to the next lower income group as a result of decline in market price . . ." (Ratcliff, 1949:321–322). Notice that this definition comprises three interacting components: change in occupancy (turnover); declining price; and declining income. Alternative simplifications have been proposed in order to measure the changes indicated by this definition.

Change in Price of Units

The best-known filtering theories have focused on the prices of housing units, disregarding the turnover process and changes in characteristics of occupants. Among the earliest, Fisher and Winnick (1951) concluded that price is the key variable in the filtering definition, but they attacked the presumption that filtering can be measured by change in rent *simply expressed in constant dollars*. They cited evidence produced by Leo Grebler to show that real rents can remain stable even while a neighborhood is falling in relative desirability. Instead, they argued for a relative index of filtering: *"Filtering is defined as a change over time in the position of a given dwelling unit or group of dwelling units within the distribution of housing rents and prices in the community as a whole"* (Fisher and Winnick, 1951:52; emphasis in the original).

Despite the persuasive power of this logic, Lowry (1960) returned to a real-value definition of filtering, emphasizing change in price in constant dollars. Lowry also explicitly excluded mobility behavior and incomes from his definition. His focus was on the suppliers' evaluation of current costs and revenues.

Uncertainty about whether or not lower-income people benefit from filtering has engendered political debate for decades. A frequent argument is that filtering "does not work" because quality declines in tandem with price. Lowry (1960) focused on the relationship between price and value, reasoning that landlords' rational response to falling revenues is to undermaintain their units, thus permitting older houses to filter down in quality. He asserted: "The effectiveness of filtering as a means of raising housing standards thus hinges on the speed of value-decline relative to quality-decline" (p. 364).

Adding a further dimension to filtering—housing quality—we may summarize the conventional understanding of the filtering concept by three dimensions that are linked in principle: quality, price, and income. Despite Lowry's claims, it is not certain that quality decline will keep pace with falling price; undermaintenance takes its toll over time and may not have serious effects until major dwelling components, such as the roof, wear out. It also is not certain that income will decline in tandem with price; this adjustment depends on turnover in the unit and residential mobility. Given that many households occupy their units for decades or longer, the adjustment of income to price decline may be very sticky, particularly in the owner-occupied market.

Change in Occupancy or Income

The interaction between the price-filtering of dwellings over time and the occupancy behavior of households is much less understood. The filtering models discussed above have disregarded the longitudinal behavior of households. Instead, the models assume that changes in occupancy and income are implied by falling price. However, this underestimates the complexity, and the importance, of the occupancy-transition process.

The most common approach for introducing occupancy transition over time is a neighborhood life-cycle model used to describe stages in the filtering process (Hoover and Vernon, 1959; Birch, 1971). I will address this method in depth in a following section.

In another well-developed approach, studies have traced the vacancy chains initiated by new construction, seeking to identify who benefits (Lansing, Clifton, and Morgan, 1969; Sands and Bower, 1976). Each person who moves into a unit is asked where he or she came from, and the surveyers work backward until the chain reaches a unit that was not left vacant (such as when a young person moves out of the parents' home or the unit was demolished). Although the chains tend to reach progressively lower-income households, the decline is not great, and the chains themselves are typically only three to five steps long.

An alternative perspective is to trace the sequence of moves by the same household or individual, often termed the housing career or housing life cycle (Kendig, 1984). Elsewhere I have applied this perspective to the question of filtering by introducing an "upward mobility" model of the filtering process (Myers, 1983). In simplest terms, new dwellings are added to the market at the top of the quality and price hierarchy, drifting downward with time. In contrast, new households are formed at the bottom of the quality and price hierarchy, moving upward in the market over time. This process is recognized also by Bourne (1981), who aptly characterizes it as analogous to walking up a down escalator. Reflecting similar observations by Birch (1971), Figure 12.1 diagrams this interaction between supply and demand in filtering.

The upward mobility component has not been incorporated by housing economists because it violates their assumptions. Instead of assuming income groups must wait passively for housing to decline in value and fall into their range, the upward mobility model stresses the active movement of cohorts upward over time. This violates economic models' *ceteris paribus* assumption regarding income and tastes. Any upward mobility tends to be viewed as social mobility that is an exception to the

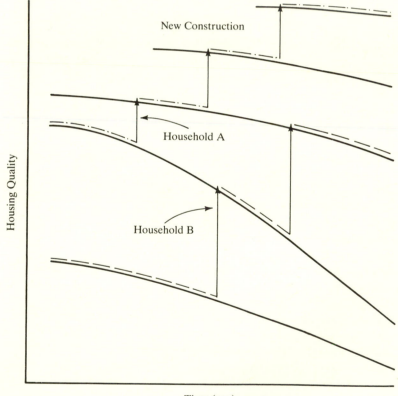

Figure 12.1 Schematic Relationship between Upwardly Mobile Housing Careers and Declining Submarkets

fundamental economic relationships. In contrast, *from a demographic perspective, we view upward mobility as the rule, not an exception.*

Evidence is assembled in Myers, 1983, to show how pervasive is upward mobility, characterizing all income classes and age groups, with the sole exception of households facing marital disruption. So strong is the upward movement toward single-family homeownership by existing households, that in a single year (1977) three-quarters of a million apartments faced abandonment. These units were subsequently occupied, however, by newly formed households entering at the bottom of the market to replace the upward departed movers.

In summation, filtering is a complex process with many interacting components. At root it is the longitudinal joining of supply and demand, and therefore time is a critical aspect of filtering. The next section reviews the three dimensions of time that must be addressed if we are to develop a stronger model of filtering.

Three Dimensions of Time

Demographers recognize three dimensions of time: age (life cycle), cohort (longitudinal group membership), and period (historical time). Any two of the dimensions determine the third (Mason et al., 1973; Palmore, 1978). For example, at a given point in history a set of ages determines a set of birth cohorts. Age measures the length of each cohort's progress through its own life cycle. The classic fallacy to be avoided is the mistaken inference that an age profile of behavioral states at one point in time defines the likely path to be followed by all cohorts as they grow older. Such cross-sectional, "life cycle" models overlook the strong differences often found between cohorts' true, longitudinal life cycles.

The application of the three dimensions to demographic analysis is well-established. Period effects are those that impact all age groups at the same time, such as changes in the economy, war, or new technology like television and microwave ovens. Period effects also include the current rate of population growth and other competitive conditions experienced by population members. Life-cycle effects involve the aging of people. Certain biological changes are well-recognized, and social changes also occur with aging (Riley et al., 1972). Cohort effects refer to unique differences between cohorts that persist over time. For example, the small cohort size of the generation born during the depression made for less competition in school, the labor force, and the housing market, leading to the label "the good times cohort" (Herter, 1977).

Each of the three dimensions has clear expression in analysis of houses and neighborhoods as well. Period effects are represented by current market conditions and prevailing tax laws or government regulations. Life-cycle effects involve changes occurring to dwellings as they age. And cohort effects involve differences between vintages other than their differences due to age alone. The novelty of applying this perspective to houses and neighborhoods requires that I explain it more fully below.

Period Effects

Housing market analysts are most familiar with period effects. Current market conditions play a major role in the planning of new construction and in making other decisions regarding investment and rehabilitation of existing structures. The current and expected yield on investments is the prime criterion. The critical variables for judging this are interest rates, current rental rates or sales prices, current rates of appreciation, and costs of land and construction. Although the level of unsatisfied demand shapes the volume of construction, it is the composition of demand by age or family type and income level that dictates what kinds of dwellings are built. Campbell's (1966) seminal work illustrates clearly how changing demographic forces over the past century have directed construction.

The other major set of period effects in addition to market conditions is the role of government programs, government tax laws, and other regulations. These government effects are changeable from period to period, as when depreciation schedules for tax purposes are made more lenient or when the treatment of capital gains is altered. The federal government has wielded major influence also through the introduction of new subsidy programs aiding movement to the suburbs (such as the VA and FHA mortgages) and programs encouraging historic preservation and renovation. Local governments add further market effects through the imposition of zoning changes, the administration of property taxes, and major infrastructure improvements such as roadways and utilities.

In general, government programs and market conditions are so closely intertwined that urban land economists treat them together (Ratcliff, 1949). The point to be emphasized here is that these effects change from period to period. The sudden introduction of a new government program or a new market condition can lead to a sudden change in filtering.

Life-Cycle Effects

Filtering theorists have focused mostly on life-cycle effects, as reviewed in the next section. Three major categories occur with the aging of dwellings.

With increasing age all dwellings suffer deterioration. Painting work first is required, a relatively superficial, but still expensive, repair. After a decade or two, more costly deterioration may require carpentry repairs, reroofing, or replacement of heating and plumbing systems.

With passing time, the dwelling will grow increasingly outdated for reasons of technology, fashion, or its match to household needs. Over the postwar decades, standards for bathrooms and kitchens have steadily evolved, as have standards for heating and cooling systems. A 1950-vintage house maintained in "like-new" condition would still be falling in relative desirability because of obsolescence. Older buildings may also fall out of fashion for purely aesthetic reasons, or less commonly they may fall back into fashion. Dwellings constructed to meet current needs also become less desirable as needs change. For example, a large house for a large family may become a white elephant if the current market consists of small households with little time for housework.

A final life-cycle effect concerns the likelihood, due to the passage of time, of occupancy or ownership transition. At such transition points abrupt filtering shifts are most likely (Meier, 1983). There are discrete holding-period limits. The owner of a large mansion will one day die. During the tenure of his occupancy, market conditions will have changed and problems of deterioration or increased maintenance will have mounted. Obsolescence will also be a factor discouraging new occupants. Upon eventual death of the owner, the property will likely be subdivided or converted. Even in the case of modest 1950s houses, evidence shows that turnover increases the rate of maintenance or remodeling (Myers, 1984). And in the case of rental property we also suspect that the holding-period limit due to tax depreciation schedules periodically will encourage resale and reevaluation of the property's optimal use.

Cohort Effects

Life-cycle effects are often confused with cohort differences. Rather than compare dwellings of different ages, cohort effects describe differences in the rates at which different vintage dwellings are filtering. For example, how much have 1950s houses changed in their first 30 years compared with the experience of 1920s houses?

Cohort effects are strongly felt in housing because each era's construction is so different. Both the volume and style of construction vary markedly, such that each vintage is an artifact of conditions prevailing during its period of construction. In a notable work, Adams (1970) lays out a comprehensive model for reading the current structure of cities as a series of vintages built under different conditions. Adams stresses the prevailing transportation mode of the era as a determinant of lot size, and he shows how the periodic sharp drop-offs in construction serve to demarcate discrete bands of dwellings built in different styles and densities.

The Fallacy of a Life-Cycle Filtering Model

One of the most popular devices scholars have used to describe filtering in cities is the notion of a neighborhood life cycle. First codified by Hoover and Vernon (1959) in a study of the New York City area, this five-stage neighborhood life cycle has been widely referenced and expanded upon (e.g., Birch, 1971; Andrews, 1971; Bourne, 1981). The stages include subdivision and buildup, transition into intensive land use, conversion and downgrading, thinning out, and finally renewal.

This classical model of longitudinal change is based upon observations at a single point in history. The life cycle is inferred by comparing neighborhoods of different ages and then assuming that each neighborhood follows the pathway implied by those age differences. The danger in this practice is that true cohorts or vintages are confused with cross-sectional age differences. When Hoover and Vernon looked upon New York City in the mid-1950s, they saw a cross-section of vintages whose individual life cycles had been impacted by unique historical events. Ample evidence can be marshaled to question the wisdom of this life-cycle approach.

One means to avoid the fallacy of the life-cycle approach is to define cohorts of neighborhoods based on the year in which they were first built up (reaching a density of two units per acre), a method pioneered by Duncan, Sabagh, and Van Arsdol (1962). In the most thorough and clearest application of the neighborhood cohort method, Guest (1974) found little evidence of status decline between 1940 and 1970 for different vintage neighborhoods. Older neighborhoods maintained constant status levels near the bottom in ranking, whereas newer neighborhoods were added at the top. The life cycle inferred from the cross-section did not represent the true longitudinal life cycle of vintages.

Despite this evidence, the life-cycle model maintains its attraction because it is a simple device for organizing complex temporal changes. In one of the fullest explications, Bourne (1981:table 2.1) presents a life-cycle typology of stages showing parallel events among both houses and households. The assumption is that various changes occur in parallel lock-step, irrespective of historical time or unique vintage differences.

Urban scholars may benefit from a more critical interpretation of the life-cycle filtering model. Closer examination is required of how historical conditions impact on filtering processes, not only with regard to current market conditions, but also in terms of their imprint on the life cycles of each unique vintage of houses and neighborhoods.

The foremost reason why the simple life-cycle model fails to describe filtering experience adequately is the dramatic "roller coaster" effect of changing historical conditions. These changes impact filtering not only through current market adjustments but also because conditions of earlier eras are imprinted on vintages built in that earlier time. Our tendency is to assume that events of the past decade or two are "normal" conditions; hence, unwittingly our normal theories are predicated upon a unique historical context. The difficulty is that changes in period conditions disrupt the stable market context necessary for deciphering filtering processes that can be termed normal.

Variations in the Population Growth Rate

Population growth constitutes one of the most influential period effects. Variation in the total growth rate, its sources, and its age profile, creates a most unstable basis for judging normal filtering patterns. Alonso's (1980) principal argument why urban analysts must pay close attention to "the population factor" is that changes during the 1970s have eliminated the normal growth conditions assumed by traditional theories of urban structure. Slowing metropolitan growth, changing family structure, and aging of the baby boom are three of the main factors he identified as threatening traditional theories of urban growth and structure.

Yet in a prescient essay, Homer Hoyt (1940) argued much earlier that traditional growth patterns had already given way to a new pattern of urban decentralization. He pointed to the cessation of central-business-district growth following the crash of 1929 and other factors, particularly the rise of trucking for manufacturers, as diminishing the competition for centrally located land. Hoyt also called attention to the impact of sharply curtailed immigration to the United States. He saw cutting off the waves of immigrant residents as robbing central-city neighborhoods of replacements required in the past to fill vacancies left by the upwardly mobile. The diminishment of immigrant demand, also cited by Campbell (1966), would leave a vacuum undermining values in central neighborhoods.

A new era of filtering in U.S. cities was spawned in the late 1940s and 1950s as black residents from the South moved north for jobs and sought residences in the weakened central-city market. The racial difference set up a color signal of neighborhood change, closely monitored by realtors and residents. New "laws" were proposed regarding tipping points of racial change and the inevitability of racial succession. In fact, as noted by Taeuber and Taeuber (1965), Downs (1960), and others, these laws of neighborhood change were dependent upon the rate at which black population was growing relative to white population. By the 1970s, black migration to the North had sharply subsided and the furor over racially changing neighborhoods dissipated.

Historical fluctuations in birth rates have yielded different-sized cohorts, dramatized by the maturing baby-boom generation. The sharp change in the number of adults turning age 30 has been a principal cause of gentrification of the 1970s and 1980s. Less widely recognized has been the effect of the cohorts born prior to the baby boom (in the 1930s). Because their sizes were smaller than those of their predecessors born in the 1920s, there weren't enough households in these 1930s cohorts to fill vacancies left by earlier travelers, thus further weakening the central-city markets and making the subsequent arrival of babyboomers all the more dramatic (Goetze and Colton, 1980).

Economic Cycles

Fluctuations in the economy create other impacts on the context of filtering, particularly through the regulation of new construction. Because housing is so bulky and durable, it is expensive to construct. Builders, landlords, and homeowners must borrow large amounts of capital to finance housing production and acquisition. The financial feasibility of assuming this much debt depends upon the interest rate of the loan. Thus the housing-supply sector is extremely sensitive to the rise and fall of interest rates over the business cycle.

Adams (1970) documents how the periodic drop-off in construction activity serves to demarcate different eras of housing construction. Each vintage reflects the volume and nature of the prevailing demand, servicing that demand with dwelling configurations that reflect prevailing transport patterns, building technology, and fashion.

The Great Depression and the post–World War II economic expansion represent two of the most clear-cut economic forces on filtering. The depression reduced construction for a longer period than other recessions of this century. The prolonged construction slump during the 1930s and 1940s prevented awareness of the loss of inner-city demand, identified by Hoyt (1940), because the rate of outward movement to new housing in the suburbs was dramatically slowed. However, the construction shortfall of this era created other problems that accelerated filtering later. Downs (1977) observes that many more households were added in the 1930s and 1940s than new units were constructed. In the 1920s, 24.5 percent more housing was built than was required by household growth; however, in the 1930s and 1940s, many fewer units were built than were required by the increase in households: shortfalls of 64.6 percent and 59.5 percent, respectively. The differences were made up by converting existing housing units into multiple units.

Following World War II the nation suffered a severe housing shortage. Much of the stock was old and outdated, and the inner-city neighborhoods were crowded by the conversions to multiple units required during the depression. After two decades of war and depression, the burgeoning numbers of young families were pressing for a return to an idealized "normal" life behind a white picket fence in the suburbs. New housing was being demanded for a new life style (Downs, 1977). Family-formation behaviors swung sharply to unprecedented early ages of marriage and childbearing as the decade of the baby boom unfolded.

Rapid economic growth made possible a dramatic postwar rise in family income. Levy and Michel (1985) document how the average male achieved an increase in real earnings of 118 percent as he matured from age 25 to 35 between 1949 and 1959. (In contrast, between 1973 and 1983 male earnings increased by a meager 16 percent over the same age span.)

Technological Change

It scarcely needs emphasis how great has been the technological change over the course of this century. Yet we often lose sight of the implications for housing markets. Transportation technology has been a principal influence on patterns of land development throughout the nation's history (Hoyt, 1960). Adams (1970) details how housing development closely matches the prevailing mode of transport, as discussed previously.

The role of the automobile is especially important, not only for making more land accessible for housing, but also for causing obsolescence of pre-1920 construction. Guest (1974) speculates that, although his neighborhood cohort analysis revealed no downward filtering after 1940, it is possible that some of the oldest neighborhoods may have suffered an earlier, one-time drop when the automobile was first introduced. If we incorporate Adams's (1970) observations that those earlier vintages were built in the era of walking and street car transportation, a better understanding emerges. Lacking provision for garages and parking, those dwellings whose lot configurations did not permit retrofitting became rapidly outmoded. To a lesser degree, even 1930s dwellings with one-car garages have been in jeopardy, because the market expectation by the 1960s was for middle-class single-family houses to have two-car garages and room for two more cars in a wide driveway. How else to care for the transportation needs of husband and wife, plus boats, lawn equipment, and teenagers' needs? The alternative is cars parked on the streets and lawns, a distinct sign of a "substandard" neighborhood.

The construction of housing and its mechanical equipment and plumbing all reflect contemporary technological norms and stylistic fashion. It was relatively easy to add wiring for electricity to gas-lighting-era housing, but it is much more expensive to retrofit plumbing for added bathrooms or to renovate kitchens with modern cabinetry and appliances. Without these changes, older houses grow outdated and become less competitive as standards continue to evolve. For example, as recently as 1977, only 16.4 percent of single-family houses built pre-1940 and 25.0 percent of houses built in the 1940s and 1950s had at least two bathrooms. This contrasts with 68.3 percent of houses built in the 1970s. Similarly, only 8.6 percent of houses built pre-1940 and 22.2 percent of houses built in the 1940s and 1950s had central air conditioning installed, whereas this is true of 60.9 percent of 1970s houses (Myers, 1982: table 3).

Housing of earlier eras is also marked by much less efficient energy conservation, not simply because of technological limitations, but because prior to the energy crisis of the 1970s this was a low-priority concern during construction. Insulation in the attic is easily added, but not so in the walls, and it is expensive to replace windows and other fittings.

In sum, it is clear that technology and building standards of earlier eras leave a relatively permanent mark on housing units, placing older units at a disadvantage. Only in cases where the older architectural style, or fashion, has superredeeming value, or where the location of the older unit has a premium site value for residential use, will we likely find older homes that remain competitive with modern new construction.

Government Programs and Policies

A final set of changing historical conditions involves the government programs and policies in each period. Oftentimes these involve highly visible changes, because they are debated politically aforehand and put in place by conscious purpose. For this reason, we run the risk of overestimating their contribution to the filtering context. In practice, it is difficult to separate the impacts of government from underlying market forces; the two so often are intertwined.

Among the most potent government influences on filtering in the post–World War II era are the innovative FHA and VA mortgage insurance programs (Checkoway, 1980), the federal system of interstate highways and metropolitan freeways, and local zoning restrictions (Downs, 1977). Other programs such as urban renewal, court-ordered school busing for racial integration, and federal tax credits for historic preservation also are of influence.

Not wishing to dwell on each and every government program, I will state the broad point: the introduction of a new program or policy unsettles the existing order. Filtering activity may accelerate in the short term as part of an equilibrating process. It would be unwise to view this adjustment period as part of the normal process of filtering.

For example, the new federal mortgage programs made homeownership achievable to families at a much younger age than before by reducing the required downpayment and lowering the monthly mortgage payments. Moreover, FHA policies favored new construction over existing neighborhoods. (And the new freeway system opened up vast amounts of cheap land in the suburbs). As a consequence, middle-class, would-be residents of rental units in older neighborhoods were abruptly siphoned off in the early postwar era. This accelerated movement to the suburbs cannot be viewed as a "normal" operation of filtering. It took a decade or more for equilibrium to be restored.

Reevaluating Traditional Assumptions about Filtering

To illustrate the utility of an improved temporal model of filtering, let us reexamine some selected assumptions about the normal filtering behavior of dwellings and households. Which of these assumptions are historically bound and which are relatively timeless? This review applies the reason of the foregoing conceptual discussion, together with a smattering of historical evidence. The conclusions reached may serve as hypotheses for subsequent research.

Place of the Elderly in the Housing Life Cycle

First, it often is assumed that the housing life cycle of the middle class involves living in apartments in the city as young adults, followed by a move to single-family houses in the suburbs, and ending frequently in elderly years with a return to apartment living in the city. Only recently has it been recognized that elderly are "moving" to the suburbs by virtue of their aging in place.

This simple housing life cycle dates from observations made in the 1950s (Abu-Lughod and Foley, 1966). These observations were cross-sectional; that is, households were compared at a given point in time. The most likely reason that elderly were found in the city is that they always had lived there. The suburbs were too new to have hosted the current generation of elderly when they were age 30 or so. Thus there could not be direct evidence linking the suburbs with a complete housing life cycle.

Perhaps some elderly did actually move from single-family houses in the city to apartments. Yet this may be a reflection of the large size of the older vintage houses they likely had been occupying. In contrast, the early postwar suburbs were built up with small houses that are much better suited for elderly occupancy. Not only are these smaller, but also many are even single-level ranch style, eliminating the nuisance of stair climbing. In fact, Pitkin and Masnick (1980) show evidence that elderly of earlier generations were much more likely to trade down from their single-family house than are those who reached age 30 after 1940.

In sum, the elderly stage of the housing life cycle has been misread. Today we find a great many elderly aging in place in the suburbs, potentially undermaintaining their houses (Myers, 1984), but we do not really know how much of a change this poses in the normal context for the filtering of their houses and neighborhoods.

Cutting Up Old Units

A major axiom of the life-cycle filtering model is that houses will be converted to more intensive use as they grow older. This expectation derives from Hoover and Vernon's (1959) assessment of the age cross-section in the New York City area and has been faithfully handed down in the filtering literature. Indeed, the recent upsurge of accessory apartments in middle-class neighborhoods seems to reflect a contemporary expression of the expected life-cycle progression.

In fact, we may reason that unique historical events encouraged conversions to multiple units, creating the impression that this is an expected life-cycle stage. Hoover and Vernon's original observation reflects the outcome of one-time events earlier in the century. As reported above, the shortfall of construction during the 1930s and 1940s meant over half again as many households were formed as new units were built. The solution to this constraint was to convert older dwellings to multiple units. And the older units available at that time were of a vintage when houses were typically very large (eight or more rooms). These large old homes had been outmoded for single-family use by middle-class families, because their lots were not configured to accommodate the automobiles owned by such families. Given the falling household sizes in this century and the shortfall of new construction, conversion of these large old homes was a rational solution.

Should conversion be expected of other vintages in different eras as well? The 1940s and 1950s houses were much smaller than their predecessors, making conversion more difficult. And in the absence of another major construction shortfall such as that experienced in the 1930s and 1940s, we would not anticipate demand for conversion. Indeed, rising costs of homeownership have made these 1940s and 1950s houses seem relatively more affordable and desirable to young homebuyers (Myers, 1984). Hence, demand remains strong to preserve these units in single-family use.

The recent proliferation of accessory apartments in former single-family homes seems to violate this conclusion. Yet we note that these conversions are ancillary to the main unit of the home, with owner-occupancy retained. Moreover, the space restrictions noted for 1940s and 1950s houses still apply, making accessory apartments viable only for older vintages or for 1960s and 1970s houses. In fact, the demand for these units is directed again by unique historical conditions. Homeowners facing the soaring housing prices of the 1970s were motivated to seek extra sources of rental income to help with mortgage payments. Conversely, on the tenant side, the arrival of the baby-boom generation at adulthood spurred a surge in demand for small rental units. Zoning restrictions and absence of developable land prevented builders from meeting this demand in large portions of the urban area. The accessory-unit providers have met this unsatisfied demand. However, that demand for small rental units is now tapering off in most cities, because the baby-boom generation has been absorbed into the market and is passing into the homeownership stage. Instead, by the late 1980s most urban areas experienced substantial overconstruction of new apartment complexes, producing large surpluses of vacant rental units that will depress demand for accessory-unit conversions in the future.

Middle-Class Flight and Dwelling Deterioration

A further axiom of filtering theory is the belief that middle-class flight to new housing in the suburbs is part of a normal process causing older housing to run down. Again, the strength of this phenomenon depends upon the historical circumstances. In this regard, the early postwar period was anomalous and not a stable environment for deciphering normal patterns. A number of factors created unique conditions in the 1950s.

Two decades of depression and war, followed by economic boom, served first to compress and then to decompress housing demand, with violent repercussions. Moreover, as Hoyt (1940) observed early on, the seeds for decentralization had already been sown. As discussed above, young families experienced dramatic income growth during the first decade after the war (Levy and Michel, 1985), enabling many to leave behind their outdated quarters in cramped inner-city neighborhoods. Aided by the revolutionary FHA and VA mortgage programs (Checkoway, 1980), and by the new mass-production of homes in large tract developments (Eichler, 1982), families could buy new homes at a much younger age than before. The result was a sudden surge toward the suburbs.

Not only was the outward movement of middle-class families accelerated, but their potential numbers in the city were depressed by a peculiar wrinkle in the nation's age structure. As Goetze and Colton (1980) observe, fewer persons were born in the late 1920s and 1930s than in prior decades. Thus as families moved out of the city during the 1950s, there was a shortage of young households to fill the vacancies they left behind. When combined with the curtailment of immigration that had occurred 20 years earlier, creating an absence of second-generation children who would now be entering the market, the traditional population base of the inner city was severely weakened, as Hoyt (1940) prophesied.

Older neighborhoods suffered a sudden and dramatic loss of middle-class residents. In the case of St. Louis, Lowry (1980) describes a "decanting" of the urban population that was previously pent up in densely packed older neighborhoods of outdated housing. The result of the sudden decompression was a collapse of St. Louis's inner-city demand by white families and a destabilization of the whole housing market. As noted previously, much of the slack in northern cities was taken up by black migrants from the South. Racial change was viewed by many as a cause of property deterioration rather than as the symptom of rapid depletion of demand.

In sum, the pattern of rapid social change and property deterioration was the product of extreme conditions. Compression and decompression, aided by new government programs, created an extraordinary acceleration of normal filtering.

Decline Precedes Land Use Succession

The final stage in the life-cycle filtering model is renewal, or redevelopment with a new land use. Land use succession is also a hallmark of mid-twentieth-century theory in urban land economics (Ratcliff, 1949; Andrews, 1971). The presumption of both theories is that a property must run down before it is renewed.

In temporal perspective, we might note a congruence between the pace of change in the life cycle of a property over, say, 80 years and historical change in market conditions governing use of a property. After so many years, the land use structure, transportation access, and economics surrounding a site would change greatly. By the time the property had physically deteriorated and its economic return had fallen below fixed and variable carrying costs, conditions would have ripened for a new use of the site.

Yet it is not hard to imagine cases where rapid historical change might overtake the more deliberate pace of a dwelling's downward filtration. Catanese (1986) provides an excellent illustration of such an instance in the organized buyouts of single-family neighborhoods in Atlanta for the purpose of office developments. Wholesale purchase of 40 or more properties has been orchestrated in order to assemble a large enough contiguous parcel and to warrant the zoning change required. The price differential between office and residential land has been such that homeowners have been paid two or three times their appraised residential values.

What is noteworthy about the Atlanta buyouts is that they have involved barely mature, solidly middle-class subdivisions. No more than 25 years old, the dwellings have not entered a decline stage. The explanation for the anomaly is that new freeways have been constructed since 1975 in the northern suburbs. Convergence of two other historical changes—a nationwide trend toward suburbanization of offices and a local trend toward rapid growth of the Atlanta economy—has sharply altered the "highest and best use" of certain residential districts.

In sum, property deterioration is not a requirement for land use succession. Rapid historical change may alter the market context surrounding a property more quickly than the property can deteriorate. Succession is expected whenever the return on a new use exceeds the old use by a premium sufficient to finance the transition and when zoning regulations can be revised. However, the buyout phenomenon underscores that such conditions for succession may occur, not only because the return on the former use has declined, but also because rapid historical change has sharply advanced the potential return on alternative uses.

The Anomaly of Gentrification

As a final application of the temporal conceptual model of filtering, we take up the example of gentrification. The expectation in filtering is for deterioration of properties over time and consequent downward filtration to lower-income households. This expectation is so embedded in usage of the filtering concept that the term "trickle-down" is widely used as a synonym for filtering. The emergence since 1970 of gentrification, or neighborhood revitalization, in selected neighborhoods of many cities forces a broadening of filtering theory.

How are we to explain this exception to the downward movement many expect of filtering? Of course, a few examples of neighborhoods that retained high status for many decades and never declined, such as Beacon Hill in Boston (Firey, 1947) have long been recognized, but the act of spontaneous renewal is less precedented. Andrews's (1971) model of land use succession includes a "renewal" stage, but this seems expectant of urban renewal or private redevelopment. Instead, gentrification has reclaimed existing housing structures, rehabilitating them and repositioning them to higher price levels. Even if Andrews's model is extended to include such renovation activity, we still must explain why this has occurred when it has.

In brief, the explanation likely centers on four events. First, the rising cost of housing in the 1970s created pressure on young, middle-class households to find affordable housing in bargain locations. Rising prices also justified rehabilitation activity by landlords or owner-occupants, as in Lowry's (1960) model. Second, the growth of office employment in the downtowns of certain cities created a strong attraction for educated, white-collar workers (Berry, 1985).

As a third factor, the arrival of the baby-boom generation in the housing market concentrated abnormally large amounts of demand in submarkets appealing to young adults. Traditionally, this young demand has focused in selected apartment districts of central cities, as explained by the "bright lights" theory of migration (Long and Glick, 1976). The excess of would-be tenants drove up rents in the most desirable areas, and the overflow of dwelling-seekers found housing in marginal neighborhoods on the periphery. Finally, lifestyle changes occurred among the babyboomers, such that marriages and parenthood were delayed. This meant that the oversized cohort was also prone to remain in the central city longer than previous generations, further inflating their numbers. When these city residents reached their late 20s they moved from renting to buying homes in the city, initially causing many to conclude erroneously that there was a "back to the city" movement by former suburbanites. In short, central-city markets faced a demand shock: attuned to declining demand when the small cohorts born in the late 1920s and 1930s reached adulthood (1950–65), a radical reversal occurred when the babyboomers became active after 1970.

Elsewhere, I have stressed how potent is the force of upward mobility (Myers, 1983). With so many young households entering the bottom of the housing market and then pushing upward toward larger and more expensive dwellings, the downward drift of a scarce supply of well-located central-city housing was counteracted (see Figure 12.1). Indeed, deterioration was halted and even reversed as the rise in prices permitted improved maintenance. Landlords and owner-occupants renovated properties to educated, middle-class tastes, repositioning the properties in higher-priced brackets, where supply was most scarce.

In sum, gentrification is an outcome of normal filtering processes fed by unique historical circumstances. Gentrification does not imply the end of trickle-down; that force is only in temporary abeyance. Historical conditions will change once more; we know the bulge of young households will subside once the baby-boom generation passes on to middle age. Also, demand will be diverted away from the central city by the increased movement of office construction to the suburbs and by the large supply of vacant suburban apartments. In the early 1990s, we are likely once again to see shrinking middle-class demand in central cities, and the gains of gentrification may be rolled back.

Conclusion

An explicit focus on time yields increased understanding of urban structure and change. I have not overturned existing theories about filtering; the economics of supply and demand still rule. But a temporal framework provides a much sharper context for understanding the economics of filtering.

Application of the demographer's notion of time, with its three components of period, life cycle, and cohort, leads to important insights. We learn to appreciate the cohort effects created by pronounced differences between different vintages of houses. And we are better able to see how a variety of unique historical conditions interact to create different filtering scenarios. Perhaps of greatest importance, distinguishing the three dimensions of time clarifies the fallacy of cross-section life-cycle models of filtering. Such cross-sectional observations confuse true age effects with unique vintage (cohort) differences.

Throughout the chapter I have indicated where traditional theory about filtering is historically bound. In particular, much of our theoretical base derives from observations made in the 1950s and early 1960s. The period reflected upon is perhaps the least stable of this century. The combination of Great Depression and World War II influences followed by the 1950s explosive growth leads to a greatly accelerated filtering process. The unsettling impact of the automobile's introduction also was still being absorbed in this period by units built prior to 1920. Traditional theory dating from the 1950s deserves scrutiny for its historical bias.

The analysis of this chapter has centered on the housing stock. Where appropriate, I have made reference to population factors that impact on demand, and hence on the stock. But I have not developed the population side of the equation. A fuller temporal model of filtering would carry out a historical analysis of households' three time dimensions as well. Although this chapter points the way, the longitudinal interaction of supply and demand at the heart of filtering requires much further study.

References

Abu-Lughod, J., and M. M. Foley. 1966. The consumer votes by moving. Pp. 175–191 in W. L. C. Wheaton, G. Milgram, and M. E. Meyerson (eds.), *Urban Housing*. New York: The Free Press.

Adams, J. S. 1970. The residential structure of midwestern cities. *Annals, Association of American Geographers* 60:37–62.

Alonso, W. 1980. The population factor in urban structure. Pp. 32–51 in A. P. Solomon (ed.), *The Prospective City*. Cambridge, Mass.: MIT Press.

Andrews, R. B. 1971. *Urban Land Economics and Public Policy*. London: The Free Press.

Baer, W. C., and C. B. Williamson. 1988. The filtering of households and housing units. *Journal of Planning Literature* 3:127–152.

Berry, B. J. L. 1985. Islands of renewal in seas of decay. Pp. 69–96 in K. Bradbury and A. Downs (eds.), *The New Urban Reality*. Washington, D. C.: The Brookings Institution.

Birch, D. L. 1971. Toward a stage theory of urban growth. *Journal of the American Institute of Planners* 37:78–87.

Bourne, L. S. 1981. *The Geography of Housing*. New York: John Wiley.

Campbell, B. O. 1966. *Population Change and Building Cycles*. Urbana, Illinois: University of Illinois, Bureau of Economic Research.

Catanese, A. J. 1986. The neighborhood buyout phenomenon. *Journal of Real Estate Development* 2:45–53.

Checkoway, B. 1980. Large builders, federal housing programmes, and postwar suburbanization. *International Journal of Urban and Regional Research* 4:21–44.

Downs, A. 1960. An economic analysis of property values and race. *Land Economics* 36:181–188.

Downs, A. 1977. The impact of housing policies on family life in the U.S. since WW II. *Daedalus* 106(2):163–180.

Duncan, B., G. Sabagh, and M. D. Van Arsdol, Jr. 1962. Patterns of city growth. *American Journal of Sociology* 67:418–429.

Eichler, N. 1982. *The Merchant Builders*. Cambridge, Mass.: MIT Press.

Firey, W. 1947. *Land Use in Central Boston*. Cambridge, Mass.: Harvard University Press.

Fisher, E. M., and L. Winnick. 1951. A reformulation of the filtering concept. *Journal of Social Issues* 7:47–58.

Goetze, R., and K. W. Colton. 1980. The dynamics of neighborhoods: A fresh approach to understanding housing and neighborhood change. *Journal of the American Planning Association* 46:184–194.

Guest, A. M. 1974. Neighborhood life cycles and social status. *Economic Geography* 50:228–243.

Herter, C. L. 1977. The "good times" cohort of the 1930s. *PRB Report* 3(3):1–4.

Hoover, E. M., and R. Vernon. 1959. *Anatomy of a Metropolis*. Cambridge, Mass.: Harvard University Press.

Hoyt, H. 1940. Urban decentralization. *Journal of Land and Public Utility Economics* 16:268–276.

Hoyt, H. 1960. Changing patterns of land values. *Land Economics* 36(2):107–117.

Kendig, H. L. 1984. Housing careers, life cycle and residential mobility: implications for the housing market. *Urban Studies* 21:271–283.

Lansing, J. B., C. W. Clifton, and J. N. Morgan. 1969. *New Homes and Poor People: A Study of Chains of Moves*. Ann Arbor: University of Michigan, Institute for Social Research.

Levy, F. S., and R. C. Michel. 1985. *The Economic Future of the Baby Boom*. Research report. Washington, D.C.: The Urban Institute.

Long, L. H., and P. C. Glick. 1976. Family patterns in suburban areas: Recent trends. Pp. 39–67 in B. Schwartz (ed.), *The Changing Face of the Suburbs*. Chicago: University of Chicago Press.

Lowry, I. S. 1960. Filtering and housing standards. *Land Economics* 35:362–370.

Lowry, I. S. 1980. The dismal future of central cities. Pp. 161–203 in A. P. Solomon (ed.), *The Prospective City*. Cambridge, Mass.: MIT Press.

Mason, K. O., W. M. Mason, H. H. Winsborough, and W. K. Poole. 1973. Some methodological issues in cohort analysis of archival data. *American Sociological Review* 38:242–258.

Meier, R. B. 1983. Code enforcement and housing quality revisited: The turnover case. *Urban Affairs Quarterly* 19:255–273.

Myers, D. 1982. *Impact of Filtering Processes on the Conservation and Use of Early Postwar Single Family Homes*. Final report to the U.S. Department of Housing and Urban Development. HUD Grant No. H-5404SG.

Myers, D. 1983. Upward mobility and the filtering process. *Journal of Planning Education and Research* 2:101–112.

Myers, D. 1984. Turnover and filtering of postwar single-family houses. *Journal of the American Planning Association* 50:352–358.

Palmore, E. 1978. When can age, period, and cohort be separated? *Social Forces* 57:282–295.

Pitkin, J., and G. S. Masnick. 1980. *Projections of Housing Consumption in the U.S., 1980–2000, by a Cohort Method*. Annual Housing Survey Studies No. 9. Washington, D.C.: U.S. Government Printing Office.

Ratcliff, R. U. 1949. *Urban Land Economics*. New York: McGraw-Hill.

Riley, M., et al. (eds.). 1972. *Aging and Society.* New York: Russell Sage Foundation.

Sands, G., and L. L. Bower. 1976. *Housing Turnover and Housing Policy: Case Studies of Vacancy Chains in New York State.* New York: Praeger.

Taeuber, K. E., and A. F. Taeuber. 1965. *Negroes in Cities: Residential Segregation and Neighborhood Change.* Chicago: Aldine.

13 *Dowell Myers*

Conclusion: Future Research in Housing Demography

The preceding chapters have afforded a comprehensive sampling of research into the various subtopics of housing demography. We have described theoretical frameworks for linking housing and demographic variables, and we have illustrated the field with a good many research applications. Yet the surface of a vast set of research questions has been hardly scratched. The concluding chapter explores future avenues for research that join housing and demography.

Integration of population and housing research promises novel and important contributions to basic knowledge among both demographers and housing researchers in the social sciences. As evidenced in this book, researchers have already profited from linking the two sets of variables. Now, with a more systematic grasp of housing demography's domain, and with an introduction to exploratory efforts across diverse fields, research in the future is likely to proceed more efficiently and yield accelerated contributions to scientific knowledge.

The greatest importance of housing demography may be for research addressing questions about subnational populations, particularly counties, cities, and neighborhoods. The science of demography is largely directed toward national-level populations, affording relative neglect to topics of internal distribution and change. Because the variation of housing-stock characteristics is so extreme among subareas of urban regions, it is vital to understand how housing factors interrelate with demographic characteristics. Rising interest in applied demography, with its focus on state and local populations and on the neighborhood locations of consumers, has given particular impetus to housing-demographic research.

Despite its rich potential, the interface between population and housing remains relatively unexplored for a reason. I begin our concluding chapter with a discussion of the current barriers that have discouraged more integrative research. Recognizing these paradigmatic challenges, we are better able to craft practical arguments in support of the emerging field. We propose an agenda of housing-demographic research that may produce vital contributions to scientific knowledge.

Breaking Down the Barriers

Upon reflection it is remarkable that an area with so much promise for theoretical development and applied research should remain so neglected and underexplored by scholars. This neglect is particularly surprising in view of the widely available data bases that link sets of housing and demographic variables at the household level. Not only is the American Housing Survey the least utilized major data base in the United States, but the housing half of the decennial census is also lightly considered.

Explanations for this curious neglect were offered in the Introduction. In brief, traditional barriers between the disciplines and differences in the priorities of public and private agencies who fund research have divided research inquiries into separate realms. Earlier, Peter Rossi's experience with housing research as a sociologist was related. Despite his seminal contribution linking family life-cycle analysis to housing questions, his efforts were strongly discouraged by those in his parent discipline. He had crossed beyond the appropriate boundaries ascribed to paradigms acceptable within sociology.

Such paradigm restrictions persist to this day. In light of scarce research funds to support investigations, review panels for funding agencies may be rational in giving priority to those projects seemingly more central to their agencies' goals and objectives. Spanning the gap between housing and population is rarely a central objective of any research-funding agency. When housing-demographic interactions are at the periphery of an agency's concern, special care is required to demonstrate their importance to the agency's mandate. Pursuits of basic knowledge are likely to be supported only if focused on central issues already assumed to be important. Along the periphery of the agency's concerns, proposed research is more likely to be supported if it is less basic and more overtly tied to practical issues of concern.

Review comments from a major federal agency in the late 1980s are illustrative of difficulties to be encountered. A research proposal sought greater understanding of the changing population structure within cities by incorporating information on the nature of housing occupied by households. Broad national demographic trends could then be differentiated more finely in terms of neighborhoods with different types of housing stocks. Not only would this information enhance basic scientific knowledge about the linkage between population change and living arrangements, but it also could provide the foundation for improved methods of small-area demography (although those applied methods were not to be developed in this proposal). The proposal was approved for funding, but with a very low priority. It received no criticism on technical grounds; instead, the weakness was judged as lack of "importance." The reviewers' summary comments capsulize the issue very well:

> The proposal focuses on data demographers seldom use and on questions they seldom ask. The proposal originates from a set of facts: 1) the Census collects data on individuals/households and on housing characteristics. 2) People live in houses. 3) People and houses have ages and belong to certain cohorts. From these facts flow research possibilities. . . .
>
> While there has been some research in this area . . . it is not clear why the proposed research is important. . . . How will understanding this connection [of population and housing] contribute to broader theories of population adjustment or to public policy debates?

The proposed research failed the test of importance because it was not anchored sufficiently to the central concerns of the agency. In an era of limited resources for research support, it is insufficient to identify a neglected area of research that is of peripheral interest and holds only vague prospects of contributing to the agency's central concerns. More concrete and practical results from the research must be explicitly identified. As a result, most successful studies have ventured into housing demography at its margins, expanding from existing agency concerns and existing knowledge bases, then showing how these are incrementally improved by incorporating some of the new variables or relationships.

Important Contributions to Knowledge

This book is the first to address the emerging field of housing demography comprehensively and systematically. As such it bears a special burden of justifying the importance of the new mode of analysis. With a clearer view of the field's dimensions and potential contributions, researchers may be able to plot their investigations more strategically.

Similarly, with a clearer portrayal of the central precepts and potential value of housing-demographic research, greater support may begin to emerge from both the funding agencies and the academic community.

Integration of population and housing research can contribute to scientific knowledge on both sides of the fence by sharing insights from the other. For demographers, the contributions in this book should help researchers who study household structure, migration, and ecology to think more about the housing dimensions of their subjects. For housing analysts from other social sciences (economics, geography, and planning), the contributions presented here may help researchers to think more about the demographic processes that underlie housing dynamics.

Each of the advantages to be cited is a research opportunity, and the aggregation of these opportunities constitutes a research agenda for the emerging field. What follows is a series of 10 research topics, with brief supporting rationales, four of which might appeal especially to demographers and six of which might hold special interest for housing researchers from the social sciences. In reality, some of these topics may hold equal appeal for both groups of researchers, illustrating how central a meeting ground is the field of housing demography.

Research Opportunities for Demographers

Impact of Housing Costs
Evidence is clear that housing costs are a factor shaping household living arrangements among young unrelated individuals and the elderly. This is apparent in chapters by Ken Chew and John Pitkin. Housing costs also affect the type or quality of housing chosen by female-headed households (chapter by Daphne Spain) and by young households seeking to become homeowners. In the face of these cost constraints, the struggle to achieve desired standards of living has reciprocal impacts on the lifestyles and composition of households, as reviewed by Hal Kendig and in the Introduction. Kendig makes a forceful argument that housing careers deserve to be integrated in analyses of life course events.

The housing shelter for population is often assumed to be of inconsequential importance in the United States (but not in Eastern Europe, where housing shortages are widely blamed for depressed fertility). Yet housing is one of the two largest items in the family budget (along with food) and also serves to anchor the household in space. Only if supply were unlimited, if cost were not an issue, and if there were no differences in housing between places would housing *not* be a significant factor in behavior related to household structure.

Local Migration Is Housing Based

Considerations that direct the migration behavior of population on the national level are different from those that direct it below this level. On smaller geographic scales, particularly the county or below, migration becomes residential mobility, as shown in this book in the chapter by Eric Moore and W. A. V. Clark. Explicit attention to housing variables and how these appeal to different subgroups will improve the causal basis underlying current demographic models. More explicit causal explanation of local migration or mobility is clearly consistent with criteria for scientific progress.

Examples of research questions to explore include: First, to what degree might migration between states be impacted by growing housing-cost differentials and consequent affordability problems, such as in the New England region or California? Second, to what extent do migration rates in counties of large urban regions reflect underlying differences in their housing stock's appeal to different age groups? And third, does the rate of new house construction, which fluctuates with the business cycle, speed up or slow down mobility (by increasing or decreasing the supply of houses available to movers)?

Housing Characteristics Link to Household Characteristics

Contributions in this book also demonstrate how the nature of local housing stocks attracts households with different demographic composition. Small apartments fit small households and large single-family homes fit larger households. However, historical inertia and the aging of household compositions serve to alter the expected configurations. Chapters by James Sweet, Daphne Spain, Patricia Gober, Dowell Myers and Alan Doyle, George Masnick, John Pitkin, and John Brennan probe this linkage of household and housing characteristics in different ways.

The greater importance of linking housing and household characteristics is not description of associations at a single point in time, but rather explanation of changes over time. To measure change over time, Sweet employs repeated cross-sections, comparing 1970 and 1980 distributions, Myers and Doyle use a single cross-section of highly detailed age groups and housing vintages, and Masnick and his colleagues employ a unique cohort framework tracing occupancy groups longitudinally. It is of intrinsic scientific interest how best to model the interaction over time of joint distributions of population characteristics and housing characteristics.

Improving the Basis for Small-Area Demography

Attention to housing variables contributes to the broad scientific progress of small-area and urban demography. These subfields of general demography have relied largely on the standard methods developed for analysis of national populations. However, at the local level, sharp neighborhood differences in housing-stock characteristics intrude into the behavior of populations and must be modeled. For example, typologies of migration rates for different types of counties represent an atheoretical, noncausal method hoped to capture some of the migration differences better explained by housing differences.

The applied, housing unit method of population estimation is the sole demographic method that has emerged in recognition of housing's importance for small-area demography, although the chapter by Myers and Doyle illustrates how this method can evolve into a more richly structured framework. Greater scientific attention to housing-stock characteristics holds the key to developing a stronger theoretical base for small-area demography and should lead to important scientific advances with regard to population dynamics in urban subareas.

Housing forms the essential substructure for small-area demography. The omission of housing variables from small-area models is inefficient, because it neglects much of the information content contained in the census or administrative records. Moreover, neglect of the underlying housing factors creates the risk of spurious relationships being estimated in small areas among population variables and spatial-location variables. Mere incorporation of total housing figures, or changes therein, is insufficient to represent housing-based processes. More systematic and detailed treatment of housing relationships clearly would be wise.

Opportunities for Linking Demographic Concepts to Housing Research within the Other Social Sciences

Demographic Characteristics Shape Housing Demand
Chapters by Jim Sweet, John Pitkin, and George Masnick and his colleagues focus most directly on how demographic characteristics shape housing demand, although all the chapters have some bearing. The associations are very strong, but researchers have yet to settle on the formulation that most fully explains variations in demand. Sweet's family life-cycle model of aggregate change in housing demand improves on earlier versions, giving special emphasis to the demographic processes that shape the distribution of persons among different life-cycle categories. The chapters by Pitkin and by Masnick and his colleagues explore the advantages of alternative temporal frameworks—cohort models— for measuring change over time.

In recent years, economists have been exploring how demographic characteristics of households shape their use of income to purchase housing. More work is required to sort out the interaction between these demographic characteristics and income or wealth in the purchase of different bundles of housing services. One research frontier concerns how much the demographic effects vary in accordance with market conditions, whether over time or between places. A related frontier concerns testing the utility of demographic versus economic frameworks for projecting housing demand over longer time frames. Interest rates and other economic variables are so much more difficult to forecast with reliability that the demographic variables may be more dependable for projections of 5, 10, or more years (within which range fertility fluctuations have no impact on the number of future households).

Occupational and Educational Characteristics Shape Demand

In addition to the effects of demographic characteristics, Ken Chew demonstrates in his chapter how strongly the business mix of a region shapes the demand for separate dwelling units by unmarried young adults. Even controlling for differences in income and housing prices and for population growth, a local economy dominated by blue-collar employment will generate fewer household formations than one dominated by knowledge-intensive employment. Young adults who are more highly educated and/ or who work in highly skilled occupations appear to have substantially higher propensities to set up their own separate households.

This novel finding begs for further research into the interaction between economic structure, migration, and rates of household formation. Projections of housing demand possibly may be improved significantly if household formation rates are adjusted for occupational and educational characteristics of the different areas.

Adopting Demographers' Sensitivity to Temporal Process

A major strength of the demographic paradigm is its emphasis on time. In a shallow usage of demography, many social scientists have added static demographic characteristics to their models. The more fundamental approach is to incorporate demographers' temporal structure, such as is demonstrated for economists in this book by John Pitkin's cohort economic model or Hal Kendig's review of life course theories about housing demand. Individuals and households have histories and futures that are structured in time and influenced by economic forces along the way. Some of the forces yield immediate effects; others are lagged from many years earlier.

Such a temporal focus can be applied directly to the stock of housing as well. The chapter by William Baer addresses changes in the housing stock that occur over time, tracing the transfiguration and ultimate mortality of housing units. The chapter on filtering and time by Myers seeks to reinterpret traditional views of filtering through the lens of demographers' three-dimensional definition of time: age, period, and cohort. Housing vintages are equivalent to cohorts, formed at one period in history and impacted by market conditions of successive periods. Our "snapshot" pictures of an age cross-section of housing units capture vintages with these different histories (and with very different original characteristics). Analyses at a single point in time often misjudge the dynamics of filtering because of inattention to the underlying temporal dynamics. Substantial errors of interpretation can be avoided by borrowing demographers' more careful treatment of time.

Housing Careers Intertwined with Other Decisions in the Life Course

Not only can we study how housing choices are linked in a cumulative sequence—the career notion—but we can also study how current decisions within housing careers are contingent upon decisions in other careers (e.g., labor force, marital, or child rearing). These different life dimensions are mutually dependent because they compete for time within the household. Although careers are somewhat age scheduled, with "normal" ages for entering different stages, the old notion of a fixed set of life-cycle stages has been replaced by the newer concept of a life course (see chapter 6 by Hal Kendig). The more modern theory is more flexible, not assuming what is the normal age for entering a stage or what is the proper sequence or what behaviors should be bundled together. The key objective is to research how life course behavior has changed over time by studying changes in the contingencies of different behaviors and by measuring changes in the relative timing of different events.

We might ask a host of questions about housing demand with respect to other life course issues. For example, one major question is, How old are people when they first buy a house and has this changed from earlier generations? A second question is, How does the changing labor-force behavior of women interact with housing demand? A third question might be, What are the changes in housing demand that accompany changes in retirement ages and longevity? A final question, which has been addressed by Daphne Spain, concerns the housing circumstances of female-headed households following marital disruption: How do they handle this transition?

It deserves note that the policy implications of life course analyses are different from economic analyses. Instead of asking how income groups fare in the market place, the focus is on people's experience in years.

MYERS: *Conclusion*   305

For example, should housing assistance be offered to all persons below a given income level, or only to those of certain ages? We already target aid to the elderly, but this is a special exception. What if age were made a major criterion for measuring and judging need? Would young adults under age 25 have the same claim to special homeownership assistance as middle-aged adults of the same income who had not yet been able to afford a house on their own? Research based upon the rich notion of life course and intertwined life-career dimensions raises important new perspectives for policy makers.

Integrating Changes in Household Structure
with Changes in Residential Mobility
Researchers have long recognized that life-cycle factors are crucial for explaining residential mobility by individual households. One current frontier concerns explanation of differences in mobility between markets, as is demonstrated in the chapter by Eric Moore and W. A. V. Clark. Another concerns the aggregate impact on mobility patterns of changes in household structure over time. To what extent do changes in households over the last 15 years explain the general slowdown in mobility rates? A third research issue concerns the amount of importance to ascribe to household changes as motivators of mobility in different urban populations. For example, is it true that in traditionally low-mobility cities a much greater share of all moves are not housing motivated but involuntary, that is, dictated by demographic events of marriage, divorce, or other family change?

Integrating the Changing Life Course
with Changing Urban Patterns
Urban geographers have already contributed some of the leading work related to housing demography. Recognizing the richly differentiated, spatial distribution of the housing stock, these scholars have sought to learn more about how demographic processes interact with the fixed housing stock to create distinct social neighborhoods. The key frontier for this line of research is triggered by recognition that, at the same time as family and household behavior is rapidly changing in the nation, the classic models of who lives where in the city are being negated. In her chapter, Patricia Gober calls for a more integrated model that might link four components: the backdrop of national change in life course behavior; dynamics of residential mobility in neighborhoods; household-level dynamics of compositional change among the nonmovers; and the anchoring of these social changes with respect to a spatial landscape of housing alternatives within the city.

Conclusion

The emerging field of housing demography addresses a long-time over-sight in the social sciences. Despite strong practical and theoretical grounds, traditional barriers have discouraged the integration of housing and demographic research. This separation of the two halves of the U.S. decennial census is regretable in view of the ready availability of this major data resource. Penetrating this divide, increasing numbers of exploratory efforts have been initiated that link population and housing variables. However, the fragmented structure of communication across disciplines and a notable lack of funding support have hampered these early efforts.

Many have tinkered at the margins of housing demography, adding a housing variable here or a demographic variable there. With a few notable exceptions, these efforts have remained fairly superficial and primitive in their rediscovery of simple truths. A glaring weakness of most of the exploratory research is its lack of guidance by the cumulative experience of other scholars, a deficiency reflected in relatively barren lists of citations to other housing-demographic studies. Scattered across so many different disciplines, experimental efforts relating housing and demographic variables have gone relatively unnoticed. And there has been a distinct lack of theory focused directly on the integration of population and housing processes.

With the present work, we have tried to fill the need for greater communication and more systematic paradigm development. We have articulated a comprehensive and systematic rationale for housing demography. Our diverse set of chapters supports this, illustrating both the scope of the interdisciplinary field and the important research discoveries awaiting scholars who explore across the divide. The coining of a shared term of identity, "housing demography," may help also as a needed signpost for assembling scholars from across the social sciences.

In its ultimate expression, housing demography may become a highly ambitious and complex paradigm. Stated most briefly, researchers would address questions concerning national-level demographic change, linking these to questions about changing patterns of housing occupancy, and then bring this complex portrait down to the local level, where economic factors shape demand and where we can spatially differentiate the dynamics of housing-demographic change. It may not be possible to address such a conceptual model within a single, comprehensive research project, and its full scope is not required for every research question, yet the comprehensive vision of housing demography represents a useful model from which to extract more manageable slices for analysis.

The success of this book will be determined by whether the present collection of research can provide a useful platform for further efforts contributing to the development of this emerging field. We hope we have set the stage for greater research to come. With luck, by the end of the century all the claims about neglected research and divorce between halves of the census will have been negated.

Index

Adams, J. S., 23, 114, 281–82, 284, 285

Age groups, 36, 301; behavior of, and the baby boom, 9; studies of, and nonfamily households, 69; and housing attainment, Kendig on, 134–35, 138; and fixed age—effect models, development of, 176; and housing consumption of the elderly, 177. *See also* Age structure; Baby Boom; Cohort; Elderly

Age structure: and demographic changes underlying changing family life-cycle distribution, 41–42; and housing characteristics, Myers and Doyle on, 109–30, 237

"Aging in place," 242

Alonso, W., 283

American Housing Survey. *See* Annual Housing Survey

Analysis and Forecasting, Inc., 158

Andrews, R. B., 292

Annual Housing Survey, 24–25, 92–93, 95, 96, 116; commencement of, 10; and housing careers, life-course approach to, 148–49; and housing consumption of the elderly, 177, 182-92; Clark's use of, 205, 206–10, 216, 218, 228; and residential mobility, 205, 206–10, 216, 218, 228; infrequent use of, 298

Appreciation, housing price, 181–82, 259, 280

Australia, 134–56; the Adelaide survey, 141–44; life-history studies in, 149–51

Baby boom, 6, 7, 148, 125, 285; impact on behaviors in specific age groups, 9; and construction, 22, 115, 241; and changing life-cycle distribution, 41, 45, 46; timing and spacing of births during, 46; and the

shrinking of household sizes, 113; and cohort flow, 139; and gentrification, 284, 292, 293; and the surge in demand for rental units, 289

Baer, William, 4, 23, 25–26, 249–73, 274, 275, 303–4; on respondent error, 120

Bane, M. J., 113

Berry, B. J. L., 215

Birch, D. L., 278

Birth rates. *See* Fertility

Blue-collar culture, 70, 74, 80, 303

Boersch-Supan, A., 177

Boertlein, C. G., 210, 229

Bourne, L. S., 235, 278, 282

Brennan, John, 24, 157–73, 176, 301

Bumpass, L., 53, 113

Burchell, R. W., 19, 112

Burgess, E. W., 234

Burke, P., 253

Campbell, B. O., 280, 283

Canada, 10

Catanese, A. J., 291

Census, U.S. Bureau of, 5, 11, 15, 23, 46, 66, 98; (1980), 9–10, 43, 46, 62–63, 71–83 *passim*, 260–61; (1970), 9–10, 43, 71–83 *passim*, 189; estimates on cohabitation, 43–44; (1960), 43; reports on housing costs among renters, 94; and changes in the family life cycle, 114, 115; and housing careers, life-course analysis of, 148–49; and housing consumption of the elderly, 182–83, 185, 187, 189, 192; of Governments (1972), 187; Public Use Micro Sample tapes associated with, 205; tracts, high rates of turnover for, 243–44; *Components of Inventory*